Strategies and Lessons for Culturally Responsive Teaching: A Primer for K–12 Teachers

Roselle Kline Chartock

Massachusetts College of Liberal Arts

PEARSON

Boston   New York   San Francisco
Mexico City   Montreal   Toronto   London   Madrid   Munich   Paris
Hong Kong   Singapore   Tokyo   Cape Town   Sydney

Acquisitions Editor: Kelly Villella Canton
Series Editorial Assistant: Annalea Manalili
Senior Marketing Manager: Darcy Betts
Production Editor: Mary Beth Finch
Editorial Production Service: Omegatype Typography, Inc.
Composition Buyer: Linda Cox
Manufacturing Manager: Megan Cochran
Electronic Composition: Omegatype Typography, Inc.
Interior Design: Omegatype Typography, Inc.
Cover Administrator: Elena Sidorova

For related titles and support materials, visit our online catalog at www.pearsonhighered.com.

Between the time website information is gathered and then published, it is not unusual for some sites to have closed. Also, the transcription of URLs can result in typographical errors. The publisher would appreciate notification where these errors occur so that they may be corrected in subsequent editions.

Library of Congress Cataloging-in-Publication Data
Chartock, Roselle.
    Strategies and lessons for culturally responsive teaching : a primer for K–12 teachers
        / Roselle K. Chartock.
            p.   cm.
    Includes bibliographical references and index.
    ISBN-13: 978-0-13-171508-0 (pbk.)
    ISBN-10: 0-13-171508-9 (pbk.)
    1. Multicultural education—Curricula—United States.   2. Cultural
pluralism—Study and teaching—United States.   I. Title.
    LC1099.3.C487   2010
    370.1170973—dc22

                                                                2009021106

Credits appear on page 224, which constitutes an extension of the copyright page.

Printed in the United States of America

13   17

www.pearsonhighered.com

ISBN-10: 0-13-171508-9
ISBN-13: 978-0-13-171508-0

Dedication

For all of those teachers who believe in the richness of diversity and put this belief into practice.

About the Author

 Roselle Kline Chartock, Ed.D., is professor of education at the Massachusetts College of Liberal Arts in North Adams, Massachusetts. Prior to teaching on the college level, Dr. Chartock taught high school history and middle and elementary school. She is the author/editor of *Educational Foundations: An Anthology* (2nd edition, Merrill/Prentice Hall, 2004) and co-editor of *Can It Happen Again: Chronicles of the Holocaust* (Black Dog and Leventhal, 2001), as well as the author of several journal articles on subjects ranging from interdisciplinary approaches to curriculum development to incorporating art and music across the curriculum. At the heart of all of her publications is the goal of preparing culturally responsive teachers. Dr. Chartock resides in Great Barrington, Massachusetts, with her husband, Alan.

Contents

Chapter 5
Strategies and Lessons for Reducing Prejudice   111

Chapter 6
Strategies and Lessons for Addressing Diversity and the Needs of English Language Learners   143

Chapter 7
Strategies and Lessons for Increasing Global Perspectives   175

Preface

"Once more I proclaim the whole of America for each individual, without exception."

"All characters, movements, growth— a few noticed, myriads unnoticed."

Walt Whitman (1860, pp. 452, 160)

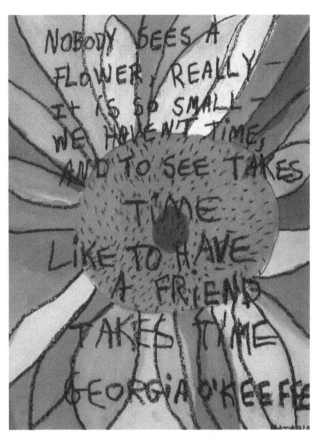

NOBODY SEES A FLOWER, REALLY — IT IS SO SMALL — WE HAVEN'T TIME, AND TO SEE TAKES TIME LIKE TO HAVE A FRIEND TAKES TIME GEORGIA O'KEEFE

Natasha Lorick: CATA 2007–2008 program year

An initial comment is warranted regarding a history-making day, November 4, 2008, when Senator Barack Obama became the first African American president of the United States. Five months earlier, on June 3, 2008, when he had secured the Democratic nomination for president by winning the requisite number of delegates to his party's convention, Senator Obama of Illinois took a historic step toward a once-improbable goal of becoming the nation's first African American president. In his speech that night in a hall in St. Paul, Minnesota, he praised Senator Hillary Clinton, who had also made history by coming closer than any other woman ever had to winning the nomination.

In her concession speech she expressed her support for Senator Obama and added, "Children today will grow up taking for granted that an African-American or a woman can, yes, become the president of the United States" (Fouhy, 2008, p. A5).

Months later on election night, November 4, 2008, after defeating Republican Senator John McCain, the newly elected President Obama walked across an outdoor stage in Chicago to thank his supporters, saying that he intended to be president of *all* the people of the United States.

After listening to the speeches on these two occasions, I wondered: To what extent did culturally responsive teaching play a role in bringing about that historic election day? In my opinion, teachers who blazed the trail of culturally responsive education deserve much of the credit for preparing citizens to look beyond race (and gender) and, in the words of Martin Luther King, Jr., to judge people not "by the color of their skin but by the content of their character." And while there is still work to be done to eradicate prejudice, we can take comfort in knowing that many systematic educational efforts to open minds to diversity have taken root. Note: Just as this book was going into production (May 2009), President Obama nominated appeals court judge, Sonia Sotomayor, for the Supreme Court, making her the first Hispanic in history to be elevated to the high court.

Theoretical Framework and Rationale

The description that follows illuminates the ways in which this text provides a unique addition to the literature of culturally responsive teaching. The intent of the text is to offer a starting point for preservice and in-service teachers who want to engage in culturally responsive practice, thereby making learning meaningful for *every* one of their students. The content and strategies are grounded in theories developed by researchers *and* practitioners who have been actively teaching and writing about multicultural education and related fields. (Banks, 2008; Beane, 2005; Chartock, 2004; Freire, 1973; Gay, 2002; Gollnick and Chinn, 2008; Nieto, 2004; Sleeter and Grant, 2007, and others).

Three tenets govern this primer. First, we can convert schools from their traditional places as institutions that mirror the prejudices within society into places where people teach and act according to the principles of multicultural awareness, acceptance, appreciation, and action. Second, culturally relevant curricula must be considered a vital component of every student's education and equally as important as knowledge about history, science, mathematics, and literature; the skills of reading and writing; and attitudes such as honesty and love of learning are for preparing democratic citizens. Third, teachers are change agents, rather than mere technicians, who can open the minds and hearts of their students and inspire them to reach their full potential and to make a difference in their schools, their communities, and the world.

Although as educators we often believe ourselves to be open-minded, we too generally view others through our own frames of reference and cultural lenses. That's quite natural. To overcome these limitations (and they *can* be overcome), we need strategies that will help us and our students to expand our perceptions of others and that allow us to walk, however briefly, in their shoes. That's what culturally responsive teaching is all about. This book, containing highly motivating, interdisciplinary, classroom-tested strategies that are suitable for, or adaptable to various grade levels and subject specialties, offers students interdisciplinary, activity-oriented approaches for becoming culturally competent.

There are many reasons for integrating culturally responsive teaching, an approach inclusive of both multicultural education (related to diversity within the United States) and global education (related to diversity in the world), across all grade levels:

- Diversity in America continues to grow; every day the planet shrinks as technology, travel, and immigration bring the world's cultures closer together.
- Intolerance and ignorance continue to plague this society, not only in the form of blatant hate groups, which numbered 762 in 2004 (SPLC, 2005, p. 3), but especially in the form of preconceived notions, both inside and outside of schools, toward certain groups and/or individuals.
- For many years a hidden bias has lurked in school texts marked by the absence of the roles and contributions of members of America's *microcultures,* minority groups based on race, religion, ethnicity, class, gender (and sexual orientation), language, and ability. When culturally diverse learners feel invisible because of their absence from the cur-

riculum, the result may be low self-esteem that ultimately prevents them from becoming successful learners.

Still another reason for including culturally responsive teaching strategies across the curriculum is the role they can play in encouraging learners to become actively involved in their own learning *and* in society's continuing struggle to bring about "liberty and justice for all." Schools play a vital role in building healthy communities in which people can pursue their individual interests while working cooperatively with others to make their world a better place in which to live.

A number of teacher education organizations, content-related professional associations, and departments of education have published documents supporting multicultural education and equity; in fact, some of these organizations were in the forefront of establishing such perspectives over 30 years ago. For example, in 1973 the American Association of Colleges for Teacher Education (AACTE) expressed their view that "multicultural education rejects the view that schools should seek to melt away cultural differences or the view that schools should merely tolerate cultural pluralism" (AACTE, 1973, p. 264). The association strongly acknowledged cultural diversity as a fact of life in America and affirmed diversity as a valuable resource that should be preserved and extended. Proponents of culturally responsive teaching concur with this view (Banks, 2008; Cochran-Smith, 2004; Diller and Moule, 2005; Finkelstein et al, 1998; Garcia and Pugh, 1992; Gollnick and Chinn, 2004; Hawley and Jackson, 1995; Sleeter and Grant, 2007).

Organizational and Pedagogical Features of the Text

This primer contains **over 40 culturally responsive lessons and teaching strategies** and several units of instruction that have been divided by themes into six chapters. The lessons and strategies incorporate many of the objectives in Bloom's hierarchy. Additionally, a matrix appears inside the cover that identifies the content area, grade level, and teaching principles for each lesson.

The lesson format satisfies the criteria for curriculum planning established by Ralph Tyler (1949), a pioneer in the field of curriculum development. He posed four questions that serve as a basis for organizing instruction: (1) What educational *purposes* should schools seek to attain? (2) How can *learning experiences* be selected that are likely to be useful in attaining these objectives? (And here Tyler expects the curriculum planner to be *well-informed about the nature of the learners for whom the objectives are being established.*) (3) How can learning experiences be *organized* for effective instruction? (4) Finally, how can the effectiveness of learning experiences be *evaluated*? There is an intrinsic connection between Tyler's questions and the design of the culturally responsive lessons and strategies presented in this text.

The sequence within Chapters 2–7 is as follows: (1) a brief discussion of the chapter theme and purpose, (2) a vignette related to the theme, (3) examples of pertinent current research, (4) guiding principles linked to the chapter theme along with classroom applications of each principle, and (5) detailed lesson plans and units of instruction, most of which can be adapted to several grade levels and subject areas. Located after each lesson plan objective in Chapters 3–7 are abbreviations that indicate standards established by the major professional organizations. By referring to the key in Appendix A teachers will be able to identify the meaning of the abbreviations. In addition to lessons, **sample units of instruction** appear in Chapters 3–7. A **summary chart of the teaching principles and their applications** follows the lessons and strategies and instructional units in each chapter.

Visuals, including political cartoons and diagrams and works of art throughout the book, reinforce and expand learning. The chapter opening pictures were created by participants in the Community Access to the Arts (CATA) Program, based in Great Barrington,

Massachusetts. CATA is a nonprofit arts organization that seeks to lessen the stigma of difference and disabilities through shared experiences in the visual and performing arts. CATAdirect, another CATA program, employs artists with disabilities in the arts and crafts industry (www.communityaccesstothearts.org). I believe that incorporating the art of CATA participants is appropriate and, in fact, inspiring, considering the goals of culturally responsive teaching.

A **Links** section at the end of most chapters provides questions to help the user review, reflect, and record his/her observations and feelings about the chapter content that may, in many cases, lead to follow-up investigations. Such a record, in the form of a written or audio journal, can be an effective self-teaching device because it helps you to construct knowledge and gain significant personal insights. Hopefully, your responses to the questions in this Links sections will help *you* to identify *your* values and educational purpose.

While keeping a journal is a very effective strategy for becoming a reflective teacher, there are other methods you might want to consider, including having yourself videotaped, inviting a peer to observe your teaching and interaction with students, carrying on mini-action-research projects in the classroom related to multicultural and diversity issues, and, of course, engaging in ongoing dialogue with your peers about culturally responsive teaching.

After the Links section are the chapter References, followed by **Recommended Resources** that provide students/teachers with sources to consult as they further investigate the topics of each chapter.

The four **Appendixes** provide more resources for teachers. Appendix A, "Key to National Standards Issued by Professional Organizations Representing Major Disciplines," presents standards that are addressed in each of the lessons. Appendix B, "Interstate New Teachers Assessment and Support Consortium (INTASC) Standards," presents the knowledge, dispositions, and performances deemed essential for all teachers regardless of their specialty area or grade level. Appendix C, "Gardner's Multiple Intelligences," explains the nine intelligences, which are apparent in most of the lessons and strategies in this text. Appendix D, "Bloom's Taxonomy of Educational Objectives," will assist teachers as they help their students progress from lower to higher levels of thinking (cognitive domain), feeling (affective domain), and doing (psychomotor skills domain).

Key Concepts of the Chapters

Chapter 1, "Introduction," includes an explanation of culturally responsive teaching (CRT) and key definitions associated with this approach that dispel any of the myths associated with it. The chapter covers the origin and background of CRT as it relates to the growth of multicultural education and includes a discussion of some of the roadblocks that account for the challenges to integrating diversity across the curriculum.

Chapter 2, "Strategies and Lessons for Preparing to Become a Culturally Responsive Teacher," offers teachers several strategies for assessing *their own* knowledge, attitudes, and skills related to diversity *before* going on to teach them to their students. While these strategies are intended for use by the preservice and in-service teachers themselves, they can also be adapted for use in K–12 classrooms. Because teacher attitudes are the most significant variable in providing all students an equal opportunity to learn, the goal of this chapter is to prepare teachers to enter their classrooms without any assumptions about their students' abilities and backgrounds, and with an increased awareness of their *own*. The chapter also includes a critical discussion of the controversial Elementary and Secondary Education Act (2001), or No Child Left Behind Act (NCLB), and how diverse groups of students are affected by its provisions. While this law has come under fire for its major testing requirements and its lack of funding for and fairness to certain groups of students, proponents have praised its underlying purpose: to provide excellent education and qualified teachers in all classrooms.

The teaching principles in this text should assist teachers in overcoming the challenges to culturally responsive teaching caused by NCLB. Lastly, the chapter provides a listing of several professional organizations and government agencies that currently support the inclusion of diversity education within the curriculum.

Chapter 3, "Strategies and Lessons for Building the Classroom-as-Community," offers ideas for enhancing relationships and interactions that take place between teachers and students; among the students themselves; and among school, family, and community. Each classroom of students is itself a cultural entity, a community with its own identity and ways of operating. Teachers can use several of this chapter's activities, such as Sample Unit 1, "Representing Our Diverse Community in a Calendar," to help nurture relationships among the students, their families, the school, and the larger community by involving *all* of them in a productive research project. When strategies require students to work in teams and to take responsibility for their own learning, they begin the civic practice of democratic decision-making that will serve them for a lifetime as they live as members of diverse communities.

Chapter 4, "Strategies and Lessons for Increasing Knowledge about Diversity," provides students with ways of learning about several microcultures, including those based on race, religion, ethnicity, class, gender (and sexual orientation), language, and exceptionality. The teacher-tested strategies in this chapter are broadly constructed so that they can be applied to learning about any one or more of these cultures depending on the focus the teacher chooses. Lesson 1, "Multicultural Bingo," for example, provides a matrix into which the teacher can place questions based on any area of study. Sample Unit 1, "A Heritage, USA, or Heritage, My Community Luncheon" engages students in exploring the diversity around them and culminates in a luncheon inclusive of the cultures in their own community (or the nation). To assist teachers in implementing these lessons and creating new ones, Chapter 4 includes Bloom's Taxonomy of Objectives in three domains: cognitive, affective, and psychomotor.

Chapter 5, "Strategies and Lessons for Reducing Prejudice," directly addresses the problem of prejudice as one of the causes of poverty, violence, and unequal treatment experienced by certain groups perceived as different within our society. Students will be able to engage in activities that include, among others, exploring the biology of race and implementing questionnaires that promote dialogue about stereotypes among students and teachers. Whatever the content of a teacher's subject area may be, the context can become even more meaningful if the teacher can find direct or indirect ways to simultaneously teach his or her students about prejudice. The strategies in this chapter will show teachers how to do this no matter their discipline or the age of their students.

Chapter 6, "Strategies and Lessons for Addressing Diversity and the Needs of English Language Learners," incorporates some basic principles and simple strategies to guide regular classroom teachers as they assist their English language learners (ELLs) in acquiring social, linguistic, and academic skills and knowledge. Demographic changes in the United States have brought to the forefront many issues related to language and education and how best to address the needs of ELLs. Because fewer than 15 percent of America's schools provide specialized programs such as ESL (English as a second language) or bilingual education, most ELLs are mainstreamed or assigned to regular classrooms where only English is spoken and with teachers who have not been trained in the field of second language acquisition. Each of the lessons, which are also appropriate for students whose native language is English, can be adapted to the appropriate language level of the students. All lessons involve the four modes of language: listening, speaking, reading, and writing. Additionally, the chapter suggests strategies for identifying the strengths and needs of the students in terms of these four modes so teachers can better plan instruction.

Chapter 7, "Strategies and Lessons for Increasing Global Perspectives," promotes strategies and lessons that facilitate global studies across the content areas. For example, Lesson 1, "The World in a Chocolate Bar" (in which students learn about economic connections to other countries), Lesson 4, "Endangered Species" (a science-related activity), and units such as "Local Links to the World" (which involves a variety of field experiences) can be easily integrated into the regular subject matter of math, science, literature, and history courses. Global studies are important for preparing students to participate in an increasingly inter-connected world. As a result of growing technological development and interdependence, Americans are linked socially, economically, and politically to diverse cultures around the world. However, our connections with other parts of the globe are not always what they could be in terms of understanding and appreciation of cultural differences. While **ethnocentrism,** the prejudiced belief that one's nation is superior to all others, still exists, and can potentially lead to war and grave social problems, not all schools include global studies in their curriculum. Often, those that do, cover it in less than one semester. One of the goals of this chapter is to help teachers dispel ethnocentric attitudes and help students recognize their identities as citizens of the world.

Teachers will discover that by carrying out all or many of these highly motivating, standards-based strategies, they will be able to teach their students important lessons about themselves and others, and, at the same time, demonstrate how exciting and meaningful such learning can be at this particular time in our history.

Acknowledgments

There are many people I want to thank for their hard work and dedication to the task of com-pleting this book. They all share the belief that underlies the content and lessons herein: that humanity is characterized by infinite variety, and these differences are what enrich our lives.

Penelope Lord and Barbara Dean are among those who share this belief. They were not only amazingly skillful typists, but they both read the book with care and assured me, time and again, that the content was essential for teachers and students alike, if we expect them to participate in making their communities and the world more peaceful places in which to live and thrive. They are in so many ways very special people.

My colleagues at the Massachusetts College of Liberal Arts (MCLA), Ann Scott, Margaret Chang, and Christine Woodcock, as a well as Linda Reardon at Sullivan Elementary School in North Adams, Massachusetts, and friends from both near and far, contributed useful ideas and moral support, all of which lent momentum to my efforts. And Sarah Sullivan, a former student and now a wonderful teacher herself, ably assisted as did Angelo Vuagniaux, whose skills and persistence were invaluable.

I had the good fortune of beginning the project with the guidance and wisdom of Pearson editor Debbie Stollenwerk. After completing the first half of the book with me, Debbie turned the project over to Darcy Betts's able hands. Kelly Villella-Canton was there with energy and insights for the completion of the book. Editorial assistant Annalea Manalili was always there to answer my questions and very promptly, I might add. The Pearson team generously devoted their time and attention in order to shape the text into a work that could be easily accessed by both preservice and in-service teachers on a multitude of levels. And a shout out must also go to Kayla Hewitt and others behind the scenes at Omegatype Typography, who were extremely helpful during the final stages of this project.

I am also grateful to the reviewers of the manuscript, those faculty who were willing to apply their academic experience and expertise, without which I could not have fine-tuned many parts of the book. I respect them immensely and thank them for their dedication and ongoing contributions to culturally responsive teaching. These reviewers include: Margarita Berta-Avila, California State University, Sacramento; Elinor Brown, University of Kentucky; Janelle Burge, University of Missouri–Kansas City; Jioanna Carjuzaa, Linfield College; Candice Carter, University of North Florida; Hussein Fereshteh, Bloomsburg University of Penn-sylvania; Barbara Fields, Park University; Michael Glassman, Ohio State University; Nancy Hadaway, University of Texas–Arlington; JoAnn Hohenbrink, Ohio Dominican University; Roy Howard, Western New Mexico University; Ana Maria Klein, State University of New York–Fredonia; Carolyn Miller, Estrella Mountain Community College; Craig Shieber, City

University of Seattle; Walter Ullrich, California State University, Fresno; Lisa William-White, California State University, Sacramento.

The teachers in my graduate course, Multicultural Education, at MCLA, were especially helpful during the process of evaluating which learning experiences would be most appropriate for inclusion in Chapter 2, "Strategies and Lessons for Preparing to Become a Culturally Responsive Teacher." These students implemented all of the activities and were honest about which ones inspired them the most and in what ways some of the experiences could be developed differently.

During my 43 years of teaching on all levels, I designed and taught many of the lessons included in the book. The feedback from my students at Mamaroneck Avenue School, Hommocks School in Larchmont, New York (1966–1971), and Monument Mountain Regional High School in Great Barrington, Massachusetts (1971–1986) helped me to determine which lessons were most effective in terms of content and methods. Their responsiveness and curiosity continue to inspire me.

I am thankful to the Literacy Network of South Berkshire for resources related to educating English language learners (Chapter 6), and Judy Waters, in particular, for sharing the books she found to be most useful and practical in preparing tutors at the Literacy Network.

For the wonderful artwork in this text I want to thank both the artists of Community Access to the Arts (CATA) and its director and founder, Sandy Newman. She stands as one who has put into practice the belief that no matter their differences or disabilities, all individuals possess talents and deserve to be treated with dignity and respect. The lessons and their artwork in this text convey the idea that all students can learn and thrive if they are recognized as individuals.

And finally, to my greatest supports in life, my husband, Alan, and Jonas and Sarah, my amazing children, who, in their own professional lives do me proud by working—in a variety of ways—for social justice and educational opportunities for those who have been traditionally underserved. Alan, my mate for life, has spent his life teaching, speaking, and writing about politics with the underlying purpose of bringing about justice, fairness, and honesty in a world where these values are not always practiced. I am constantly in awe of his courage and willingness to stand up and tell it like it is.

I hope in some small way that this book will make a difference, as those people mentioned here have done within their respective environments.

References

American Association of Colleges for Teacher Education Commission on Multicultural Education. (1973). "No One Model American." *Journal of Teacher Education, 24*(4), pp. 264–265.

Banks, J. A. (2008). *An Introduction to Multicultural Education.* Boston: Pearson.

Beane, J. A. (2005). *A Reason to Teach: Creating Classrooms of Dignity and Hope.* Portsmouth, NH: Heinemann.

Chartock, R. K. (Ed.). (2004). *Educational Foundations: An Anthology.* Columbus, OH: Merrill/Prentice Hall.

Cochran-Smith, M. (2004). *Walking the Road: Race, Diversity, and Social Justice in Teacher Education (Multicultural Education).* New York: Teachers College Press.

Diller, J. V., and J. Moule. (2005). *Cultural Competence: A Primer for Educators.* Belmont, CA: Thomson Wadsworth.

Esquith, R. (2004). *There Are No Shortcuts.* New York: Anchor Books.

Finkelstein, B., et al. (1998). *Discovering Culture in Education.* Washington, DC: ERIC Clearinghouse on Assessment and Evaluation.

Freire, P. (1973). *Pedagogy of the Oppressed.* New York: Seabury.

Garcia, J., and S. L. Pugh. (1992). "Multicultural Education in Teacher Preparation Programs: A Political or an Educational Concept?" *Phi Delta Kappan, 74*(4), pp. 214–219.

Gay, G. (2002). *Culturally Responsive Teaching.* New York: Teachers College Press.

Gollnick, D. M., and P. C. Chinn. (2008). *Multicultural Education in a Pluralistic Society* (8th ed.). Boston: Allyn and Bacon.

Hawley, W. D., and A. Jackson (Eds.). (1995). *Toward a Common Destiny: Improving Race and Ethnic Relations in America.* San Francisco: Jossey-Bass.

Nieto, S. (2004). *Affirming Diversity: The Sociopolitical Context of Multicultural Education.* Boston: Allyn and Bacon.

Northwest Regional Educational Laboratory. (December 2005). *Classroom to Community and Back: Using Culturally Responsive Standards-Based Teaching to Strengthen Family and Community Partnerships and Increase Student Achievement.* Portland, OR: NWREL.

Sleeter, C. E., and C. A. Grant. (2007). *Making Choices for Multicultural Education: Five Approaches to Race, Class and Gender.* Danvers, MA: Wiley.

Tyler, R. (1949). *Basic Principles of Curriculum and Instruction.* Chicago: University of Chicago Press.

Whitman, W. (1860). "So Long!" and "Chants Democratic." *Leaves of Grass.* Boston: Thayer and Eldridge.

Chapter One

Introduction

Teresa Thomas, CATA 2007–2008 program year

"Diversity need not mean adversity. Our bonds transcend our differences."

David Gewirtzman, Holocaust survivor,
in a speech given November 20, 2005

Background of Culturally Responsive Teaching

Fact: The United States has always been a diverse nation.

Fact: The dominant majority has discriminated against groups who differed from them.

Fact: Unequal treatment of people because of differences is inconsistent with the democratic values contained in the Constitution.

These three facts help to explain, in part, the conditions that have led to periodic explosions of protest throughout U.S history demanding that the dominant majority become more responsive to the diverse cultures within their midst. Among the most familiar of such reform movements were the antislavery crusade of the nineteenth century and the Progressive Movement of the early twentieth. A more recent example was the drive for civil rights during the latter half of the last century, which led to many societal changes, especially in education. One such change was the introduction of *culturally responsive teaching* (CRT), whose primary goal is to achieve a pluralistic democracy, in which equal rights and educational opportunities will, once and for all, be shared with those who have hitherto been excluded.

Reform efforts within the sphere of education took the form of restructuring schools and teacher education in ways that would enable students of all ages to participate actively in building a democracy based on social justice for all (Banks and McGee Banks, 2005; Gay, 2002; Gollnick and Chinn, 2005; Ladson-Billings, 1995; Nieto, 1999, 2004; Spring, 1997; Suzuki, 1979; Wlodkowski and Ginsberg, 1995.)

Results of these efforts included laws such as PL 94-142 (Education for All Handicapped Children Act, 1975) and court decisions, including *Brown v. Board of Education* (1954) in which separate and supposedly equal educational facilities based on race were determined to be inherently unequal. (See Chapter 4 for other laws and decisions.) While these reforms have remedied some educational inequities, current realities create formidable obstacles to the success of these well-meaning policies.

1. As institutions reflecting attitudes within the larger society, schools continue to be afflicted by racism and other forms of discrimination.

2. Although 40 percent of the nation's pupils are minorities, 95 percent of their teachers are white (Frankenberg, Lee, and Orfield, 2003; Watkins, 1989). And in 2002, W. B. Harvey noted that 85 percent of *preservice* teachers were white, with few of them having had the opportunity for learning about and interacting with minorities (minorities referring here to groups based on differences in class, race, religion, ethnicity, language, gender, and ability).

3. There is persistent inequality in the funding of public schools attended by most children of color and the poor.

4. Overplacement of African American and Latino children and English language learners in special education and lower-level curriculum tracks continues.

5. Due to the increased resegregation throughout the United States for both African American and Latino students (Orfield and Lee, 2004), the racial achievement gap has widened (Frankenberg et al., 2003). Other potential consequences of resegregation could be a reversal of the social benefits of integrated schools identified by Braddock and Eitle (2004) in their review of the literature. Such benefits have included among both African American and white students a reduction of prejudice and stereotyping and an increase in interracial friendships.

6. The nature of expanded federal and state testing has resulted in discrimination against certain groups of students, particularly English language learners and students with learning disabilities, as well as against the schools they attend (see also Chapter 2).

As long as these realities continue—whether based on apathy or prejudice—children from certain nondominant cultures will suffer the kinds of indignities that prevent them from success in school and consequently in life.

On a more hopeful note, there are currently signs of increased recognition within a variety of different sectors on the need for culturally responsive teaching. Publishers, for example, are competing to provide materials and literature about the what, whys, and how-to's of culturally responsive teaching. Government agencies and professional education associations have created content standards that specify the need for integrating multicultural and global studies curricula across the disciplines. Workshops and professional development courses are being offered by school systems and colleges to assist pre- and in-service teachers in exploring their attitudes about other cultures and how their own backgrounds may affect their interactions with diverse students. Private foundations are contributing to schools—among them public charter schools—that have developed programs for addressing the needs of inner-city children (Tough, 2008). Even the controversial federal No Child Left Behind Act (Elementary and Secondary Education Act; see Chapter 2) includes such provisions as additional funding for underserviced schools and providing quality teachers for *all* students. Although many of these good intentions have yet to be fulfilled and funded, there is—at least on paper—an awareness about the current need for change.

While these actions within both public and private sectors to eliminate educational inequities and promote culturally responsive teaching are steps in the right direction, changes are slow in coming, and there are roadblocks along the way. But this author believes that positive change happens one teacher at a time. This text was written with that idea in mind.

Culture Wars and Other Roadblocks

Although there have been some real successes in integrating diversity across the K–12 curriculum, as will be discussed throughout the remainder of the book, restructuring efforts have by no means been consistent or universally accepted. Misconceptions and prejudices persist, for example, in many places across the United States among those who do not recognize the duality of purpose inherent in culturally responsive approaches, which seek to emphasize *both* the commonalities within American society *and* its diversity.

The ongoing so-called *culture wars* are a clear indication that culturally responsive teaching, a concept often associated with multicultural education, is an issue that continues to divide people, with conservatives (traditionalists) taking the position that first and foremost, teachers should aim to assimilate diverse groups by conveying American values and shared practices (Bennett, 1992; Bloom, A., 1987; Cheney, 1995), while liberals (multiculturalists) generally support a belief in cultural pluralism, that is, teaching about the unique and culturally diverse communities within the United States along with values that all groups share as Americans (Banks and McGee Banks, 2005; Grant and Gomez, 1996; Shor, 1987). Conservatives often accuse liberals of *political correctness*, a view characterized as an overabundance of sensitivity and tolerance toward differences. "Because some, in their zeal for such tolerance, have appeared to be intolerant themselves, this perspective has taken on negative connotations: 'P.C.' is how the right wing labels this otherwise constructive attitude" (Chartock, 2004, p. 317).

Another misconception that opponents of culturally responsive approaches harbor is the idea that it is mainly the poverty in which many children live that accounts for their failure in school. While the conditions in which many children of the poor live—conditions that deprive them of decent nutrition, medical care and other necessities—may account for some of their educational problems, "racism and other forms of discrimination play a central role in educational failure, as does the related phenomenon of low expectations" (Nieto, 2000, p. 49).

A battle of words between two academics—one liberal and the other conservative—exemplifies these so-called culture wars. The late Lawrence W. Levine (1997) countered conservative Allan Bloom's (1987) assertion that the ideal curriculum was represented by the Western canon based on Eurocentric values and history. Levine argued that this canon never existed and that changes in curricula to broaden courses to include other cultures were big steps forward. Levine used his experiences as the son of Eastern European immigrants to support his argument that today's model is not the American melting pot but a cultural mosaic in which discrete ethnic groups persist and interact with other groups. He noted that he could, for example, have both Moses and Lincoln as forefathers, both Joshua and Joe Lewis as warrior heroes, and the Torah and the U.S. Constitution for his moral foundations (Levine, 1997). New immigrants continue to follow in Levine's footsteps, albeit with their own references.

Teachers are in a position to help end the "culture wars" by activating the dual purposes of culturally responsive teaching. As change agents they can help students learn about themselves, about diverse others at home *and* abroad, and about "a common vision of liberty, equality, and justice that . . . remains the only guarantee that a multicultural society will live in democracy and mutual respect" (Gagnon, 1991).

Another major roadblock to integrating diversity across the curriculum—which has also divided people according to their political perspectives—is the Elementary and Secondary Education Act, also known as the No Child Left Behind Act (NCLB). Those on the political left as well as many moderates see the testing provisions of this act as reinforcing the unequal and unfair treatment of certain groups, including children with special needs, English language learners, and students whose socioeconomic status has placed them in underserviced schools. While the intent is to hold schools accountable for overall student achievement and to close existing achievement gaps, there is ongoing debate about the methods by which these goals can best be achieved. NCLB will no doubt remain a roadblock on the path to respecting diversity for the foreseeable future unless and until the act shows signs of fulfilling its promises (see Chapter 2). One purpose of this book is to help teachers overcome the obstacles posed by this controversial act.

Some Definitions

Culturally responsive teaching is based on the assumption that culture is central to student learning. *Culture* refers to "integrated patterns of human behavior that include language, thoughts, communication, actions, customs, beliefs, values, and norms of racial, ethnic, religious, or social groups" (State Action for Educational Leadership Project, 2005).

Culture has also been defined as

a way of life, especially as it relates to the socially transmitted habits, customs, traditions and beliefs that characterize a particular group of people at a particular time. Culture is the lens through which we look at the world. It is the context within which we operate and make sense of the world and it influences how we process learning, solve problems, and teach. (Northwest Regional Educational Laboratory, 2005, p. 6)

A case in point regarding the power of culture on students' lives can be seen in the efforts of Geoffrey Canada. He has, for the past several years, been trying to transform an entire community with his Harlem Children's Zone, a network of early intervention programs and schools. In order to bring positive changes to their youth, he wants "Harlem's parents to adopt what he calls middle-class [cultural] values," including not only pride and devotion to the neighborhood "but also focused on success, learning, working hard, getting to college" (Tough, 2008, p. 125), values that would enable Harlem's African American and Hispanic students to escape the culturally influenced cycle of poverty.

Canada wants to plant the seeds that will nurture aspirations for a better life among young people, which is, in fact, also one of the objectives of culturally responsive teaching, as well as of multicultural education (addressing the United States as a diverse society) and global education (addressing the world as a diverse place). The primary goals they all share are (1) creating a sense of understanding and respect for differences, (2) overcoming prejudice and discrimination, (3) providing an understanding of the dynamics of racism, (4) replacing historical and cultural distortions about diverse groups with accurate information, (5) ensuring that all students receive equitable benefits from the educational system (Drum and Howard, 1989), and finally, (6) promoting self-respect and respect for others.

Experts in the field of culturally responsive teaching have defined the concept in ways that make clear their general agreement on its meaning and purpose. Ladson-Billings (1995) calls CRT an approach that empowers students intellectually, socially, emotionally, and politically by using cultural referents to impart knowledge, skills, and attitudes. The use of cultural referents in teaching can bridge and explain the mainstream culture, while valuing and recognizing the students' own culture.

Hollins (1996) explains that the link between culture and classroom instruction is derived from evidence that cultural practices shape thinking processes, which then serve as tools for learning within and outside of school. Thus, according to Nieto (2000), culturally responsive education recognizes, respects, and uses students' identities and backgrounds as meaningful sources for creating optimal learning environments.

The project of the Northwest Regional Educational Laboratory (NWREL), *Classroom to Community and Back* (2005), is an excellent source for ways to use "culturally responsive, standards-based teaching to strengthen family and community partnerships and increase student achievement" (Northwest Regional Educational Laboratory, 2005). NWREL's School-Family-Community Partnerships Team has defined culturally responsive teaching as an approach that "infuses family customs—as well as community culture and expectations—throughout the teaching and learning environment" and is built on a foundation of knowledge and understanding of "your own and your students' family and community culture" (2005, p. 5).

> Becoming culturally responsive is an ongoing process that evolves as we learn more about ourselves, our world and other cultures. To become culturally responsive, first look at your own culture—especially if it is part of our country's dominant culture—from the worldview of others; have an open mind to what you don't understand; and be ready to learn new ways of looking at and doing things. (Northwest Regional Educational Laboratory, 2005, p. 6)

Villegas and Lucas (2002) refer to the expansion of cultural awareness as gaining "sociocultural consciousness," or gaining an awareness that "one's worldview is not universal but is profoundly shaped by one's life experiences" (p. 27). They offer by way of example how a white upper-middle-class man raised in a wealthy northeastern suburban community experiences the world very differently from a poor Mexican American woman raised in East Los Angeles. They emphasize that both preservice and in-service teachers need to inspect their own beliefs about students from nondominant groups and confront negative attitudes they might have toward these students (p. 38).

In a culturally responsive classroom the needs and interests of all students from all backgrounds would be addressed within a climate of respect for differences. Diller and Moule (2005) believe that culturally responsive teaching by culturally competent educators means successfully teaching students who come from cultures different from their own and entails mastering certain personal and interpersonal awarenesses and sensitivities, learning specific bodies of knowledge, and mastering a set of skills that, taken together, underlie effective cross-cultural teaching.

In a culturally responsive environment, lessons "blend information on how students can become more comfortable with American culture with ways that other students can become culturally responsive to members of diverse cultures" (Stickey, 2003).

Wlodkowski and Ginsberg (1995) issue an appropriate warning here on making assumptions about someone's cultural affiliation. They note that the most obvious cultural characteristics that people observe are physical. "Physical characteristics, however, provide a cursory sense of who we are. Our families, friends, jobs, organizational ties, and lifestyles draw upon a repertoire of behaviors, obstructing a clear view of who we might be culturally" (p. 5). They stress that our unique personal histories and psychological traits interact dynamically to distinguish us from other members of our *own* cultural groups. "The subtle complexity of who we are makes it difficult to define human beings according to narrow, static lists of expected characteristics" (p. 6).

Principles That Guide Culturally Responsive Teaching

On the Education Alliance at Brown University (2006) website there is posted a synthesis of several principles that guide culturally responsive teaching, all of which can be observed in the lessons and units of instruction in this primer:

1. *Communication of high expectations.* Both teachers and schools convey the message that students will succeed (Gay, 2002; Ladson-Billings, 1994; Tomlinson, 1999; Williams, 1996) while appropriately challenging them to think critically (see Appendix D for Bloom's taxonomy).

2. *Utilization of diverse learning strategies.* Teachers incorporate cooperative learning and differentiated teaching that recognizes different learning styles (Gay, 2002). (See Appendix C for Gardner's multiple intelligences.) Active teaching methods promote engagement by requiring students to play an active role in shaping and developing the curriculum and related activities (Banks, 2005; Oakes and Lipton, 1999; Tomlinson, 1999).

3. *Teacher as facilitator.* The teacher's role is one of guide, mediator, and knowledge consultant as well as instructor (Banks and McGee Banks, 2005; Ladson-Billings, 1994; Villegas, 1991)

4. *Positive perspectives on parents and families of culturally and linguistically diverse students.* There is ongoing participation by not only students and teachers but also parents and community members on issues important to them, along with inclusion of these individuals and issues in classroom curriculum and activities (Delgado-Gaitan and Trueba, 1991; Hollins, 1996).

5. *Cultural sensitivity.* Teachers gain knowledge of the cultures represented in their classrooms and translate this knowledge into instructional practice (Banks, 2001; Nieto, 1999; Villegas, 1991).

6. *Reshaping the curriculum.* Curriculum should be designed so that it is interdisciplinary (Banks, 2001) and connected to students' real lives (Chion-Kenny, 1994), while challenging students to develop higher-order knowledge and skills (Villegas, 1991) and capitalizing on students' cultural backgrounds rather than attempting to override or negate them (Abdul-Haqq, 1994).

7. *Culturally mediated instruction.* Instruction is characterized by use of knowledge within given cultures, culturally appropriate social situations for learning, and culturally valued knowledge in curriculum content. Culturally appropriate social situations refer to relationships among students and between teachers and students that are congruent with the culture of each student (McCarty, Lynch, Wallace, and Benally, 1991) and culturally valued knowledge is that which is relevant to students' lives (Banks, 2001; Hollins, 1996; Nieto, 1999).

8. *Student-centered, student-controlled classroom discourse.*   Students are given opportunity to control some portion of the lesson, providing teachers with insight into the ways that speech and negotiation are used in the home and community (Gay, 2002; Ladson-Billings, 1994; Nieto, 1999).

The culturally responsive teaching approaches that characterize the lessons and units of instruction in Chapters 2 through 7 can help to lay the philosophical foundations on which teachers can begin to create social change.

Myths about Culturally Responsive Teaching

Aldridge and colleagues (2000) have identified several common misconceptions or myths about multicultural education that are also applicable to culturally responsive teaching, and they have been adapted in this section for that purpose, along with a few additions and omissions. It should be noted again that CRT is inclusive of both multicultural curriculum (related to diversity within the United States) and global education (related to diversity in the world), so there are, indeed, similarities among all three in terms of definitions and goals and the myths that surround them. Clearly, the main similarity they all share is valuing diversity in all aspects of the classroom environment, whether content, method, perspective, personnel, students, or cultures.

It should be noted that teachers are not the only ones who need to become aware of the following myths. The general public as well, once these myths are dispelled, will be able to see the intrinsic value of culturally responsive teaching across all disciplines and grade levels so that meeting the needs and interests of *all* students will become a reality.

Myth 1

People from the same nation or region, or those who speak the same language, share a common culture (Aldridge, Calhoun, and Aman, 2000). The fact is, for example, that while most Latinos share a common language, the cultures, say, of Cuba, Mexico, Puerto Rico, and Argentina are distinctly different from one another.

Myth 2

Families from the same culture share the same values. In reality, a continuum of cultural identity exists, and, interestingly, the entire range can often be found within the same family.

Myth 3

Children's books about other cultures are usually authentic. Not necessarily. For example, a popular book, *Tikki Tikki Tembo*, offers inaccurate depictions of Chinese culture, especially in relation to names.

Myth 4

Multicultural education (culturally responsive curriculum) just includes ethnic and racial issues. In fact, such education goes beyond these issues to include concerns for gender, class, ability, language issues, and the values of cultural diversity. Furthermore, a number of texts identify additional goals for culturally responsive teaching, especially the promotion of equal opportunity in the school for all students as well as social justice for all peoples beyond the school environment, human rights, and respect for all no matter their differences (Banks, 1994; Davidman and Davidman, 1997; Gollnick and Chinn, 2005; Sleeter, 1996).

Myth 5

The seasonal/holiday approach is appropriate for teaching multicultural education. This approach involves incorporating culturally responsive curricula at certain times of the year based on a holiday (e.g., studying Native Americans in November when Thanksgiving occurs or learning about Martin Luther King, Jr., during Black History Month or at the time of his birthday). Ironically, Aldridge notes that students often come away from such teaching with even more biases. When all Americans are sufficiently a part of courses of study and daily instruction, notes Aldridge and colleagues (2000), there will be no need for these special months or weeks.

Myth 6

Multicultural education (culturally responsive education) should be taught separately. Such an approach, like the holiday focus just mentioned, sends the message that certain groups are still on the fringes of the society. Culturally responsive curriculum should actually be an organic component of *all* disciplines, regardless of the fact that its presence has traditionally been overlooked.

Myth 7

Multiculturalism is divisive. It is not multiculturalism or culturally responsive teaching approaches that are divisive, but rather intolerance and prejudice toward people or groups who are different in some way. Multicultural education (culturally responsive teaching) can assist in teaching students of all ages about tolerance and the idea that "we are all alike and all different in certain ways" (Aldridge et al., 2000) and that our identities are usually influenced by others and thus change over time.

Myth 8

Historical accuracy suffers in multicultural education. There is no question that some curricula promote certain cultural perspectives. For example, Eurocentric curriculum teaches that Western civilization started in Greece as opposed to Egypt, as asserted by Afrocentric curriculum. In order to help students seek historical accuracy, they need to be taught how to investigate controversial questions and do extensive research when confronted with discrepancies in historical literature.

Myth 9

Most people identify with one culture. The fact is that many students come from families that are multicultural. Attention therefore needs to be given in school not only to the existence of differences between groups, but *within* groups as well, so that children from such families, as well as others, view this as a common phenomenon within the United States.

Myth 10

There are cultural group learning styles. Based on research among five major cultural groups in the United States—African Americans, European Americans, Asian Americans, Hispanic Americans, and Native Americans—Dunn and Griggs (1995) concluded that there are instead cross-cultural and intracultural similarities and differences among all peoples, which are enriching when understood and channeled positively. Teaching students using a variety of diverse methods that address their specific needs while having high expectations are the greater determinants of success among minority students. Whether you agree with Dunn and Griggs or not, it would be wise to consult other studies that have been done on the learning styles of particular cultural groups.

Beyond the Myths

No matter the depth of one's commitment to culturally responsive teaching, we are all subject to misconceptions about its meaning and purpose. You are more likely to move beyond these myths if you make a continual effort to examine your own beliefs and attitudes about diversity and seek objective, research-based studies related to diversity and culturally responsive approaches. This primer seeks to assist you in fulfilling these important goals.

References

Abdul-Haqq, I. (1994). "Culturally Responsive Curriculum" Washington, DC: Educational Resources Information Center. (ERIC Digest ED 370936)

Aldridge, J., C. Calhoun, and R. Aman. (Spring 2000). "15 Misconceptions about Multicultural Education," *Focus on Elementary, 12*(3). Retrieved from www.acei.org/misconceptions.htm

Banks, J. A. (1994). *An Introduction to Multicultural Education*. Boston: Allyn and Bacon.

Banks, J. A., and C. M. Banks. (2005). *Multicultural Education: Issues and Perspectives* (5th ed.). Hoboken, NJ: John Wiley & Sons.

Bennett, W. J. (1992). *The Devaluing of America: The Fight for Our Culture and Our Children*. New York: Simon & Schuster.

Bloom, A. (1987). *The Closing of the American Mind*. New York: Simon & Schuster.

Braddock, J. H., II, and T. M. Eitle (2004). "The Effects of School Desegregation." In J. A. Banks and C. A. M. Banks (Eds.), *Handbook of Research on Multicultural Education* (pp. 828–843). San Francisco: Jossey-Bass.

Chartock, R. K. (2004). *Educational Foundations: An Anthology*. Upper Saddle River, NJ: Pearson Education.

Cheney, L. V. (1995). *Telling the Truth: Why Our Schools, Culture and Country Have Stopped Making Sense and What We Can Do about It*. New York: Simon & Schuster.

Chion-Kenny, L. (1994). "Weaving Real Life Images and Experiences into Native Education." *R & D Preview, 9*(1), pp. 4–5.

Davidman, L., and P. Davidman. (1997). *Teaching with a Multicultural Perspective: A Practical Guide* (2nd ed.). New York: Longman.

Delgado-Gaitan, C., and H. Trueba. (1991). *Crossing Cultural Borders: Education for Immigrant Families in America*. London: Falmer Press.

Diller, J. V., and J. Moule. (2005). *Cultural Competence: A Primer for Educators*. Belmont, CA: Thomson Higher Education.

Dunn, R., and S. A. Griggs. (1995). *Multiculturalism and Learning Styles: Teaching and Counseling Adolescents*. Westport, CT: Praeger.

Education Alliance at Brown University. (2006). *Culturally Responsive Teaching*. Retrieved from http://knowledgeloom.org/crt/index.jsp

Frankenberg, E., C. Lee, and G. Orfield. (January 2003). *A Multicultural Society with Segregated Schools: Are We Losing the Dream?* Cambridge, MA: The Civil Rights Project, Harvard University.

Gagnon, P. A. (June 1991). "History: The Best Multicultural Education." *History Matters*. Westlake, OH: National Council for History Education.

Gay, G. (2002). *Culturally Responsive Teaching: Theory, Research and Practice*. New York: Teachers College Press.

Gollnick, D. M., and P. C. Chinn. (2005). *Education in a Pluralistic Society*. Columbus, OH: Merrill.

Grant, C. A., and M. L. Gomez. (1996). *Making Schooling Multicultural: Campus and Classroom*. Upper Saddle River, NJ: Prentice-Hall.

Harvey, W. B. (2002). *Minorities in Higher Education, 2001–2002: 19th Annual Report*. Washington, DC: America's Council on Education.

Hollins, E. R. (1996). *Culture in School Learning*. Mahwah, NJ: Lawrence Erlbaum.

Ladson-Billings, G. (1994). *The Dreamkeepers: Successful Teachers of African American Children*. San Francisco: Jossey-Bass.

Ladson-Billings, G. (1995). "Toward a Theory of Culturally Relevant Pedagogy." *American Education Research Journal, 32*(3), pp. 465–491.

Levine, L. W. (1997). *The Opening of the American Mind: Canons, Culture and History*. New York: Houghton Mifflin.

McCarty, T. C., R. H. Lynch, S. Wallace, and A. Benally. (1991). "Classroom Inquiry and Navajo Learning Styles: A Call for Reassessment." *Anthropology and Education Quarterly, 22*(1), pp. 42–59.

Nieto, S. (1999). *The Light in Their Eyes: Creating Multicultural Learning Opportunities.* New York: Teachers College Press.

Nieto, S. (2000). *Affirming Diversity* (3rd ed.). New York: Longman.

Nieto, S. (2004). *Affirming Diversity: The Sociopolitical Context of Multicultural Education* (4th ed.). Boston: Allyn & Bacon.

Northwest Regional Educational Laboratory. (2005). *Culturally Responsive Practices for Student Success: A Regional Sampler* (By Request Series). Portland, OR: Author.

Northwest Regional Educational Laboratory, School-Family-Community Partnerships Team. (2005). *Classroom to Community and Back.* Portland, OR: Author.

Oakes, J., and M. Lipton. (1999). *Teaching to Change the World.* Boston: McGraw-Hill.

Orfield, G., and C. Lee. (January 2004). *Brown at 50: King's Dream or Plessy's Nightmare?* Cambridge, MA: The Civil Rights Project, Harvard University.

Shor, I. (1987). *Culture Wars: School and Society in the Conservative Restoration, 1969–1984.* New York: Routledge.

Sleeter, C. (1996). *Multicultural Education as Social Activism.* Albany: State University of New York Press.

Spring, J. (1997). *Deculturalization and the Struggle for Equality* (2nd ed.). New York: McGraw-Hill.

State Action for Educational Leadership Project (SAELP) in Oregon. (2005). *A List of Resources on Cultural Competency.* Retrieved from www.ode.state.or.us/opportunities/grants/saelp/resrcescultcomp.aspx

Suzuki, B. (1979). "Multicultural Education: What's It All About?" *Integrated Education, 17,* pp. 43–50.

Tomlinson, C. A. (1999). *The Differentiated Classroom: Responding to the Needs of All Learners.* Alexandria, VA: Association for Supervision and Curriculum Development.

Tough, P. (2008). *Whatever It Takes.* New York: Houghton Mifflin.

Villegas, A. M. (1991). *Culturally Responsive Pedagogy for the 1990s and Beyond.* Washington, DC: ERIC Clearinghouse on Teacher Education.

Villegas, A. M., and T. Lucas. (2002). *Educating Culturally Responsive Teachers: A Coherent Approach.* Albany: State University of New York Press.

Watkins, B. T. (December 13, 1989). "Colleges Urged to Train Future Schoolteachers to Deal With Expected 'Influx of Immigrants.'" *The Chronicle of Higher Education,* p. A41.

Williams, B. (1996). *Closing the Achievement Gap.* Alexandria, VA: Association for Supervision and Curriculum Development.

Wlodkowski, R. J., and M. B. Ginsberg. (1995). *Diversity and Motivation: Culturally Responsive Teaching.* San Francisco: Jossey-Bass.

Recommended Resources

Banks, J. A., and C. A. M. Banks. (Eds.). (1995). *Handbook of Research on Multicultural Education.* New York: Macmillan.

Gollnick, D. M., and P. C. Chinn. (2008). *Multicultural Education in a Pluralistic Society* (8th ed.). Columbus, OH: Pearson.

Irvine, J. (2003). *Educating Teachers for Diversity: Seeing with a Cultural Eye.* New York: Teachers College Press.

Michie, G. (2005). *See You When We Get There: Teaching for Change in Urban Schools.* New York: Teachers College Press.

Parker, W. C. (2002). *Teaching Democracy: Unity and Diversity in Public Life.* New York: Teachers College Press.

Sheets, R. H. (2005). *Diversity Pedagogy: Examining the Role of Culture in the Teaching-Learning Process.* Boston: Allyn & Bacon.

Journals

Multicultural Education
Caddo Gap Press, Inc. 3145 Geary Blvd., Suite 275, San Francisco, CA, 94118 (415)750–9978. Journal of the National Association for Multicultural Education (NAME).

Multicultural Review
Greenwood Publishing Group, Inc., P.O. Box 5007, Westport, CT, 06881–5007.

Teaching Tolerance
Southern Poverty Law Center, 400 Washington Ave., Montgomery, AL, 36104.

Websites

Culturally Responsive Teaching (Brown University)

www.lab.brown.edu
Provides information and strategies to adapt teaching so that it meets the needs of all students.

Diverse Schools: "Skewing Myths About Diverse Schools"

www.washingtonpost.com
Presents discussion by education columnist Jay Matthews of author and parent Eileen Gale Kugler's debunking of seven myths that frighten concerned parents away from diverse schools. (*Washington Post,* August 2004)

Diversity Calendar

www.kumc.edu/diversity (University of Kansas)
Shows ethnic, national, and religious days in a monthly listing.

Diversity Web

www.diversityweb.org
Describes a resource center for higher education (part of a larger communication initiative titled Diversity Works) whose purpose is to create new pathways for diversity collaboration and connection through the Internet as well as more traditional forms of print communication.

Educating Teachers for Diversity

www.ncrel.org (North Central Regional Educational Laboratory)
Addresses the crucial issue of preparing future teachers to advance "meaningful, engaged learning for all students, regardless of their race, gender, ethnic heritage, or cultural background."

Equity and Diversity Resources

www.enc.org/topics/equity (Eisenhower National Clearinghouse)
Presents articles, checklists, and other resources regarding equity and diversity in the schools.

Glossary of Terms Related to Judaism

www.philo.ucdavis.edu/zope/home/bruce (University of Pennsylvania, prepared initially by Robert A. Kraft)
Provides definitions and historical backgrounds of people, places, and things.

Multicultural Education and Ethnic Groups: Selected Internet Sources

www.library.csustan.edu/boyer/multicultural/main.htm (California State University Stanislaus Library)
Blends a variety of Internet resources on multicultural education and diversity, including websites for school teachers, bibliographies, biographies, as well as Web articles on ethnic cooking, religion, and various other topics.

Reading Resources: Celebrate Reading 365 Days a Year—Multicultural Web Resources

www.nea.org/webresources/readmulticult0509.htm
Promotes multiculturalism through literature that opens a window on world cultures for students.

Tolerance.org's Resources for Teachers, Administrators, and Counselors (a project of the Southern Poverty Law Center)

www.tolerance.org/teach/index/jsp
Encourages people everywhere to resist hate and nurture tolerance; provides the following teaching resources free on request:
- *Teaching Tolerance* magazine subscription (one copy per issue)
- *Responding to Hate at School* booklet (available in bulk)

Scholastic: Diversity Lesson Plans

www.teacher.scholastic.com/professional/teachdive/index.htm
Features lesson plans, activities, and professional resources to assist teachers in coping with the challenges of the diverse classroom.

Chapter Two

Strategies and Lessons for Preparing to Become a Culturally Responsive Teacher

Kate Ryan, CATA 2007–2008 program year

"The first thing is to be honest with yourself. You can never have an impact on society if you have not changed yourself."

Nelson Mandela, former president of South Africa and 1993 Nobel Peace Prize winner

"Sí, se puede: Yes, we can!"

Barack Obama's campaign slogan, 2008

*T*he purpose of this chapter is to offer you opportunities for examining your own attitudes and knowledge about diversity, on the assumption that, equipped with self-knowledge, you will be more effective in integrating the lessons and strategies in this book.

Besides providing you with activities to help you explore your personal connections to diversity, this chapter offers background information that will serve as a foundation on which to build your knowledge base. For example, you will learn about several national organizations that have acknowledged a need for culturally responsive practice. You will also find two charts containing the positions of several of these organizations and the diversity-related standards they have published.

Other foundational issues addressed in Chapter 2 include discussions of the internal debates and tensions related to the role and importance of multicultural curricula, the myths associated with diversity education, and the meaning of white privilege, as well as some of the other obstacles that you may face as you introduce diversity curricula. All of these issues, plus a critical discussion of the No Child Left Behind Act (2001), are intended to help prepare you for culturally responsive teaching.

Finally, following the research and principles in this chapter, you'll find lessons and strategies that will help you explore your current attitudes and knowledge about diversity. But it should be noted that although these activities have been designed to be carried out by you, the in-service or preservice teacher, they can also be adapted for use with your students.

What benefits do you think are possible from the following activity?

Twenty students sit in a circle, a Literature Circle, and discuss a biography, novel, or autobiography that they have recently completed. Each book presented the story of a person's life and how that person was influenced by their culture and environment. The students ask and answer each other's questions as they compare and contrast the traditions and beliefs of the people they read about; then they compare the characters' lives to their own. They listen to one another with interest and speak with authority when they refer to specific parts of their book. The teacher asks them to share the voice of a major character by reading aloud certain sentences. The 45 minutes allotted for the Literature Circle go by quickly, and the students express excitement about continuing their discussion.

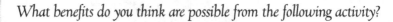

What the Research Says

ONE Developing Empathy

Studies have shown that when students have the opportunity to "walk" in another's shoes, they are better able to develop empathy. That is, they begin to recognize that those who may differ from them culturally have similar hopes, dreams and potential, no matter the labels so often attached to them (Phillion and Fang He, 2004). The author's own experiences in classrooms at multiple levels from 1966 to the present confirms this process.

The rationale for this kind of imagining experience is that if one can identify with others, one is likely to care about them. Developing empathy is important not only for K–12 students but also for pre- and in-service teachers. The preceding vignette, in which literature serves to build empathy and knowledge about culturally diverse groups, is one of many strategies you can use to help yourself prepare to teach in a culturally responsive manner, and it can also be used to help your students develop the kind of awareness necessary for ultimately bringing about social change. If you find it difficult to begin, librarians can help you locate culturally relevant novels, biographies, and autobiographies.

Reflective question: Have you ever observed—or actually developed—a strategy for helping students develop empathy?

TWO Areas of Agreement and Disagreement among Multicultural Education Proponents

In her synthesis of scholarship on multicultural education, Geneva Gay, professor of education and faculty associate of the Center for Multicultural Education at the University of Washington, Seattle, points out some of the major areas of agreement among proponents (Gay, 1994). For example, proponents of multicultural education desire to make cultural pluralism and ethnic diversity integral parts of the educational process; they agree that the content of *multicultural education curricula* should include data about ethnic identities, cultural pluralism, unequal distribution of resources and opportunities, and other sociopolitical problems stemming from long histories of oppression (Gay, 1994, p. 3). Most of all they value diversity and believe schools need to promote a comprehensive understanding of cultural groups, using interdisciplinary approaches and methods that are sensitive to the varying learning styles, backgrounds, and needs of each student.

Gay identifies these areas of agreement on multicultural education based on her research and also makes clear that there are dozens of definitions of multicultural education, with numerous rationales and goals, teaching and learning approaches, differing key principles and effects of multicultural education, as well as many reform implications (Gay, 1994, p. 17). Clearly individuals bring to this field of study their own unique frames of reference and philosophies that account for the many perspectives that Gay identifies (p. 1).

Multicultural education is a part of the larger focus referred to here as *culturally responsive teaching* (CRT), which pertains to the following:

- Strategies that educate students about the multicultural nature of their society and world.
- Strategies that encourage respect for—not simply tolerance of—diversity. (Students are more successful when they learn in an environment where they are respected.)
- Strategies that encourage students to become actively involved in building a community in which there is "liberty and justice for all." (Strategies in this book can assist you in accomplishing these goals.)

Gay is known for her work on culturally responsive teaching, which involves viewing the students' backgrounds as assets—that is, using the cultural knowledge, prior experiences, frames of reference, and performance styles of ethnically diverse students to make learning more relevant and effective for them (Gay, 2002). Schools that are culturally responsive promote such goals as:

- Establishing staffing patterns that reflect the diversity of American society.
- Teaching an unbiased, inclusive curricula.
- Empowering all students to achieve academically.
- Ensuring equity of resources and programs for all students.
- Empowering students to recognize social injustices and to devise approaches for correcting them (Bazron, Osher, and Fleischman, 2005).

Reflective question: How would *you* define multicultural education and its primary purposes?

THREE Minority Groups Growing in Numbers

The U.S. Census Bureau has projected that whites and minority groups overall will be roughly equal in size by 2050 (U.S. Census Bureau News, 2008). As of July 2007 the U.S. population was an estimated 301.6 million, with the following racial and ethnic breakdown: 199.1 million whites, 40.7 million African Americans, 15.2 million Asians, 4.5 million Native Indians and Alaskans, and 1 million Native Hawaiians and other islanders. The Census Bureau notes that Hispanics can be of any race and therefore counts "Hispanic" or "Latino" as an ethnicity rather than a race. The agency estimated 45.5 million Hispanics in the United States (or 15.1% of the population) as of July 2007, such that they now comprise the country's largest minority group.

The obvious implication of this data for schools is the need for developing culturally responsive teaching strategies and curricula that address the needs of every student—no matter their cultural differences.

Reflective question: What evidence have you personally observed that corroborates these statistics?

FOUR Debating How to Teach Multicultural Education

While multicultural curricula have expanded during the last 20 years, educators are "still at odds over how the distinctive experiences of racial and ethnic groups should be taught, and who should decide" (Zehr, November 2005).

Multicultural education formally began in the 1960s as a response to three phenomena: (1) the ongoing policy of accepting immigrants into the United States; (2) the emergence of the civil rights and women's movement, as well as other movements of the 1960s, during which minority groups asserted their right to participate equally in the greater society; and (3) the growth in numbers of minority students on college campuses.

Multicultural education has expanded from an attempt to reflect the growing diversity in American classrooms to include curricular revisions that specifically address the academic needs of all students (Sobol, 1990). Advocates say that, rather than dividing citizens along racial and cultural lines, their goals are to increase academic achievement among underserved youth while also promoting greater sensitivity to cultural differences in an attempt to reduce prejudices.

Internal Debates about the Nature of Multicultural Curricula

Despite these laudable goals, many of which are now contained in the documents of professional organizations as well as state certification regulations, educators continue to be caught up in debates related to multicultural education. One example of such a debate took place in New York State, Illinois, and New Jersey between 2002 and 2005 regarding how slavery was to be portrayed in their schools as well as who—educators, special interest groups, or legislators—would, and should, decide the issue. Amistad* commissions were established by the legislatures in these states to ensure that students were taught about the impact of slavery on people of African descent as well as slavery's ramifications for African Americans after it was outlawed.

Another interesting example emblematic of interest group efforts to influence multicultural curricula and of internal disagreements among proponents of such curricula is a 2005

Amistad is the name of a ship on which enslaved Africans were transported in 1839. A group of Africans overthrew the ship's crew and gained their freedom after successfully pressing their case before the U.S. Supreme Court (Zehr, November 2005). Steven Spielberg's film of the same name portrayed this historical event.

federal lawsuit filed in Massachusetts involving curricula mandated by a 1998 law requiring the provision to schools of materials on genocide and human rights. Among the plaintiffs was the Assembly of Turkish American Associations who argued that the law should not use *genocide* to refer to the killing of Armenians by Turks during World War I. The assembly then accused the education department of violating their free speech rights by keeping the Turkish American perspective on World War I history out of educational materials.

This controversy calls to mind Princeton philosophy professor Kwame Appiah's question: Might the treasured concept of liberty be at odds with diversity? Citing a Unesco Convention principle that affirms "equal dignity of and respect for all cultures," he asks whether we then want to include the KKK among those cultures or condone sentencing adulteresses to death by stoning as is the custom in northern Nigeria? "Vive la différence? (Long live difference?)," he asks (Appiah, 2006, p. 37). (And to that question how would *you* reply?)

Textbooks at the Center of Controversy

Still another highly published debate about appropriate materials for multicultural education took place in 1990 in California where dozens of groups, including Native Americans, African Americans, Muslims, Jews, and others objected to the way in which certain texts portrayed them (Reinhold, 1991). Finding common ground in the need for the ongoing struggle for greater equality and social justice, they all found fault with the U.S. history texts submitted by nine publishers whose content, the critics said, was still mainly Eurocentric.

Fast forward to the twenty-first century and the fifth-grade history textbook used in many schools, McGraw-Hill's *A New Nation: Adventures in Time and Place*, is a model of multicultural sensitivity (Boyer, 2005, p. 68) that presents the nation's founding as a sort of pageant of ethnicities. One of its authors, Dr. James A. Banks, one of the best-known authorities on, and proponents of, multiculturalism in education, encourages teachers to present history from the perspectives of many groups. In teaching about America's westward expansion, for example, the instructor might ask students their meaning of the word *West* and then note that for the Lakota Sioux, it had a different meaning. It wasn't *West*; it was the center of their universe, their home (Boyer, 2005, p. 68).

This same text became an object of criticism for a Christian teacher in California who opposed the authors' choice to annotate the Declaration of Independence for 10- and 11-year-olds and omit all references to "nature of God," "Creator," and "Divine Providence." While it might be easy to argue that the Declaration should not be a tool for promoting beliefs in religion, it is of great concern to this author when the historical role played by religion, in fact, Christianity, in the founding of this country is ignored. To recognize the role played by religion in early American history is certainly as important as teaching students the reasons why Thomas Jefferson favored maintaining a wall of separation between church and state. It may be that the authors were trying to be *politically correct* when they decided to omit these terms—that is, trying to follow a policy of not saying anything that might offend someone. But distinctions need to be made between terms that would, indeed, be considered intolerant of differences or hurtful and humiliating to someone and those that reflect historical realities. Teachers need to recognize the potential that political correctness has for threatening open discussion and debate on issues related to diversity.

Culturally responsive teaching need not stifle expression or questions that can lead to growth of knowledge about race, gender, religion, ethnicity, ability and language. Listening to the views of others—even when we don't agree with them—is a characteristic of tolerance.

Traditionalists versus Multiculturalists

Finally, there is the long-term debate between the traditionalists and multiculturalists. Traditionalists believe that the canon—the classics that reflect Western scholarly traditions—should remain the core of liberal arts education. Multiculturalists, on the other hand, believe that as American society becomes more racially, ethnically, and culturally diverse, a place needs to be made for multiculturalism or "divercentricity," the practice of exposing students to diverse but significant works of literature and authors, inclusive of many perspectives (Tembo, 1993, p. 55).

Rather than being an either–or situation, students need a pluralistic approach with exposure to *all* forms of knowledge without exclusive emphasis on any one. More traditional theorists like Diane Ravitch express concern that multiculturalists don't pay enough attention to commonly held American values (Ravitch, 1990). The fact is that the literature cited in Gay's monograph (noted earlier in the chapter) reflects strong support for a balanced, dualistic approach to culturally responsive teaching. By advocating *cultural pluralism*, this approach recognizes the unique cultures within the larger society and, at the same time, values the common elements binding the society together.

Ravitch is correct in warning the advocates of multiculturalism about the dangers of stereotyping members of a particular culture without consideration of each one's individuality. She is also correct in pointing out that *all* children need excellent teachers and safe environments. And she is especially right when she states that students need to be aware of how cultures influence one another. They do not exist in isolation but instead "grow and change by learning from others" (Ravitch, 1990, p. 48), what Appiah refers to—not pejoratively—as "contamination" (Appiah, 2006, p. 37).

Culturally responsive teaching should help students begin to see the interconnected nature of knowledge and that all sources may contain shortcomings, biases, and excesses in their delivery of information. With this in mind, perhaps the best advice to teachers is to help your students become healthy skeptics who ask questions and do extensive research before believing what they hear and read.

It is quite clear that for all the groups referred to earlier—teachers, theorists, legislators and interest groups—who are at odds about the content and meaning of culturally responsive teaching, there is still much work to be done in trying to reach some consensus.

Reflective question: Where do you stand on the issues that comprise the debate about teaching multicultural education?

FIVE The Role of White Power and Privilege

Understanding the role that white power and privilege has played in educating diverse students is an issue that teacher educators have been addressing more frequently (Teach for America, 2004). However, the majority of teachers in the public schools are still white, and many, if not most, have spent little time exploring racial oppression or the other consequences for their minority students of white power and skin color privilege. Some first steps for teachers to take in addressing such issues include

- Recognizing their own frames of reference and the language they use to express issues related to race.
- Confronting the subjective nature of the record of Western history.
- Acknowledging the pervasiveness of racism throughout that history.
- Identifying the educational effects of such prejudice on historically oppressed groups.

One educator, Jane Bolgatz (2005), was concerned about ways that teachers could carry the discussion of race and racism further to include issues of power and privilege. She observed a team-taught class in U.S. history and language arts and concluded that the major variables for successfully putting these issues on the table were teacher willingness to examine their own positions, modeling reflection for their students, and taking risks by opening the door to multiple conversations about race and racism. The teachers she observed were open to the students' thinking and maintained an atmosphere of respect while incorporating interdisciplinary materials that dealt explicitly with race and racism, including a poem by Lorna De Cervantes, "Poem for the Young White Man Who Asked Me How I, an Intelligent, Well-Read Person, Could Believe in the War between Races" (in Bolgatz, 2005, p. 32). Dialogue of this kind indicates to students that these topics are worthy of their attention and can play a role in helping teachers bridge the gap between discussing race and confronting issues of white power and privilege.

"Unpacking privilege" is a metaphor used to describe the process of becoming aware of how society confers status to certain groups based on their identity and how those advantages shape our experiences, attitudes, and actions. Such privileges may be conferred on the dominant or mainstream majority because they are white, or male, or affluent, straight, able-bodied, Christian, or speakers of English. The phrase "unpacking privilege" was popularized in part by Peggy McIntosh at the Wellesley College Center for Research on Women (McIntosh, 1988). She defines *white privilege* as "an invisible package of unearned assets that I can count on cashing in each day, but about which I was 'meant' to remain oblivious. White privilege is like an invisible weightless knapsack of special provisions" (McIntosh, 1988). McIntosh's work can stimulate the kind of self-examination that can lead to an awareness of the origins of power and its effects on lives both within and outside of schools.

Reflective question: What is *your* view about the role white privilege (and power) has played in your education as well as the education of diverse students?

SIX Mandates Issued for Development of Diversity-Related Curricula

Several state departments of education, as well as a number of professional organizations and various researchers, have issued mandates—or strong support—for the development of diversity-related curricula. The certification standards related to diversity that state departments of education have issued share similarities. For example, the Maine *Initial Teacher Certification Standards* (Maine Department of Education, 2003), summarized below, reflect those issued by other state departments of education as well as professional organizations (see Table 2.1). Future teachers therefore need to learn effective ways of applying these standards so as to bring about awareness of diversity. The strategies in this primer can help preservice and in-service teachers meet these standards as well as the goals established by professional content-based organizations (see Table 2.2 on p. 21).

Summary of the Maine *Initial Teacher Certification Standards* (2003)

Like most state teacher certification standards, Maine's standards require teachers to "promote equity" and "demonstrate an awareness of and commitment to ethical and legal responsibilities of a teacher" (Maine Department of Education, 2003). Section 9 of the Maine standards calls for teachers to "interact with all students in an equitable manner" and not discriminate on account of "race, color, sex, physical or mental disability, religion, ancestry or national origin." Section 9 also requires that the candidate "understand how beliefs, values, traditions and requirements of various religious groups interact with school." Mentioned twice is the requirement that the teacher "treat others with respect and honor the dignity of all people" (2003).

Reflective question: What are some of the similarities and differences among the mandates listed in Tables 2.1 and 2.2 for developing diversity-related curricula?

Table 2.1   Three Professional Organizations That Play a Role in Establishing Diversity Standards

Organization	Position on Diversity
NCATE (National Council for the Accreditation of Teacher Education)	Establishes professional standards for the accreditation of schools, colleges, and departments of education. One of the standards is "developing a classroom and school climate that values diversity" (NCATE, 2005, p. 29), learning multicultural content that nurtures respect toward students and colleagues from diverse backgrounds, and commitment to equal educational opportunity.
NAE (National Academy of Education)	Based at New York University in New York City, NAE issued a book in February 2005, *Preparing Teachers for a Changing World,* which stated that there should be material preparing preservice teachers to teach students of different cultural and linguistic backgrounds and to connect those diverse learners to the subjects being taught (Jacobson, 2005, p. 10). "For this connection to occur, teachers must know their students—who they are, what they care about, what languages they speak, what customs and traditions are valued in their homes," the book says. "Opportunities to learn about diversity should not be isolated to a course or two," it adds, "but spread throughout the curriculum" (Jacobson, 2005, p. 10).
NAME (National Association of Multicultural Education)	Disseminates materials related to diversity so that teachers can help their students raise their achievement levels, their self-concept, and their desire to cooperate with others. Through its conferences for teachers and its journal, *Multicultural Perspectives,* NAME shares current research and pedagogy related to culturally responsive teaching. Their areas of concern range from research on "Black Students, White Teachers" to "Making Theater for Social Justice" (NAME, 2005) to issues related to gender, disability, and religious tolerance.

SEVEN   The No Child Left Behind Act

All of the nation's schools are evaluated annually under the provisions of the Elementary and Secondary Education Act (ESEA). Revised in 2001 when it became popularly known as the "No Child Left Behind Act" (NCLB), it continues to be a source of controversy.

Below are questions frequently asked about NCLB and answers to those questions. Along with an explanation of its intent are reasons why NCLB has been an object of constant debate and, in some cases, a "burgeoning rebellion" (Garan, 2005, p. 38). During the past few years, it should be noted, there has been an overwhelming proliferation of articles about the controversy. Words of praise and protest appear on a daily basis in both education-related news sources such as *Education Week* (www.edweek.org) as well as prominent newspapers including the *New York Times* (www.nytimes.org). One of the greatest concerns among teachers regarding NCLB is the belief that its emphasis on testing makes culturally responsive teaching and community building more difficult. That concern, in fact, was a primary springboard for this book—to help make culturally responsive teaching *less* difficult in light of the challenges posed by the NCLB Act.

What Is the No Child Left Behind Act?

The NCLB Act is the 2001 revision of the Elementary and Secondary Education Act and was passed with the intent of holding schools accountable for overall student achievement. Few have argued with its overarching goals of providing children with a quality education

Table 2.2   Diversity Standards of Professional Organizations That Represent the Major Disciplines

Organization	Beliefs/Standards Related to Diversity
NSTA (National Science Teachers' Association)	Expresses in its standards (2003) the beliefs that science teachers should construct curriculum that demonstrates provisions for and awareness of student differences and should use a variety of ways for delivering instruction and that culturally responsive teaching can help science come alive for students, especially those who have traditionally resisted this field. NSTA's Standard 7 (Science in the Community) specifies that examples and "investigations based on students' personal experiences and on cultural contexts promote curiosity and help students build a personally meaningful framework for science" (Atwater, 1994). The association advises teachers about what to do when values of the community, often religious values, directly conflict with tenets of science; they advise that teachers study the composition of the community and the beliefs held by its members. It notes that teachers should not feel forced to compromise the values and ethics of what they teach, but rather should find ways to accommodate these deeply held beliefs, for example, by examining the role of belief in all human thought (Atwater, 1994).
NCTM (National Council of Teachers of Mathematics)	In their standards NCTM states as the first goal: "Learning to Value Mathematics: Students should have numerous and varied experiences related to the cultural, historical evolution of mathematics" (NCTM, 2000). An example of such an experience would be learning about the lunar and solar calendar of the Anasazi, the highly developed numeration system of the Mayans, and the numerical codes of the Inca quipu.
NCTE (National Council of Teachers of English)	In its *Standards for the English Language Arts* (2005), NCTE recommends that students read a wide range of print and nonprint texts to build an understanding about themselves and of the cultures of the United States and the world. Other culturally responsive standards include developing "an understanding of and respect for diversity in language use and dialects across cultures, ethnic groups, geographic regions and social roles" (NCTE, 2005). In terms of students whose first language is not English, "make use of their first language to build competency in the English language arts and to develop understanding of content-related curriculum."
NCSS (National Council for the Social Studies)	In its *National Standards for Social Studies Teachers* (1999), NCSS (www.ncss.org, www.ncate.org) lists 20 standards. The first 10 are referred to as "thematic standards," the first being "Culture and Cultural Diversity," the ninth, "Global Connections" (NCSS, 1999). One of the standards for all grade levels involves teachers being able to give "examples and describe the importance of cultural unity and diversity within and across groups" (NCSS, 1999) by assisting learners in acquiring knowledge of "the values of the many people who have contributed to the development of the continent of North America," and "knowledge of the history and values of diverse civilizations."

Note: The standards established by the professional organizations representing the major disciplines are tied to the objectives of the lessons and strategies included in Chapters 3–7.

and closing existing achievement gaps in part through the promised additional funding for poor schools.

Under the act, all students in grades 3 through 8 and in one grade in high school must be tested once a year in reading and mathematics. Students are expected to score at the "proficient" level or above on state-administered math and English tests by 2014 and to make "adequate yearly progress" (AYP) toward that goal until then. And the federal government requires that all students, including subgroups such as students with special needs, improve by that margin (AYP) every year.

Because the goal of the law is to close the achievement gap between African American and Hispanic students and their white peers, the mandate includes breaking down performance data for these groups as well as for special needs students and English language learners, all of whom must meet AYP standards. A school that fails to make AYP for two consecutive years is labeled "in need of improvement." Districts and schools characterized as such have two years to improve their scores with help and money from the state. If they fail to improve after two years, the sanctioned schools must give parents the choice of sending their children to another school in the district, with transportation costs paid out of Title I federal dollars, which are funds allocated to schools serving a requisite number of low-income students. After five years, a school faces "corrective action." After seven years, a school must be "restructured," with options including state takeover, conversion to a charter school, management by a private company, or other unspecified major restructuring (Barrett, 2005, p. 14). The law was scheduled to be debated and reauthorized in 2007, but as of 2009, has yet to be reauthorized. President Obama has made reauthorization a priority.

(For a complete list of the provisions of the Act see the website www.nclb.gov.)

Why Is NCLB a Source of Controversy?

Criticism of the NCLB Act abounds (Barrett, 2005; Brooks and Thompson, 2005; Brown, 2005; Garan, 2005; Keller, November 2005; Olson, 2005; Samuels, 2005; Zehr, June 2005). A report issued by the National Conference of State Legislators (NCSL) in February 2005 contains a summary of the more typical complaints (Hoff, 2005, pp. 1, 20) and areas of concern. The NCSL leaders urged Congress and the U.S. Department of Education to give states broader authority to define student-achievement goals and more latitude in devising strategies to help students reach those goals, especially special education students for whom, the report says, states should be allowed to set separate AYP goals (Hoff, 2005, pp. 1, 20). NCSL also wants states to be able to determine "when to require students with limited English proficiency to be tested in English" (Hoff, 2005, p. 20). Finally they seek a doubling of current funding levels for Title I programs under the law.

A major criticism from education circles is that the act establishes standardized testing as the major means of evaluating schools when these tests don't reflect what students have been taught but rather what they bring to school. In other words, these tests only yield the socioeconomic status (SES) "score" of a school's students (Popham, 2005, p. 40). That's why there is frequently such a strong relationship between a school's standardized test scores and the economic and social makeup of the school's student body.

Another cause for complaint has been expressed by Reg Weaver, president of the National Education Association (NEA), the nation's largest teacher's union, who said that the federal government was breaking the law by demanding changes in schools without fully funding the NCLB Act (Keller, July 2005, p. 16).

In May 2005, Utah became the first state to openly and completely opt out of the NCLB in favor of the state's own standards, resulting in a potential loss of $76,000,000 in federal funding (Brown, 2005, p. 44). Connecticut filed a lawsuit against the federal government, arguing that the NCLB is an unfunded mandate. "As state attorney general Richard Blumenthal put it, 'This mindless rigidity harms our taxpayers, but most of all our children'" (Brown, 2005, p. 43).

The most common state response to NCLB has been the request for a waiver, a plea for some rule bending. Forty states have requested leniency on almost every aspect of the mandates, including levels of teacher qualifications, timing of tests, determination of pass levels for different groups of students, and tutoring requirements. Former Secretary of Education Margaret Spellings addressed some of these criticisms by allowing some flexibility in the testing of special education students (Samuels, 2005, p. 22), as well as in some other areas, such as the date for states to meet requirements for highly qualified teachers and an allowance for delaying sanctions to schools directly affected by Hurricane Katrina. In 2004 former Education Secretary Rod Paige had consented to some flexibility in "the testing of English language learners and students with special needs" (Keller, November 2005, p. 18).

A report was issued in 2005 by a national group of legal, political, education, and civil rights advocates to spur discussion of the value of racial and ethnic diversity in schools. Entitled *With All Deliberate Speed—Achievement, Citizenship and Diversity in American Education,* the report urged that the reauthorization of the No Child Left Behind Act "take into account the benefits of diversity," which it deemed to be as important as increasing academic achievement. The paper also suggested that for teachers to be considered highly qualified under the federal law, they should be required to have cultural diversity training (Reid, 2005, p. 5). These recommendations certainly appear to be in line with the original intent of the law—to educate *all* children. However, the debate will likely continue as to how best to achieve this worthy goal, and whether or not the potential costs of the law—in terms of money, students' self-esteem, and the possible loss of quality-of-life curricula—will diminish even further the support for this law in the future.

Reflective question: How can the three potential costs of the NCLB Act just mentioned be ameliorated so as to allow this act to simultaneously promote diversity while also promoting academic achievement?

Principles and Applications for
Becoming a Culturally Responsive Teacher

Principle ONE

Culturally responsive teachers model certain behaviors, many of which can be replicated by their students.

Teachers who are culturally responsive

- Use materials and curricula that reflect the students' backgrounds and their needs and interests.
- Display images that might be familiar to students.
- Maintain caring relationships reflecting their understanding of the child's difficulties while not condoning bad behavior.
- View each child as someone who can teach others by bringing their own stories and experiences to the class.
- Provide equal opportunities for all students to fulfill their potential regardless of race, religion, ethnicity, gender, class, and abilities.
- Avoid stereotypes and help students recognize that members of the same group frequently differ in many ways.
- Encourage respect for differences.
- Avoid making assumptions about groups of people and the origins of their cultural characteristics and practices.
- View children not as victims but as unique individuals worthy of respect.
- Help students identify how they are different and alike in terms of their past and present experiences and identities.

- Converse with minority parents and other representatives of cultural groups about how they would like to see their concerns discussed and taught in the schools.
- Teach their students about prejudice and intolerance by discussing their meaning and consequences and how they affect *all* people, not only the victims but those *with* the prejudices as well.
- Go beyond teaching historical content and respect for difference by *modeling* such attitudes in their classrooms.
- Show students ways they can actively work to bring about social justice and equal opportunity for everyone within their school and community.
- Encourage students to keep an open mind, to question, to seek the truth.
- Support cultural pluralism, the idea that people can maintain the unique characteristics of their native culture, or microculture, while at the same time adapting to the common practices and values of the United States, the macroculture (see Figure 2.1).

Culturally responsive teaching can bring about many positive results, including

- Strengthening students' self-concept and reducing behavior problems (for example, by not misinterpreting cultural difference for misbehavior as in the case of a white teacher expecting a Latino student to look him or her in the eye, when the fact may be that the Hispanic student has been taught that this is a sign of disrespect).
- Building a stronger connection among students, parents, and the schools, especially after studies have shown the many benefits of parental involvement, including reduced absenteeism and greater academic motivation (Henderson and Berla, 1994; Jordan, Orozco, and Averett, 2001).
- Increasing the academic success of ethnically diverse students—for example, when the class contributions of diverse students are valued and recognized by teachers, student learning increases (Brooks and Thompson, 2005).

Figure 2.1   A Cartoon Showing Unity within Diversity

Source: Auth, T. (December 23, 2004). "A Christmas Carol." © 2004 The Philadelphia Inquirer. Reprinted by permission of Universal Press Syndicate. All rights reserved.

Principle TWO

 Some minority students may be reluctant to succeed academically. Teachers, without making assumptions, should investigate possible reasons for this behavior so they can help the student overcome any reluctance.

One reason some minority teenagers may be reluctant to do well in school could be related to their fear of losing popularity among their peers for "acting white" (Viadero, 2005, p. 14). The "acting white," or "cultural opposition" theory, emerged in the 1980s, when sociologists coined the term to describe how African American students in a District of Columbia high school dismissed achievement-oriented behavior as "acting white." A Harvard University economist, Roland Fryer, offered evidence to bolster this theory in his study, "An Empirical Analysis of 'Acting White.'" Fryer, himself an African American, shows that this phenomenon is indeed a problem, although *not* for students in all-black schools or among high-achieving minority students at private schools who remained as popular as other minority students with lower grades. It was, however, true for minority students, including Hispanic students, who attended integrated public schools (Tierney, 2005).

Fryer noted that it may be a class problem more than a race issue, since the phenomenon arises when a group comes into contact with another group whose members have historically been high achievers. In an integrated school, when members of a group that has been fundamentally disadvantaged get good grades, it can be a signal that they're being disloyal by joining the other group. "As a result," says Fryer, "minority students face a cruel choice" at precisely the kinds of suburban schools that are supposed to be eliminating minority disadvantages, causing some African American and Latino students to not reach their full potential (qtd. in Tierney, 2005).

There is criticism of the study by some scholars who have tested the "acting white" idea. For example, James Ainsworth, an associate professor of sociology at Georgia State University, believes that the theory blames the victim and takes attention away from the real issue, the structural inequalities in education for African American and white students (Viadero, 2005, p. 14). Others argue that Fryer's work distracts attention from the many other socioeconomic causes of the achievement gap that separates African American and Latino students from higher-achieving students.

A constructive response to this situation might include programs that convey to minority children the idea that academic achievement is not synonymous with trying to "act white," but rather clearly show their possibilities for achievement with hard work, effort, and practice. Moreover, with the election of Barack Obama in 2008, the idea that being bookish means you're "acting white" may have finally been put to rest. Interestingly, in his speech at the Democratic Convention in 2004, Obama challenged the myth that holding a book is "acting white" (McWhorter, 2008, p. 16).

Another reason that may account for a student's reluctance to succeed academically may have to do with how the curriculum is presented. By now, most teachers have heard about and perhaps read Howard Gardner's work on *multiple intelligences* (Gardner, 1983). The value of his identification of the inherent differences in children's strengths and learning styles is that it emphasizes the need for teachers to learn about the abilities and aptitudes of each of their students beyond their verbal and mathematical paper-and-pencil skills. Recognizing the talents of each student outside of these more typical aptitudes enables the teacher to reach all students by tapping into their unique strengths, which can then become the vehicle for expanding their knowledge in the more traditional areas most often measured by standardized tests.

The sometimes controversial work of Ruby Payne may help teachers identify possible reasons for a student's reluctance to achieve in school. She explains the hidden rules of students who come from what she calls "generational poverty." These rules are completely different from the hidden rules of the middle class that govern most schools (Payne, 1996).

Payne defines generational poverty as being in poverty for two generations or longer. She insists that teachers need to understand the hidden rules of students from poverty and then teach them the rules that will make them successful at school and at work. "We can neither excuse them nor scold them for not knowing," she writes. "As educators, we must teach them and provide support, assistance, and high expectations" (Payne, 1996).

For example, some of those hidden rules, according to Payne, can be seen in the differences in students' response to discipline. Students of generational poverty may laugh when disciplined because it is a way to save face, whereas among the middle class, a reprimand is usually taken seriously (at least the pretense is there), without smiling, and with some deference to authority.

By understanding the hidden rules of generational poverty and being able to teach the hidden rules of the middle class, teachers can help enable students from poverty to choose appropriate responses if they so desire and thus be able to demonstrate that they are no less capable or intelligent than their middle class peers (Payne, 1996).

The work of Fryer, Gardner, and Payne show that there can be a variety of causes for academic failure. Teachers need to carefully investigate reasons that can explain a student's reluctance to succeed before assuming that the student lacks interest or intelligence.

Principle THREE

 Students preparing to become culturally responsive teachers should be aware of a number of brick walls—or barriers—they may face on their path to appreciating diversity.

These "brick walls" refer to preconceptions in teachers' minds that close them off from new ideas on diversity, such as those expressed by Rahima Wade's teacher education students at the University of Iowa (1998), most of whom were white. Her intent was to help them confront their own attitudes towards diversity before going into the classroom. (Which of the "walls" in the following list do *you* identify with and why? What are some ways to knock down these walls? Are there other barriers that you personally will need to address?)

1. "I don't have any prejudices" (Wade, 1998, p. 85). Many of Wade's white teacher education students were adamant that they held no prejudices and would treat all children equally, thus not needing to explore their views on working with diverse populations.

2. "My attitudes won't affect my students" (p. 85). Even those students who recognized their own prejudices insisted that they would not let these attitudes interfere with their teaching. Wade asserts that most of them were not yet aware of how words, body language, choice of curricular materials, and so many other aspects of their teaching are a direct reflection of their beliefs and attitudes. "They also do not yet understand the power that teachers have to affect the self-esteem and learning potential of their students."

3. "I'm not going to teach 'those' students" (p. 85). The students who said this were planning to teach in areas where there were few if any students of color, but, notes Wade, these preservice teachers still needed to learn the importance of multicultural education for students of all ethnic and cultural backgrounds and to address the sociocultural factors influencing both their teaching behaviors *and* students' learning styles.

4. "All I have to do is teach about countries and cultures" (p. 85). Wade notes that few of her students have ever considered lessons on prejudice, discrimination, power, racism, or social action.

5. "Life is fine—we don't need to change anything" (p. 85). Wade notes that many white teacher education students grew up in supportive rural or suburban communities with good schools. They may be unaware of the importance of working for social justice and the common good.

Strategies and Lessons for
Preparing to Become a Culturally Responsive Teacher

The lessons and strategies in this section have been designed to help you *examine your own attitudes* about, and experiences with, diversity. The assumption here is that those teachers who confront their attitudes and values are better able to help their students gain insight about themselves and others.

As you carry out these activities, including the cultural immersion experience (Lesson 4) and the inventory on personal experiences with prejudice (Lesson 2), you will notice that the objectives of culturally responsive teaching go beyond simply helping your students accept and appreciate diversity to include building community both within the school and beyond, based on mutual respect, justice, and truth.

These lessons can also help you knock down the "brick walls" and avoid the misconceptions that so often hinder the implementation of culturally responsive teaching. All of the lessons will help enable you to apply the three principles previously presented.

And one more thing. Before you embark on this journey, sit down and think really hard about just one incident that hurt you or someone else, when you or they were on the receiving end of a discriminatory act, when someone laughed at you or someone else for being different in some way, or, on the other hand, when you acted in a way you'd rather forget. Then carry out all or some of the following activities, alone or with your peers, with the goal of seeing beyond your comfort level, beyond *your* frame of reference.

Lesson 1: Cultural Autobiography and Identity Collage

For teachers preparing to implement culturally responsive practice, one of the most useful first steps is to explore your own cultural influences and connections. The truth is that in order to be an effective teacher in *any* context, it is helpful to look within and reflect on how your cultural identity (or identities) and attitudes may indirectly affect what and how you teach. Those unintended influences on your teaching—often referred to as "the hidden curriculum"—can enhance, but also interfere with, the quality of your teaching and your students' learning.

The strategy below provides a way for you to examine your cultural influences, experiences, and values. You may choose to do one or both of the activities that comprise Lesson 1.

Objectives

You will be able to

1. Reflect on your identity, experiences and values as they relate to diversity.
2. Explain the insights you gained as a result of completing a written "cultural autobiography" and "identity collage."
3. Recognize the ways that your identity might be influencing the content and method of your teaching.

Materials

- Photos (from magazines or newspapers, Internet images, or personal photos)
- (Optional) Artifacts from your life or original sketches

Procedures

1. Reflect on how writing a cultural autobiography can lead to discovering ideas and sensitivities that can be useful to you as you embark on culturally responsive teaching (or any kind of teaching, for that matter).

2. Write a cultural autobiography that includes descriptions of and references to your identity in terms of

   - Your race, religion, ethnicity, abilities, gender, and class, as well as your educational and neighborhood environments.
   - How all of these factors have affected who you are, what you believe, and how you act.
   - Two memorable experiences in which you came into contact with others different from yourself.
   - Prejudices you think you may have, the origins of those views, how you have expressed them, and whether you have changed them (or not).
   - Any other ideas that may seem applicable.

3. (Optional) Peruse magazines in class and notice pictures that reflect aspects of your identity. Then for sharing with peers, create an identity collage that reflects your identity in terms of the characteristics you mentioned in your cultural autobiography. (A variation might involve doing a collage that reflects your response to the content of Chapter 1.) You may do original sketches or use photos from newspapers, magazines, the Internet, or from your own personal photo albums (which can be copied if you don't want to use the originals). You can even attach small personal artifacts.

4. During the next class (for preservice teachers) you may be able to share your cultural autobiographies and collages informally in a round table discussion during which you compare and contrast your responses to the four topics (in item 2 above). As part of that sharing experience you may also discuss

   - Incidents you have experienced (or seen) in school in which you (or others) had a teacher who did or did not behave in a way indicating that they had examined their beliefs and values as they related to diversity.
   - How you believe this activity has helped or will help you prepare to become a culturally responsive teacher.

Assessment

(Self-assessment or assessment by peers or instructor)

- The cultural autobiography and the degree to which the criteria were met
- The identity collage
- Contribution to class discussion

Extension

1. You may expand your knowledge about your identity by beginning genealogical searches for your cultural roots. You might begin by trying to find answers to the following questions:

   - When did your ancestors first come to America? (John F. Kennedy is often quoted as saying, "We all got off a boat," though in more recent times it is more likely to have been a plane.)
   - Where did your ancestors come from?
   - Where did they settle and what did they do? You might begin this research by interviewing your oldest living relative, which this author did several years ago, learning numerous details related to ancestral history.

2. One way of sharing your cultural autobiography is by doing a Globe Toss. Find a plastic balloon with a map of the globe imprinted on it. In class, toss the balloon to someone. After catching it, the person states his or her name and expresses some details about personal cultural identity or, if known, points to his or her ancestors' country of origin on the globe. This person then tosses the balloon to someone else, and so on, until everyone has held the "ball." The original balloon tosser can be either the first or last to share this information.

Lesson 2: Inventory: Personal Experiences with Prejudice

Teachers who confront their prejudices are less likely to bring them into the classroom. The inventory in Figure 2.2 comprises several questions that will help you examine your attitudes and experiences regarding prejudice and how they may have influenced your views about diversity-related issues.

Note: This author distributes the inventory to students, asking them to respond to the questions and telling them that they can remain anonymous. She then collects the questionnaires and collates their answers so she can report back to them during the next class on the percentage of students who responded in a certain way to each question—for example, "About 90 percent of you said you had heard a prejudiced remark in your home." She encourages students to express their views as she shares her findings. What usually happens during the ensuing discussion is that many students feel comfortable enough to say, "That's my answer, and this is what I experienced."

Objectives

You will be able to

1. Examine your attitudes related to diversity-related issues.
2. Reflect on experiences you have had with prejudice and how these may have influenced your attitudes about diversity.
3. (Optional) Compare and contrast your attitudes with those of your peers.
4. Reflect on the significance of this inventory as it relates to your position as a teacher.

Materials

- The inventory in Figure 2.2

Procedures

1. Read the preceding introductory remarks so you understand the purpose of the inventory.
2. Answer all (or a selected portion) of the questions in Figure 2.2 on a separate piece of paper.
3. (Optional) Share your responses with your peers and, if possible, try to determine why answers were similar or different. Together assess how knowledge gained from the discussion might be useful to you.

Assessment

- Completion of the inventory
- Participation in follow-up discussion

Figure 2.2   Inventory: Experiences with Prejudice

Please respond to each question and provide brief explanations where appropriate.

1. Have you ever been on the receiving end of a prejudiced remark or act? If so, describe the situation and how you felt. What was your response, if any?
2. Have you ever heard a culturally insensitive remark or witnessed firsthand an act of prejudice

   - Within your family?
   - In your school?
   - In the community?
   - In the media?
   - Somewhere else?

   If so, please describe these incidents. If not, have you heard about such remarks or behavior? What, if any, was your reaction to these situations?
3. Have you ever expressed a prejudiced remark or acted in a discriminatory manner against an innocent person or group? If so, please identify the circumstances.
4. Have you ever been in a situation where you were in the minority? If so, please describe what happened and how you felt.
5. What would you do if a friend told you a racist joke? Why?
6. Do you think most people carry some form of prejudice toward other cultures (even if they won't admit it)?
7. Would you ever date a person who was different from you in race, religion, ethnicity, or ability?
8. Should race ever be a factor in hiring or college admissions in an attempt to correct past discrimination?
9. a. Have you ever taken a course in which you learned about the nature of prejudice or about historical examples of prejudice related to race, religion, ethnicity, gender, class, or ability? Please explain.
   b. Have you ever taught lessons on any historical examples of prejudice? If so, describe very briefly.
10. Please agree or disagree with the following statements and include brief comments after each one:

    - I feel more comfortable with people of my own race.
    - Television shows are full of racial stereotypes.
    - Students are not really honest when they talk about race and diversity.
    - Prejudices will always exist.
    - Students of all races are, in general, treated equally in my school.

11. a. Are there any organizations in your school or community that are working on ways to reduce prejudice and cultural insensitivity? If so, can you identify them and briefly describe their efforts?
    b. Would you consider joining such a group? Why or why not?
12. Do you want to express any other comments related to the concept of prejudice?

Lesson 3: Defining Culture

Culture means many things. It can refer to a particular field such as literature, music, art, and related areas, or to a group's history, institutions, artifacts, values, and behaviors. It can also be defined as a group's way of thinking, feeling, and believing, or that which constitutes the pooled learning of a group (Kluckhohn, 1959, p. 25). Ruth Benedict, noted anthropologist, said simply, "Culture is that which binds men [people] together" (qtd. in Kluckhohn, 1959, p. 27). (See also the definition for culture in Chapter 1.)

Because cultures and ethnic groups are usually *ethnocentric*, that is, centered on their own ways of being and seeing the world, with a belief in their inherent superiority over others, it is important to learn about *others'* cultures and ways of seeing, as difficult as that might be.

The following exercise can help you confront the challenges posed by trying to go beyond cultural frames of reference to discover others' cultural values and behaviors, a crucial step in becoming a culturally responsive teacher. (This exercise is most successful if completed with your peers.)

Objectives

You will be able to

1. Define the basic attributes of culture.
2. Apply those basic attributes to specific examples of cultural behaviors.
3. Evaluate the importance of trying to overcome the challenges posed by learning about cultures different from your own.

Materials

- Blackboard or chart paper

Procedures

1. Begin your discussion of culture by asking each person to describe two beliefs that people in the United States generally hold in common. (Or two common American cultural behaviors.) Share answers and try to reach a consensus; offer a basis for your responses.
2. Place on the board some attributes of culture—for example, it is learned; it is shared by a group of people within a common geographical or social context; it is necessary for people to know certain values and behaviors if they want to fit in with the cultural group. Then discuss whether the beliefs you and your peers identified in step 1 fit the attributes you indicated in step 2. Next discuss some of the following questions that may help you to consider certain cultural norms within the United States:

   - How important is getting an education?
   - What professions are most respected?
   - How do people greet one another?
   - What are the ways young people show respect to elders?

   Now discuss the ways these norms differ in some other cultures with which you might be familiar.
3. After you complete steps 1 and 2, reflect on some of the difficulties that were involved in reaching a consensus on the values and behaviors that typify American culture. Then think about how much greater is the challenge of learning about *another* cultural group within this country or other countries.
4. Now reflect on how this exercise relates to defining culture. Review the meanings of culture and relate them to examples of American cultural values and behaviors. Then consider why learning about different cultures can often be challenging but worth pursuing.

Assessment

- Your participation in the exercise and contributions to discussion
- (Optional) Written paper responding to the data in step 4 above.

Extension

Do research on the origins of some of the cultural values and behaviors in the United States.

Lesson 4: Cultural Immersion Experience

Below are several suggestions for carrying out a cultural immersion experience, an activity that logically follows Lesson 3, in which you learned the definition of the concept of culture and how difficult it can be to grasp all aspects of a culture. This activity will give you the chance to observe carefully and gather information about a culture with which you are not familiar.

Objectives

You will be able to

1. Immerse yourself in a cultural environment with which you are not familiar, doing so for a minimum of two hours.
2. Observe the physical as well as less tangible characteristics and interactions within that environment.
3. Compare and contrast the culture in which you are immersing yourself with your own cultural zones.
4. Gain insights about the culture in which you are briefly immersed and what it feels like to walk in the shoes of members of that culture, or at least to come close to doing so.
5. Describe the experience in detail (perhaps also sketching or photographing aspects of the experience).
6. Evaluate in writing the cultural immersion experience in terms of its professional as well as personal value to you (or as a student learning about other cultures).

Materials

- (Optional) A list of suggested places in which you can carry out the cultural immersion experience (see step 3 below)

Procedures

1. Reflect on—or begin discussing with peers—this question: Have you ever been placed in an environment different from those in which you normally work, play, live, or carry on regular activities? If so, describe those experiences briefly.
2. Read the objectives of this strategy.
3. Identify a microculture (a culture within the larger culture of America) with which you are not familiar or with whom you have not spent much time. Consider the following immersion options, and after choosing *one* of them (or another not listed), carry out the objectives listed above:
   - Spend a day at a school that is very different from the one in which you teach or which you have attended.
   - Sit in a house of worship in which the religion and congregation are unfamiliar to you (e.g., Hindu temple, synagogue, mosque).

- Attend a wedding or funeral in which the ceremony, dress, or other customs differ from those practiced in your culture.
- Participate in a holiday meal connected to a religion different from your own (e.g., Passover seder, Native American feast).
- Sit in or assist in a kitchen of an ethnic restaurant. Interview the cooks if possible and ask about the foods and how they connect to their culture.
- Sit in on a foreign language class or English as a second language class.
- Walk around and talk with people in an unfamiliar neighborhood; observe the signs, the kinds of stores, and other public places; listen to the languages being spoken and note other parts of the environment. For example, notice objects in the windows of stores that may display certain kinds of food (e.g., sushi or salami).
- Attend a cultural festival in your area.
- Spend time in a museum that houses exhibits depicting other cultures.
- Visit a workplace (e.g., factory where there are workers from another culture).

Assessment

- A written description and evaluation of your cultural immersion experience
- A discussion with peers during which you share your cultural immersion experiences

---

Lesson 5: Learning about Culturally Responsive Teaching from Film

Watching films about teachers in culturally diverse classrooms and films related to diversity is an excellent way to learn about culturally responsive teaching. Several such films are described in Tables 2.3 and 2.4; all are likely to be available from local video stores or on the Internet. (*Note:* You may also try to locate culturally diverse schools in your area—perhaps you're even teaching in one—and observe your colleagues' teaching strategies.)

Objectives

You will be able to

1. Watch one or more films related to diversity.
2. Write synopses of the films.
3. Evaluate the lessons the films can offer in terms of preparing you for culturally responsive teaching.

Materials

- The film(s) chosen for viewing (see Tables 2.3 and 2.4)

Procedures

1. Watch one (or more) of the films listed in the tables (outside of class or with peers in class).
2. Record in your journal responses to the following questions:
   - What did you learn about culturally responsive teaching from the film(s)?
   - Was the film effective in conveying some of the causes, conditions, and effects of prejudice? Explain.

Table 2.3 Films Depicting Teachers in Culturally Diverse Classrooms

Name of Film	Brief Summary of Film
Children of a Lesser God (1986)	James Leeds is a new speech teacher at a school for the deaf. He encounters Sarah, a former pupil who refuses to read his lips, only using signs.
Dangerous Minds (1995)	Based on a true story by Lou Anne Johnson who teaches in a Northern California high school in which she defies all the rules, creates her own curriculum, and helps a class of tough inner-city teenagers who are desperate to connect with someone who cares about them.
In and Out (1997)	This film focuses on a Midwestern teacher who questions his sexuality after a former student makes a comment about him at the Academy Awards. This romantic comedy touches on important issues of self-discovery and diversity as well as tolerance.
Mad Hot Ballroom (2005)	This documentary tells the story of students from several New York City elementary schools who learn ballroom dancing as well as the merengue, rumba, and tango and compete in a citywide dance competition. The film provides unique insights into the cultural diversity that is New York City. There are many lessons here for the beginning teacher.
Stand and Deliver (1988)	Based on the true story of math teacher Jaime Escalante, this film depicts his success with disadvantaged students at Garfield High School in East Los Angeles, where he built a calculus program rivaled by only the best private schools.
Up the Down Staircase (1967)	Sylvia Barrett is a rookie teacher in New York's inner-city Calvin Coolidge High School. Her classes are overcrowded, and she tries her best to address the needs of her often troubled students. By the end of this realistic film, it is clear that her methods and perseverance are finally paying off.
The Chorus (*Les Choristes*) (2004)	This French film (with subtitles) takes place in 1949 at the Fond De L'Etang School for difficult boys. Their new teacher seems to understand how to treat children with compassion, respect, and a gentleness that transforms their unruly behavior.
The Front of the Class (2008)	This film is based on the true story of Brad Cohen, who overcomes his disability—Tourette's Syndrome—to become an award-winning elementary teacher. There are many lessons to be learned from this film, including that it's okay to be different and that no matter your difference, you can fulfill your dreams and goals. (The film also shows Cohen teaching in a diverse classroom.)

- What teaching methods appeared to be successful?
- How might you use one of these films in your classroom? Explain.

3. (Optional) After you have viewed a film and recorded responses in your journal, carry on a large-group (or small-group) discussion. If you watch more than one film, you might write a paper in which you compare two or more of the films in terms of the given questions.

Assessment

- Your synopses of the films and responses to the questions given
- Participation in discussions about the film(s)
- (Optional) Paper comparing two or more films

Table 2.4   A Sample of Multicultural Films

Name of Film	Brief Summary of Film
The Color of Fear (1995, Stirfry Productions)	This documentary sits eight men down with each other to examine racism. It explores what it means to be white and what it means to be a person of color. It turns out that much of what the group talks about in the context of racism is actually fear.
The Joy Luck Club (1993)	Based on the bestseller by Amy Tan, the film is about the experiences of four women who emigrated from China to the United States and how these experiences affected their relationships with their American-born daughters.
Rize (Lion's Gate Films, 2005)	This is a dance documentary that reveals a phenomenon that has come out of the streets of South Central Los Angeles. Sometimes referred to as "clowning" or "krumping," the dance is an expression born from oppression. It is both aggressive and very fast moving and reflects moves indigenous to African tribal rituals, though it has gone beyond African American culture in that there is also an Asian troupe.
Eye of the Storm (1968)	This well-known documentary takes the viewer into teacher Jane Elliot's third-grade classroom in an elementary school in Iowa, as she carries out her "brown eyes–blue eyes" experiment to help her students understand what it feels like to be discriminated against.
Crash (2005)	This award-winning film provides an unflinching look at the complexities of racial conflict in America and challenges viewers to question their own prejudices. Set in diverse, post-9/11 Los Angeles, this film examines fear and intolerance from several perspectives.

Note: Teachers and students can learn from these films about diversity as well as the prejudices that continue to exist within the United States. Many other films are listed on the Multicultural Film and Movie Reviews website, www.edchange.org/multicultural/filmreviews.html

Lesson 6: The Face: Do You See What I See?*

What we see, hear, smell, taste, and feel may differ for each of us. Perception refers to our *interpretation* of sensory information. A dandelion may be a weed to you, but a flower to someone else. The categories "black" and "white" may mean different things to different people, depending, for example, on whether one is white or black. What these categories mean to us influences how we perceive differences. We often filter out certain stimuli and add others to make "reality" fit our images, a process referred to as selective perception (Sociological Resources, 1969, pp. 2, 3).

Whether you see a glass as half full or half empty (see Figure 2.3) depends on your frame of reference, which is determined by such things as your interests, needs, cultural background, and expectations. The purpose of this cartoon is to prove that point while injecting some humor at the same time. See also Figure 2.4 ("Wife and Mother-in-Law"), which is the focus of this activity.

*Adapted from Sociological Resources for the Social Studies. (1969). "Perception." *Images of People* (pp. 2, 3). Boston: Allyn & Bacon.

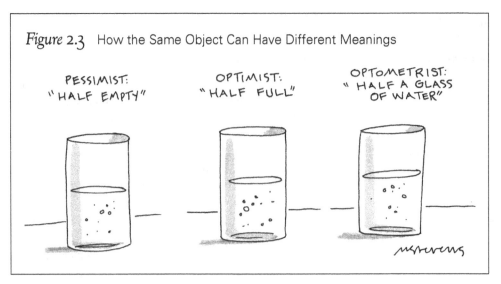

Figure 2.3   How the Same Object Can Have Different Meanings

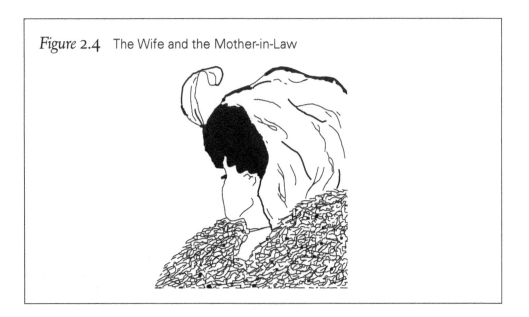

Figure 2.4   The Wife and the Mother-in-Law

Objectives

You will be able to

1. Identify the image(s) in the figure labeled "The Wife and the Mother-in-Law."
2. Discuss why you (and your peers) may have perceived different faces within the image.
3. Make connections between this activity and the idea that your frame of reference affects your perceptions, and your perceptions, in turn, affect your attitudes toward others and the way you behave toward them.

Materials

- The image of "The Wife and the Mother-in-Law" (Figure 2.4)
- The water glasses cartoon (Figure 2.3)

Procedures

1. Read the introductory remarks to this exercise.
2. Look at the image of "The Wife and the Mother-in-Law" and describe what you see. Note the following characteristics: old, large-nosed woman in profile or young, small-nosed, elegantly dressed young woman the back of whose head is turned toward viewer. If you see one woman, you may not be able to see the other immediately. But once you have seen both, linking perception to the stimuli of the ink marks, one way or another, you will be able to see either woman at will. If you make an effort, you may even be able to see both at once.

Assessment

- Notes in your journal describing this strategy and its meaning in terms of culturally responsive teaching
- Your explanation of the relationship between Figure 2.3 (the cartoon with the water glasses) and the way your perceptions may influence your attitudes and behavior towards *your* students

---

Lesson 7: Role-Playing Scenarios

You may be confronted with situations in your classroom that test your ability to deal effectively with cultural diversity. This section presents three scenarios. Imagine the roles of the people mentioned in the scenarios (or with your peers, assume those roles). If you carry out the role-playing with peers, take turns playing the various roles. After your peers have indicated how they would respond to the situation, discuss which response would, in fact, be the best one. Add to these scenarios by bringing to class real-life dilemmas you have observed or actually experienced in the classroom so that further role-playing can take place. (*Note:* Feel free to change the descriptions of the people in the scenarios.)

Objectives

You will be able to

- Use role-playing (or imagining situations) to solve problems you may be confronted with in the classroom.
- Compare and contrast the different responses to problem situations.
- Discuss the responses that appear to be most effective and how they might be applied in similar situations.

Materials

- The three scenarios that follow

Procedures

1. Read the brief introduction to this activity and then read the three scenarios.

2. If you do this activity alone, simply place yourself in each scenario and imagine what you might do in each case. If you do the activity with peers, then follow the guidelines listed in the Introduction and Objectives above.

Assessment

- Reflection on or participation in the role-playing and the discussion following the role-plays
- The notes taken in response to each role-play observed

The Scenarios

(Feel free to change the age level, ethnicity, race, or other aspects of the "players" in each scenario.)

Scenario 1

In an integrated school, you teach a class with five African American students. You are white and are concerned about the possibility of being called "prejudiced," so you are especially sensitive to these five students and their needs. Several of your white students notice your behavior and accuse you of "playing favorites" and of actually being antiwhite. How would you handle this situation?

Scenario 2

You are a white teacher with high standards and expectations of all of your students. You have three Hispanic students in your class and one of them is having some behavior problems. You are direct in asking her to stop disrupting the class. She continues, and you then ask her to sit in the back of the class. She says out loud, "You're picking on me 'cause I'm not white." How would you handle this situation?

Scenario 3

You are an African American teacher meeting with parents of an African American child in your class. You tell them you are concerned about the child's resistance to learning standard English; you also explain that you accept the students' use of Black English but want him or her to demonstrate knowledge of standard English that will help him or her succeed in other environments. The parents show no sign of concern or cooperation with your requests for help. How would you handle this situation?

Lesson 8: Multiculturalism in the Headlines

The daily newspaper as well as news sites on the Internet are an excellent source of information about culturally relevant issues both within and outside of schools. Locate at least one article each week related to some aspect of diversity—people and events, legislation, education, prejudice—and write a synopsis of the article. Reflect on how the knowledge you are gaining might be useful as you develop culturally responsive attitudes and teaching approaches (or, in class, discuss with peers how these articles might expand your knowledge of culturally relevant issues).

Keep in mind that the truth is elusive and the media don't always get things right. What you read in one newspaper or journal or on the Internet may not be accurate. Find out what several different sources have to say about an issue and the frames of reference of these sources before accepting the stories as true. One way, for example, of determining the accuracy of certain details is noting where sources on opposite ends of the political spectrum agree.

Objectives

You will be able to

1. Locate news sources and current articles related to diversity and culturally responsive education.
2. Analyze one or more articles each week and write succinct synopses, including the date of each source, name of the source, and three to five key ideas.
3. Reflect on the connections that your articles have to culturally relevant issues that can inform your teaching (or share your summaries with peers and discuss these connections).
4. Keep a log of your summaries in a section of your binder or other type of folder for future reference.

Materials

- Binder or other place for filing the news summaries you write

Procedures

1. Locate two or three news articles related to diversity. (If you do this activity with peers, have copies for them.)
2. Identify main idea of each article, the five Ws (who, what, when, where, why important), and key details.
3. Analyze the articles. (If done with peers, compare analyses and opinions about the key ideas in each article.)
4. Every week, read and write a summary of at least one article related to an aspect of diversity. Such research will prove useful as you assume the role of culturally responsive teacher.

Assessment

- One or more summaries of current news stories related to diversity
- Participation in the discussion of the article summaries in class
- A binder or other filing device containing your weekly summaries

 ## LINKS: Recording in Your Journal

Now that you have completed this chapter on "Preparing to Become a Culturally Responsive Teacher," reflect on the following questions and enter your responses in your journal.

1. Before reading this chapter, what were some questions you had about culturally responsive teaching? What questions remain? How will you seek answers to them?
2. What experiences in your background do you think will help or hinder you on your path to becoming a culturally responsive teacher?
3. Reflect on the research and principles presented in this chapter:

   a. What research surprised you? And what implications does this research have in terms of your own behavior?

b. What are the costs and benefits of the No Child Left Behind Act in terms of its effectiveness in improving education for poor and minority students?

c. Which aspects of the principles had the most meaning for you? Why?

4. Which strategies—including the vignette at the beginning of Chapter 2—do you think you could adapt in your own classroom? And in what curricular context would they be most appropriate?

5. Can you think of another strategy that would be useful in preparing you for culturally responsive teaching? If so, consider writing it in the form of a lesson plan and having your peers respond to it.

References

Appiah, K. A. (January 1, 2006). "The Case for Contamination." *The New York Times Magazine*, pp. 30–37, 52.

Atwater, M. M. (1994). "Cultural Diversity in the Learning and Teaching of Science." In Gabel, D. (Ed.), *Handbook of Research on Teaching and Learning of Science* (pp. 558–576). New York: Macmillan.

Barrett, L. (August/September 2005). "A Manufactured Crisis." *MTA Today*, pp. 6, 14.

Bazron, B., D. Osher, and S. Fleischman. (September 2005). "Creating Culturally Responsive Schools." *Educational Leadership, 63*(1), pp. 83–84.

Bolgatz, J. (2005). "Teachers Initiating Conversations about Race and Racism in a High School Class." *Multicultural Perspectives, 7*(3), pp. 28–35.

Boyer, P. J. (March 21, 2005). "Jesus in the Classroom." *The New Yorker*, pp. 62–71.

Brooks, J. G., and E. G. Thompson. (September 2005). "Social Justice in the Classroom." *Educational Leadership, 63*(1), pp. 48–52.

Brown, J. (November 2005). "It's Revolting." *Edutopia*, pp. 43–44.

Garan, E. M. (November 9, 2005). "Will Katrina Topple the No Child Left Behind Law?" *Education Week, 25*(11), pp. 36, 38.

Gardner, H. (1983). *Frames of Mind: The Theory of Multiple Intelligences*. New York: Basic Books.

Gay, G. (1994). "A Synthesis of Scholarship in Multicultural Education." North Central Regional Educational Laboratory (NCREL) *Urban Education Monograph Series*. Available online at www.ncrcl.org/sdrs/areas/issues/educatrs/leadrship/urbaned.htm.

Gay, G. (2002). *Culturally Responsive Teaching: Theory, Research and Practice*. New York: Teachers College Press.

Henderson, A.T., and N. Berla. (1994). *A New Generation of Evidence: The Family Is Critical to Student Achievement*. St. Louis, MO: Danforth Foundation and Flint, MI: Mott Foundation.

Hoff, D. J. (March 2, 2005). "NCLB Law Needs Work, Legislators Assert." *Education Week, 24*(25), pp. 1, 20.

Jacobson, L. (March 2, 2005). "Book Spells Out 'Core Curriculum for Teacher Training.'" *Education Week, 24*(25), p. 10.

Jordon, C., E. Orozco, and A. Averett. (2001). *Emerging Issues in School, Family and Community Connections*. Austin, TX: Southwest Educational Development Laboratory.

Keller, B. (July 13, 2005). "Weaver Calls on Delegates to Make Covenant with Nation." *Education Week, 24*(42), p. 16.

Keller, B. (November 2, 2005). "States Given Extra Year on Teachers." *Education Week, 25*(10), pp. 1, 18.

Kluckhohn, C. (1959). *Mirror for Man*. New York: Fawcett World Library.

Maine Department of Education. (2003). *Initial Teacher Certification Standards*. Augusta, ME: Author.

McIntosh, P. (1988). "White Privilege and Male Privilege: A Personal Account of Coming to See Correspondences through Work in Women's Studies" (Working paper). Wellesley, MA: Wellesley College Center for Research on Women.

McWhorter, J. (November 17, 2008). "Revenge of the Black Nerd," *New York Magazine*, p. 16.

National Association for Multicultural Education. (November 2005). *NAME Conference Catalog* (pp. 9, 10). Washington, DC: Author.

National Council for Accreditation of Teacher Education (2005). *Professional Standards for the Accreditation of Teacher Education*. Washington, DC: Author.

National Council for the Social Studies. (1999). *Program Standards for the Initial Preparation of Social Studies Teachers*. Washington, DC: National Council for Accreditation of Teacher Education and the National Council for the Social Studies.

National Council of Teachers of English. (2005). *Standards for the English Language Arts*. Urbana, IL: Author.

National Council of Teachers of Mathematics. (2000). *Principles and Standards for School Mathematics*. Reston, VA: Author.

National Science Teachers Association. (2003). *Standards for Science Teacher Preparation*. Arlington, VA: Author.

Olson, L. (July 13, 2005). "Requests Win More Leeway under NCLB." *Education Week, 24*(42), pp. 1, 20.

Payne, R. K. (March 1996). "Understanding and Working with Students and Adults from Poverty." *Instructional Leader, 9*(2).

Phillion, J. A., and M. F. He. (2004). "Using Life-Based Literary Narratives in Multicultural Teacher Education." *Multicultural Perspectives, 6*(3), pp. 3–9.

Popham, W. J. (April/May 2005). "For Assessment." *Edutopia*, p. 40.

Ravitch, D. (Spring 1990). "Diversity and Democracy." *American Educator*, pp. 16, 18–20, 46–48.

Reid, K. S. (November 30, 2005). "National Panel Says Diversity Is Overlooked Issue in Schools." *Education Week, 25*(13), p. 5.

Reinhold, R. (September 29, 1991). "Class Struggle." *The New York Times Magazine*, pp. 26–29, 46–47, 52.

Samuels, C. A. (May 18, 2005). "Special Education Test Flexibility Detailed." *Education Week, 24*(37), p. 22.

Sobol, T. (1990). "Understanding Diversity." *Educational Leadership, 48*(3), pp. 27–30.

Sociological Resources for the Social Studies. (1969). "Perception." *Images of People* (pp. 2–4). Boston: Allyn & Bacon and The American Sociological Association.

Teach for America. (2004). *Diversity, Community and Achievement*. New York: Author.

Tembo, M. S. (Spring 1993). "Being Oversensitive About Nothing: The Potential Impact of 'Political Correctness'

and Multiculturalism on Knowledge." *Proteus: A Journal of Ideas, 10*(1).

Tierney, J. (November 19, 2005). "Got Each Other's Backs, or Holding Each Other Back?" *New York Times*, p. A27.

U.S. Department of Commerce. (2008). *U.S. Census Bureau News*. Retrieved May 1, 2008, from www.census.gov

Viadero, D. (November 16, 2005). "Minority Students' Popularity Found to Fall Off as Grades Rise." *Education Week, 25*(12), p. 14. Available online at www.edweek.org/links

Wade, R. (February 1998). "Brick Walls and Breakthroughs; Talking About Diversity with White Teacher Education Students." *Social Education, 62*(2), pp. 84–87.

Walsh, Mark (September 14, 2005). "Rehnquist Had Lasting Influence on School Cases." *Education Week, 25*(3), pp. 31, 33.

Zehr, M. A. (June 15, 2005). "State Testing of English Learners Scrutinized." *Education Week, 24*(40), pp. 3, 12.

Zehr, M. A. (November 2, 2005). "States Still Grappling with Multicultural Curricula." *Education Week, 25*(10), pp. 1, 20.

Recommended Resources

Banks, J. A. (2005). *Cultural Diversity and Education: Foundations, Curriculum and Teaching* (5th ed.). Boston: Allyn & Bacon.

Cushner, K., et al. (2008). *Human Diversity in Education: An Integrative Approach*. New York: McGraw-Hill.

Dozier, C., et al. (2005). *Critical Literacy/Critical Teaching: Tools for Preparing Responsive Teachers* (Language and Literacy Series). New York: Teachers College Press.

Heacox, D. (2001). *Differentiating Instruction in the Regular Classroom: How to Reach and Teach ALL Learners, Grades 3–12*. Minneapolis, MN: Free Spirit Publishing.

Irvine, J. J. (2003). *Educating Teachers for Diversity: Seeing With a Cultural Eye*. Multicultural Education, 15. New York: Teachers College Press.

Ladson-Billings, G. (1994). *The Dreamkeepers: Successful Teachers of African-American Children*. San Francisco: Jossey-Bass.

Ramirez, R., et al. (2008). *Diverse Learners in the Mainstream Classroom: Strategies for Supporting All Students across Content Areas*. Portsmouth, NH: Heinemann.

Timpson, W. M. (Ed.). (2003). *Teaching Diversity: Challenges and Complexities, Identities and Integrity*. Madison, WI: Atwood Publishing.

Timpson, W. M. (Ed.). (2005). *147 Practical Tips for Teaching Diversity*. Madison, WI: Atwood Publishing.

Video

"No Child Left Behind" (2005). 56 minutes. Film Maker: Lerone Wilson. Website: www.boondogglefilms.net Wilson points out some of the positive results of NCLB, such as its success in closing achievement gaps, raising some test scores, and bringing to the forefront the subject of education. However, he also identifies some of its problems, including the weight it gives to standardized tests in judging students' achievements, the lack of funding of the mandate, and the issues of fairness to poor children, special needs children, and English learners.

Chapter Three

Strategies and Lessons for Building the Classroom-as-Community

Joanne King, CATA 2007–2008 program year

"There is more than a verbal tie between the words common, community, and communication . . ."

John Dewey, 1916

The purpose of this chapter is to provide lessons and strategies that can contribute to the building of learning communities where the needs and interests of all students are addressed and where culturally responsive school-family-community partnerships are developed. An examination of 80 research studies and literature reviews found a connection between family involvement and student success in a number of different areas, including academic achievement and social skills (Henderson and Mapp, 2002) among students of all ages and across all economic, racial/ethnic, and educational backgrounds.

In a classroom that functions as a *community of learners*, there are lively cooperative activities as well as opportunities for individual pursuits. Students work with others—often in heterogeneous groups—to solve problems and practice civic engagement skills that include sharing ideas and listening to diverse views. By communicating with one another and cooperating on projects and other activities, students can often achieve more than they would if working alone. In addition, they are practicing democratic participatory skills that they can apply outside of the classroom as citizens of their town or city, their state, and the nation.

Teachers can help to shape this type of healthy and intellectually rich environment by involving parents and the community as partners in helping students develop strong work habits, respect for differences, and the self-discipline necessary to successfully address a variety of educational activities.

Preceding the chapter's lessons and units of instruction, you will find brief references to the research and six educational principles relevant to establishing communities of diverse learners within and outside of the schoolroom.

Can you see yourself as a teacher in the following scenario? Why or why not?

It's September, the first day of school in Lexington, Massachusetts, and the fourth graders walk eagerly into their classroom. They look around and notice that the room is empty. There are no desks or chairs or posters on the wall. There's nothing written on the blackboard. There are no welcoming messages or images on the bulletin board like the ones in all the other rooms. Empty.

That's because Steven Levy had written a summer letter to the students who would become his fourth-grade class and asked them to think about their ideal classroom. When they arrived in September, they found an empty room. *They* would be building their own curriculum.

Levy's idea of building the classroom-as-community was to start with the students themselves. Their task was to decide together what they'd need and what they wanted in order to function and enjoy their year in fourth grade. With Levy's guidance and advice, they would be answering these questions through research and discussion before finally reaching a consensus (Levy, 1996).

While this approach to building classroom-as-community may seem unusual, Levy, who was selected in 1993 as Massachusetts Teacher of the Year, can vouch for its effectiveness in terms of directly demonstrating to students that *they* can think, plan, work together, compromise, and ultimately become the decision makers, accountable, in part, for what takes place in *their* educational environment. The process is empowering and also provides excellent preparation for their future as active members of various communities. Levy's starting-from-scratch approach may not be the easiest path to classroom community building, but it can and does work (Levy, 1996). His approach is one of the many ways that a class made up of diverse students can learn to respect one another as they work together on a common goal.

 **What the Research Says**

ONE Cooperative Learning Defined

Cooperative learning is a teaching strategy in which small groups (a) use a variety of learning activities to improve their understanding of subject matter, (b) interact in responsible ways, and (c) develop social skills through sharing of common goals.

There are literally hundreds of cooperative learning strategies. While they may differ as to the number and nature of the students within each grouping, the roles to be played by each member of the group, and the techniques they employ in teaching, learning, and helping one another, these strategies usually involve a pair or group of three or more students working together and actively accepting responsibility for their own learning.

Students working in groups is a common technique, but what distinguishes a cooperative learning approach are three characteristics:

1. Positive interdependence as well as individual accountability
2. The practice and monitoring of social interaction skills that have been described and carefully reviewed before the group work begins
3. An allotment of time for group processing of how effectively the groups worked together to complete the established goals and discussion of ways to improve the group process along with reflection by students of their own and others' behaviors

Reflective question: Evaluate each of these characteristics of cooperative learning. Do they make sense to you? Why or why not?

In terms of the preparation process for cooperative learning, researchers emphasize the importance of helping students develop interpersonal skills and they agree that the desirable behaviors—that is, keeping an open mind, listening to each other, not interrupting, sharing information—have to be named and practiced repeatedly in a consistent manner (Johnson, Johnson, and Holubec, 1988).

More than 70 major studies by federally sponsored research centers, field-initiated investigations, and local districts examining their own practices, have demonstrated cooperative learning's effectiveness on a range of outcomes: student achievement, improved relations among different ethnic groups, and mainstreaming students with learning disabilities (Balkcom, 1992).

The two following examples of cooperative learning can be used with any subject and almost any grade (see also the jigsaw approach, discussed later in this chapter under Principle 2).

- *Group Investigation Model.* Many of the key features of this model were designed originally by Herbert Thelen (1954) and then extended and refined by Shlomo Sharan and his colleagues at Tel Aviv University (1984). Students work to produce a group project (see Figure 3.2, p. 51). Their research and the eventual products of their research reflect the involvement of higher-order thinking.
- *STAD (Student Teams Achievement Divisions).* STAD was developed by Robert Slavin and his colleagues at the Johns Hopkins University and is a simple, straightforward cooperative learning approach (1983). Students of varying academic abilities are assigned to four- to five-member teams and, in studying what has already been taught by the teacher, they help each other reach their highest level of achievement. Students are then tested individually. Teams earn certificates or other kinds of recognition based on the team members' degree of progress over their past records.

Reflective question: Can you see a practical application of one of these examples within the subject or grade you teach? Explain.

TWO Conflict Resolution Builds Classroom as Community

By the mid-1990s more than 7,500 public schools nationwide offered some kind of conflict resolution program (Johnson and Johnson, 1996).

The classroom as community is strengthened when there are mechanisms in place for settling conflicts. Organizations like the National Association for Mediation in Education (NAME), which merged in 1996 with the Conflict Resolution Education Network (CREnet), provide information about how school-based conflicts can be resolved. School Mediation Associates, located in Watertown, Massachusetts, offers role-plays that can help in mediation training to address conflicts involving prejudice, sexual harassment, homophobia, teacher versus students, and more.

Peer Mediation

One of the more popular conflict resolution approaches is peer mediation, whereby a cadre of students is trained to help their peers resolve disputes. Peer mediators, working alone or in pairs, do not impose solutions; they assist their classmates in working out their own solution to the conflict. The steps commonly taken are as follows:

1. The mediator and disputants come together (based either on the disputants seeking mediation or a teacher referring the parties to a mediator).
2. Once the disputants agree to participate, the mediator establishes some ground rules (e.g., no interrupting or put-downs).
3. Each disputant tells the mediator his or her side of the story.
4. The mediator paraphrases or summarizes what he or she hears and asks clarifying questions.
5. The mediator encourages the disputants to brainstorm as a way to resolve the conflict.
6. Once there is agreement on the best solution, they may put it in writing and sign the agreement.

The mediator may check later on to make sure the agreement is working.

Conflicts that lend themselves to peer mediation may include playground fights, arguments over whose turn it is to use the classroom computer, or anger stemming from name-calling or other relationship issues. Conflicts that require adult involvement—such as serious violence, illegal activity, and weapons—are less appropriate for handling by peer mediators.

A study that looked at one peer mediation model was implemented in six elementary schools in the same urban school district (Bickmore, 2001). The program was designed to foster leadership among diverse young people and to develop their capacities to be responsible citizens by giving them tangible responsibility, that is, the power to initiate and carry out peer conflict management activities. At the very most, such programs have been found to successfully achieve those goals and at the very least have been effective in teaching students integrative negotiation and mediation procedures that they can apply throughout their lives.

Reflective question: Have you ever participated in a conflict resolution process? If yes, how does it compare with those just described? If not, can you see yourself using one of these models? Explain.

Principles and Applications for
Building the Classroom-as-Community

The following research-based principles will not only provide a rationale for the lesson plans and units of instruction located in the last section of the chapter, but they will also help you understand the lessons' objectives and procedures. Each principle reflects the theme of this chapter.

Principle ONE

Students of all backgrounds and income levels are more likely to have success in school when classroom community building involves strong parent–teacher communication and partnership.

In "A New Wave of Evidence: The Impact of School, Family, and Community Connections on Student Achievement," published in 2002 by the Southwest Educational Development Laboratory, Anne T. Henderson and Karen Mapp reviewed years of research on parental involvement and concluded unequivocally that when parents are involved in school, students of all backgrounds and economic levels do better.

The federal government has recognized the importance of parental involvement in schools by including such a provision in the No Child Left Behind Act and in requiring that schools receiving Title I money have a comprehensive parent-involvement policy (Furger, 2006, p. 48).

While it is clear that parents are the child's first teachers and, as the child gets older, continue to shape his or her character and academic development (Berkowitz and Bier, 2005), they don't always feel welcome in carrying that influence into their child's school or don't know how to get involved in the classroom. Conversely, there are teachers and students who view parental involvement as intrusive or don't know how to take advantage of parental skills. Such concerns can be resolved when there are organized efforts to reach parents with concrete ways they can collaborate in meaningful projects. When students see their parents contributing to their education and helping schools carry out their objectives, they are, at the same time, learning a lesson in community participation and democratic citizenship, a lesson they will carry with them into adulthood (Berkowitz and Bier, 2005, pp. 64–69).

In terms of responding to the needs of students from diverse cultures, research supports the connection between student success and strong teacher–parent communication (Bazron, Osher, and Fleischman, 2005, pp. 83–84). Other reasons for strengthening such parent–teacher interaction include the following:

- Teachers can learn about potentially difficult transitions students may experience when returning to school from their homes after a weekend or vacation. Stress caused by the change from immersion in their home culture to the school's can be eased if teachers collaborate with families early on so they can create methods for reducing difficulties (Bazron et al., 2005, p. 84).
- Teachers can also help their students become successful learners by assisting parents in gaining *cultural capital*, that is, the skills for negotiating the education system and knowledge of the norms of behavior that govern schools (Briscoe, Smith, and McClain, 2003).

Communicating with minority parents, especially new immigrants, is best carried out by talking directly to parents rather than in writing. One example of this kind of direct parent–school collaboration took place in a school district located in the Navajo Nation and resulted in the creation of a traditional sweat lodge that helped students reflect on their behavior, while at the same time reconnecting to a communal spiritual practice (Bazron et al., 2005, p. 84).

Before listing several ways for involving parents in the classroom community, it should be noted that parental involvement is not always constructive. For example, there have been cases in which parents have become so abusive in their encounters with teachers or administrators that they have been asked to leave the school or have been refused access (Strauss, 2006, p. A6). According to current research, some parents can be "needy, overanxious, and sometimes just plain pesky—and schools of every level are trying to find ways to deal with them" (Strauss, 2006, p. A6).

Classroom Applications and Strategies

• In a study about the success of partnerships among the schools, the community, and parents of English language learners, one of the factors accounting for success was that schools adopted a culturally sensitive model in which the students' native language and culture were viewed as a positive foundation and resource on which to build knowledge as well as facility in their new language (Grant and Wong, 2004, p. 19), as opposed to the deficit model that sees home language and culture as interfering with English acquisition.

• During parent conferences, schools can demonstrate respect for parental involvement by providing translation for all those who request or need it. Parental liaisons, those parents who are bilingual and live in the community, help to establish rapport with parents and build trust (Grant and Wong, 2004, p. 21). (See also Chapter 6.)

• Schools can create parent resource centers or drop-in centers perhaps within the library where books and other materials—as well as coffee and cake—are available to parents. In one school, in La Verne, California, a bilingual instructional aide taught parents how to use office machines and how to engage in a variety of other activities to help classroom teachers (Bradley and Anderson-Nickel, 2006, p. 16).

• In a school in Phoenix, when parents in a low-income area visit their child's teacher, they receive a voucher for one bag of groceries from a local food bank. If they have three children, they receive three bags (Bradley and Anderson-Nickel, 2006, p. 16).

• A visit to the child's home at the beginning of the school year can send a strong message that the teacher values a partnership with the parents. One example of the success of this approach began in Sacramento, California, in 1998 when the Susan B. Anthony Elementary School, working with a local community-organizing group, Sacramento Area Congregations Together, instituted a pilot program, The Parent–Teacher Home Visit Project, in which teachers visited the homes of their students twice a year. "Working in teams of two (teachers often paired up with an interpreter or the school nurse), the school staff reached out to parents and began to forge relationships with the previously marginalized community" of mostly Southeast Asian immigrant families (Furger, 2006, p. 47). Within two months of the first round of home visits, 600 family members came to school for a potluck dinner and parent meeting. The result of this program was increased student achievement and improved test scores; in addition, there were fewer student suspensions. In fact, the state of California enacted legislation to provide $15 million in annual funding for schools throughout California to conduct similar programs. Parents and educators from as far away as Boston and the South Bronx have visited Sacramento to learn about the model program (Furger, 2006, p. 47).

• Teachers can invite parents into their classrooms as tutors, presenters of information (e.g., about their jobs or hobbies), field trip chaperones, snack-time monitors, storytellers, or simply observers.

• Sudia Paloma McCaleb, who teaches at the New College of California, initiated a research project with parents of first graders. The project involved engaging in dialogues with the parents who participated in the project in their own language, which was either English or Spanish. In addition, the parents with their children coauthored books that reflected some of the themes of the dialogues, including the participants' own educational experiences, their life concerns, literary practices, and activities of the family and community. The books included family photographs and illustrations, and, in some cases, interviews conducted by the parent participant with other family members or members of their communities (McCaleb, 1994).

Principle TWO

 When students from different backgrounds, cultures, and ability levels engage in cooperative small-group learning, in which they are able to observe that their peers often make useful contributions to the group, such interactions can lead to prejudice reduction (Johnson, Johnson, and Holubec, 1988; Sharan et al., 1984).

While there are a number of strategies for carrying out cooperative learning, this section will concentrate on three in particular: the jigsaw approach, project-based learning, and the group investigation model.

Classroom Applications and Strategies

Jigsaw Approach.   Dr. Eliot Aronson, a social psychologist, author, and currently professor emeritus at the University of California in Santa Cruz, developed a cooperative learning approach that he refers to as the *jigsaw approach* (Aronson, 1978).

Following the desegregation of the Austin, Texas, schools in the early 1970s, riots had broken out among African American, Hispanic, and white students, and the district asked Dr. Aronson, then head of the social psychology department at the University of Texas, to help (Gilbert, 2001). Together with some of his graduate students, he devised a cooperative learning method:

> Fourth, fifth, and sixth graders were divided into small socially mixed groups to work on some lessons. Each student had a component to research and teach. How well the students learned — and did on the exams that followed — depended on how well they worked in the group. So it was in the students' best interest to get along and to get the best work from one another. (Gilbert, 2001)

Initially the students resented the plan, but after several weeks they began to accept it, and when measured by a psychological test, prejudice was shown to have decreased. The teachers and graduate students even observed the students of different races playing together at recess, and they noticed a significant reduction in fights and bullying. Students from all of the racial groups expressed less negative stereotyping and also appeared to be more self-confident.

See Lesson 2 in this chapter for an example in which the jigsaw structure is applied. Jigsaw uses the following procedure:

1. Divide students into groups of five or six. The groups should be diverse in terms of gender, race, ethnicity, and ability. These groups are "Expert Groups." Appoint one student from each group as the leader. (Briefly share with the students some techniques for leading.)
2. Divide the lesson for that day into five to six approximately equal parts. So, for example, if you are planning to teach about the United Nations and its various agencies, you would divide up the relevant article or chapter so that each "expert group" is responsible for an equal amount of material. (Make sure students in the expert group have direct access only to their own segment.)
3. Give students time to read over their segment at least twice so they can become familiar with it, but they need not memorize it. Together the students in their "expert groups" discuss the main points of their material, master the material, and rehearse the presentations they'll give in their "teaching groups."

4. Bring students into their teaching group and have them teach their particular segment. Encourage others in the group to ask questions about aspects they don't understand (see Figure 3.1).
5. Monitor the groups and offer assistance, if necessary.
6. At the end of the session, give a quiz on the material so that students recognize the seriousness of this process.

A high school mathematics classroom in the San Francisco Bay area was the site of an apparently successful application of Aronson's principle (that students from different backgrounds can learn to respect one another if given opportunities to work together in groups on tasks important to all of them). A study by a Stanford University professor and her graduate students sought to determine the effects on mathematics learning of, among other things, students working in groups on complex problems. Professor Jo Boaler noted that the most

Figure 3.1   Diagram of Aronson's Jigsaw Approach

Step 1: Expert Groups Students help each other learn information.	**Step 2: Teaching Groups** Students teach each other the information they mastered.
Group 1—Topic 1	*Group A*
Alisa	Alisa—Topic 1
Adam	Brittany—Topic 2
Addison	Carter—Topic 3
Aaron	David—Topic 4
Group 2—Topic 2	*Group B*
Brittany	Adam—Topic 1
Bill	Bill—Topic 2
Beth	Charity—Topic 3
Bella	Denise—Topic 4
Group 3—Topic 3	*Group C*
Carter	Addison—Topic 1
Charity	Beth—Topic 2
Chris	Chris—Topic 3
Courtney	D. J. —Topic 4
Group 4—Topic 4	*Group D*
David	Aaron—Topic 1
Denise	Bella—Topic 2
D. J.	Courtney—Topic 3
Desiree	Desiree—Topic 4

Step 3

Assessment of students' learning

1. Observe students as they work in their respective groups.
2. Give quiz on the material that students taught others and that was taught to them.
3. Debrief with the class on the value of the jigsaw approach.

successful of three schools they studied had few financial resources for a culturally and linguistically diverse school population. These students initially tested poorly relative to the two suburban schools involved in the study. But by the end of the four-year study, the students in the diverse school were outperforming the students from the other two schools. Her study concludes that one reason for this outcome was that teachers had worked hard to create classrooms that approached learning as a collective, rather than an individual, endeavor (Boaler, 2006, p. 76). The teachers had spent a lot of time reinforcing the message that everyone has different strengths and that there are many ways to be smart. "Students heard and believed that message" (Boaler, 2006, p. 77).

Project-Based Learning.   Like the jigsaw approach, *project-based learning (PBL)* involves students working as collaborators and critical thinkers who learn to communicate in writing as well as orally and learn the "values of the work ethic while meeting state or national content standards" (Pearlman, 2006, p. 52). The usual methodology, though there are many approaches to project-based learning, involves the following steps:

1. Create teams of three to five students who will work together on an in-depth project for three or more weeks.
2. Introduce a stimulating, authentic question that arouses the students' interest and establish a structure that might include certain activities and useful information. The question or problem can relate to local civic and global issues, among others.
3. Schedule dates by which target tasks are due—that is, initial project plan mapped out, drafts, other benchmarks, and finally the group's presentation to an outside panel of experts drawn from parents, faculty, and community.
4. Provide frequent assessments or feedback on the different aspects of the project, such as content, oral and written communication, cooperation, critical thinking, and other skills. A rubric can be used to delineate the criteria. Students, at the outset, should see the rubric and use it both as a guide and to self-evaluate as they work on the project (Pearlman, 2006, p. 52).

One example of a school that incorporates PBL is New Technology High School in Napa, California. Among the real-world projects students worked on in groups included presenting a plan to Congress on solving the oil crisis and addressing economic issues as a team simulating the president's economic advisors. Because of the tight planning completed before students even began their project, they were better able to direct their own learning of skills, content, and attitudes. In most cases, the projects integrated two or more subjects, and in all cases addressed the content standards on which students would be tested on their state's exit exam (Pearlman, 2006, pp. 52–53).

Project-based learning is quite similar to the group investigation model (GIM), which is summarized in Figure 3.2.

Figure 3.2   Steps for Implementing the Group Investigation Model

---

1. Students identify a topic or problem and pose a question about it.
2. Students offer initial responses to the question.
3. Each group decides what resources and tasks they will need to carry out.
4. Groups investigate and gather information from a variety of sources.
5. Students look at their findings and analyze progress.
6. Groups prepare final report and share with class.
7. Students evaluate the group's as well as their own contributions to the process.

Source: Sharan, Y., and S. Sharan. (1992). *Expanding Cooperative Learning through Group Investigation.* New York: Teachers College Press.

One aspect of group work that troubles some teachers is the extra time it takes to cover content when students are given some control over their own learning. Certain classroom management techniques can be employed to ensure that the groups use their collaborative time efficiently. For example, to move in and out of group work, Barbara J. Millis, director of faculty development at the U.S. Air Force Academy and researcher on approaches to cooperative learning, suggests the use of a quiet signal to gain students' attention. In small classes, merely calling "time" may suffice.

Teachers can also save time by using group folders. Before class, a designated group member can pick up the group's folder that may contain such materials as checklists, attendance sheets, and returned papers. During class students can add to the folders their homework and assignments completed in the group. The designated student then returns the folder to the teacher's desk.

Below are four common questions about group learning. Each question is followed by answers describing important options for facilitating the way that cooperative learning models function.

Question 1: How should students be assigned to a group? (See also the previous description of how the jigsaw approach uses a culturally responsive basis for assigning students to groups.)

One way of assigning students to a group is by using playing cards. Give students their group assignment by the number (rank) of the card. Once that is done, assign members of the group a role by the suit of their card—for example, spades = group leaders, hearts = recorders, diamonds = reporters, clubs = folder monitors. The group may stay the same for several weeks, but their roles can be rotated once a week (Millis, 2003, p. 8).

The most obvious—and the simplest way—of assigning students to a group is by having them count off by fives or fours although that again may not be the most effective approach from a culturally responsive perspective. Stein and Hurd (2000), like Aronson, believe that groups should be heterogeneous, that is, diverse in terms of gender, ethnic background and academic ability. Teacher-selected groups ensure the diversity needed for a variety of perspectives.

There may also be times when you will want to pair or group students based on their common interests. Some teachers assign students to several different groups for different purposes. One technique for helping students keep track of the groups they belong to is by having them prepare a "clock." At the beginning of the year you give each student a sheet on which there is the face of a clock. Next to each number (time slot) are four to five lines (use as many or as few as appropriate) on which they will write the names of peers in each designated group. Their "one o'clock" group may be made up of the peers that *they* have chosen to work with. The "two o'clock" slot may include the names of peers you have chosen for them to meet with to do math work, and so on. Each time slot is labeled with its purpose. Then you can simply say, "Please get into your three o'clock groups." Of course, you can always make changes in the composition or purposes of any of the groups.

Question 2: How often should the composition of the group be changed?

The permanence of a group is usually based on the nature of the task they are addressing. Clearly, if the group is working on a project, the members will stay together for several weeks. On the other hand, if one of the purposes of group work is to address short-term goals, such as discussing questions related to a chapter in a novel, then the teacher may want to change group membership frequently in order to have students get to know the views of everyone in the class. If you want groups to bond, however, you would keep them together for several weeks.

Question 3: Should every member of a group be assigned a role?

There are no hard and fast rules about the types and the number of roles to assign within a group. While the roles of leader, recorder, and reporter are among the most common, there are others. For example, if the group is discussing fiction or nonfiction, roles to consider can include passage picker, illustrator, connector, summarizer, vocabulary enricher, travel tracer, or investigator. These roles are briefly defined in Table 3.1. Over the course of a semester, students may rotate roles, eventually experiencing each one of them.

To ensure successful cooperative learning, this author suggests that you take at least 30 minutes to explain to students—or hold a discussion about—the purpose of cooperative learning (see the earlier discussion of this topic) before coaching the students on the tasks required of each role. Without such preparation, students may view group learning as simply social time.

Question 4: How should credit be allotted?

Deciding how credit is to be allotted and how each student will be held accountable is very important if cooperative learning is to be successful. In order to foster both positive interdependence and individual accountability, it is useful to have students work together on a problem and require both group feedback and another related assignment to be completed by each member of the group. You may want to establish a criterion-referenced grading scheme where peer coaching and cooperative efforts contribute toward individual achievement and grades (Millis, 2003, p. 6).

Finally, it is important for both students and teacher to monitor group and individual progress. Teachers should move from group to group observing the students' participation and progress. Such monitoring is vital if students are to stay on track and if the teacher is to be accessible should students have questions.

After the groups complete their task and share their responses with the whole class, it is useful to give them a few questions on a sheet of paper for the purpose of debriefing and evaluating the group process, such as the following examples: Did I contribute to the group?

Table 3.1   Definition of Roles in Groups Discussing Fiction and Nonfiction Selections

Role	Definition of Role
Leader or Director	Reads aloud list of questions given for discussion. May develop that list. Seeks total participation in the discussion. Keeps the group on track. Solicits input from the others.
Recorder	Takes notes that reflect the comments of the group and their conclusions. (The recorder should never interrupt the discussion but rather should try to listen and record as well as conditions allow. They may, however, ask for some clarification at the *end* of the discussion.)
Reporter	(This role may be assumed as well by the recorder.) Shares the recorder's notes with the larger class.
Passage Picker	Locates a few special sections of the reading that the group should look back on because of the humor or interest or importance. This person can read aloud the passages or ask someone else to read them or have the group read them silently.
Illustrator	Draws some kind of picture related to the reading, perhaps based on a character, a surprising event, or other aspect that was appealing.
Connector	Finds connections between the material the group is reading and the world outside or with other material the group has read.
Summarizer	Prepares a brief summary of the assigned reading, the essence of the reading, or three or four main ideas.
Vocabulary Enricher	Looks out for a few important words in the reading and presents definitions for the group.
Travel Tracer	Tracks carefully where the action takes place within the reading selection. Points out pages where each location is described.
Investigator	Digs up some background information on any topic related to the reading and presents very brief findings (Daniels, 2002; Schniedewind and Davidson, 1998, p. 55).

Did everyone in the group participate? How could the discussion have been improved or changed so that the tasks could be more successfully accomplished?

As a way of summarizing the previous discussion about cooperative learning, Johnson, Johnson and Holubec (1988) mention five basic elements for small-group learning:

- Positive interdependence: achieved by setting mutual goals, dividing materials among group members, assigning students roles, giving joint rewards
- Face-to-face interaction
- Individual accountability for mastering the assigned material
- Use of interpersonal and small-group skills: actually take time to teach skills of active listening, respect for differences of opinion, peer support, honesty, empathy, and other cooperative behaviors.
- Ample time for students to analyze how well their group is functioning and the extent to which students are employing social skills to help all group members achieve and maintain constructive relationships within the group

Principle THREE

 Building the classroom as community involves teaching about and providing opportunities for positive interactions among members of the class *and* within the larger community.

Applications and Strategies within the Classroom and School

- In order to foster a culture of community within the classroom, teachers can focus on four goals: instituting a respectful tone, establishing a bond with and among the students, creating a community that values *all* students, and helping students resolve conflicts (Teach for America, 2004, p. 101). One strategy suggested for resolving conflicts is teaching students how to use "I" statements to explain their actions and feelings to each other. For example, a student being bothered by another student might say, "I don't like it when you push my chair. I can't concentrate on my work. Please stop." Or possibly have them record their thoughts in writing prior to a discussion about the conflict. Also, teach "active listening" strategies so students feel they are being heard and understood—for example, "I hear you saying that you . . ." (Teach for America, 2004, p. 102). See also our previous discussion of conflict resolution in this chapter for more information on this topic.

- One of the many ways that KIPP (Knowledge Is Power Program) Academy Charter Schools nurture community is through repetition of maxims, such as "Team Always Beats Individual." Such maxims pervade everyday school life and serve in bringing students together.

- Adding one of the greatest moral maxims of all time, the Golden Rule, to the curriculum is one way of encouraging positive interaction both in and outside of the classroom. "Do unto others as you would have them do unto you" is a general precept shared by most of the world's religions (Damon, 2005, p. 26). Stimulating classroom discussion of this idea can inform students about the diverse times and places in which this classic maxim has been considered important as well as how it can be applied in the classroom. Some schools include the Golden Rule, or "learning by giving," by requiring a certain number of hours of *community service* with clear academic connections.

Applications and Strategies outside of the Classroom and School

Community Service.   *Community service*, or service learning, means different things to different people. Service is simply defined as an act done for the public good. The continuum runs from youth performing simple acts of charity or service, such as tutoring or visiting a home for the elderly, to youth tackling real community problems as part of their school curriculum. Service learning enables students to develop positive attitudes about diverse others within their community, improve their own self-esteem, and increase academic knowledge through direct experience. Although Maryland is the only state that mandates service learning, a growing number of states, including California, Florida, Minnesota, New Jersey, Oregon, South Carolina, Wisconsin, to name a few, actively encourage it (Smith, 2006, p. 55).

Projects nationwide run the gamut from traditional charity endeavors, such as working on local end hunger campaigns to environmental clean-ups to fund-raising to help orphanages for children with AIDS in Africa. In the Sanford School in Hockessin, Delaware, in order to honor the legacy of Martin Luther King, Jr., each grade worked on a different community service project, including such activities as knitting mittens for children in need at a local day care center, making dog biscuits for the Humane Society, painting a mural on one of the school's buildings commemorating the work of Dr. King, helping to sort and organize clothes at the local clothing bank, and weaving place mats for a local nursing home (Buttenheim, personal communication, February 2006).

Christine Read (2005), a student in this author's Education and Society course, described in a paper how her sixth-grade teacher "knew how to encourage teamwork and a sense of community" both within and outside of the classroom.

"From the beginning, Mrs. Kruger . . . did this through the physical setup of the room, with desks clustered together, facing each other, in small groups which were continually shuffled throughout the year so that by June every student had had the opportunity to get to know every other student" (Read, 2005).

She described the weekly bake sale the class held to raise money for an educational trip at the end of the year. These bake sales required from students the sharing of responsibilities, taking turns contributing baked goods, keeping track of whose turn it was to carry out the tasks that were rotated each week, including setting up the tables, taking money, and preparing deposits to go into the bank. Two other service learning activities were walking seeing-eye dogs-in-training for an organization that matched dogs up with blind owners (Read, 2005) and making origami paper cranes to decorate a gift that was auctioned off by the school to raise money for local families in need.

Wrote Ms. Read at the end of the paper, "There has never been another school year where I've felt that I've worked harder, accomplished as much, contributed more to the community, or been as connected to my fellow classmates, despite our differences. She [Mrs. Kruger] tried her best to make sure each and every one of us had something to be proud of by the end of the year" (Read, 2005, p. 3).

Dr. Rona J. Karasik, a professor of community studies at St. Cloud State University in St. Cloud, Minnesota, who has worked with students and community groups to develop and implement service learning projects since 1993, offers advice on such projects:

1. Start with course objectives. Then identify and talk to groups who might need the students' services.
2. Start small by limiting the number of community partners students will work with and the size of the project. Establish clear outcomes with the community partner.
3. Treat service learning as an integral part of the courses rather than an add-on.
4. Participation may or may not be mandatory, although there needs to be several options available for participating in the service learning project so that everyone can play a role.
5. Set a minimum number of hours, such as 20 to 30 hours per semester, although this may not be necessary if, instead, completing the task is the basic requirement.
6. Grades should be given for *learning* rather than service, using, for example, graded assignments such as papers, presentations, or portfolios that require students to integrate their service experience with specific course content (Karasik, 2006, pp. 7, 8).

Career Academies.   "Nothing matters more to kids than having people take them seriously—and nothing achieves this better than work that really matters in their community," wrote Kathleen Cushman (2005, p. 48), coauthor of *Schooling for the Real World.*

One example that illustrates her point is the establishment of career academies within high schools around the country that organize curricula around themes such as health professions, the law, or the performing arts. "These more intimate learning centers provide a natural opportunity to bring outside partners into the schools," as well as place students in workplace settings as interns or apprentices (Cushman, 2005, p. 49).

The National Academy Foundation (NAF), a national school-to-work curriculum provider, is built on the premise that students can combine academic curricula with meaningful practical experience. Their "academies," the Academy of Finance, Academy of Travel and Tourism, and Academy of Information Technology, empower inner-city high school students to become active citizens. (See www.naf.org for more information.) In the academy model businesspeople work as partners with educators to introduce young people to the world of business. This process ultimately leads students to higher education and to professions of their choosing.

Principle FOUR

Differentiated Instruction enables teachers to tailor their instruction to the needs of individual students with attention to auditory, visual, and kinetic differences, differences in ability, and differences in student interests. Such instruction uses both cooperative and independent study strategies.

Classroom Applications and Strategies

Carol Ann Tomlinson in *The Differentiated Classroom* (1999) offers six strategies for differentiating instruction. These strategies respond to the question that teachers often have about how to address the needs of students with disabilities as well as gifted and talented students:

1. Establish stations in the classroom where students can work on various tasks alone or in groups.
2. Construct agendas that list tasks a student must complete within a specified time frame.
3. Organize cooperative groups in which students complete tasks as the teacher monitors them, asking questions and assessing their understanding.
4. Assign group or independent projects lasting from three to six weeks and related to some area of the curriculum. Students can select the topics and receive guidance from the teacher.
5. Use "choice boards" whereby assignments are written on cards that are placed in hanging pockets. Students select a card and the teacher targets work toward students' needs.

Principle FIVE

"The school must itself be a community life in all which that implies. Social perceptions and interests can be developed only in a genuinely social medium—one where there is give and take in the building up of common experience" (Dewey, 1966, p. 358).

The impressive body of ideas of philosopher John Dewey reflects his call for a communal vision of education. Dewey's perspectives, even in his own time, have challenged common conceptions of what schools and education should be. The factory model of education, born in the nineteenth century and surviving until the present, neglects the principle of the school as a form of community that schooled the child for a role as a full-fledged member of a democratic society (Driscoll, 1995, pp. 214–215).

Schoolwide Application

James Comer's (2004) School Development Program restructures the school in ways that alter the notion of the school as merely an academic agency. His theory is based on the psychology of child development and an understanding of the child's social, emotional, cognitive, physical, and language development. The School Development Program (SDP)—in place in many schools around the country—consists of four components. The first component is a governance and management team representing all adults in the school community, such as the principal, two teachers, three parents, and a mental health professional. The group meets weekly to establish policies for the school in curriculum, staff development, and school climate. A second component is the mental health team, consisting of a classroom teacher, special education teacher, social worker, and school psychologist. The third component of the program is implementation of the activities planned by the teams just mentioned, and the fourth component is the parent participation program, which involves parents in the schools in several ways, from taking on the role of tutor or aide to consulting on school governance.

Comer's contribution to the radical restructuring of the school as a community that supports teachers, parents, and students is reflected in the work of others who also believe in Dewey's concept of the school as community (Bryk and Driscoll, 1988; Epstein, 1987; Rowan, 1990).

Principle SIX

 Other models exist that promote student–school–community relationships that are mutually beneficial.

Classroom Applications and Strategies

Some schools remain open to the community for use after school hours and on weekends. These community schools bring together students and local people and provide opportunities for working on all kinds of pursuits from sports activities to research in the library to knitting circles.

The Community as School model eliminates the school altogether as it places schooling many places in the community on any given day. For example, one Minnesota school, Duluth's Harbor City International Charter School, depends extensively on students using community resources as an integral part of learning (Nair, 2006, p. 31).

Whether learning takes place in the classroom, in the school after hours with community partners, or outside of the school entirely, the real meaning of building community is in making connections among diverse individuals and addressing their joint visions.

Strategies and Lessons for
Building the Classroom-as-Community

Studies have shown that by incorporating cooperative learning strategies, some of which are applied within the following lessons, students learn to relate to one another in ways that build mutual respect. When strategies require students to work together in teams and to take responsibility for their own learning, they are able to practice democratic decision making and self-reliance that will serve them for life as they take their places as members of diverse communities. Other lessons bring together the school, the family, and the community by involving all three as sources of information that students can tap in completing research projects and other assignments. Note that the parenthetical references in the objectives signify the content-based standards of several professional organizations. See Appendix A for a key to the abbreviations and listings of the specific standards.

Lesson 1: Introduction Activities

Grade Levels: K–12
Content: Communication, Language Arts
Principles: 1, 3

At the beginning of the school year, you can begin the process of building the classroom-as-community by introducing students to a number of "introduction" activities that enable them to get to know one another and that are, at the same time, fun. You probably remember engaging in such activities; use those, of course, and consider the following introduction activities as well.

Objectives

Students will be able to

1. Participate in activities that enable them to get to know their classmates (ELA 2, 4, 9, 11, 12).
2. Share information about themselves (ELA 4, 6, 11, 12).
3. Listen respectfully to the comments of their peers (ELA 2, 11).
4. Recall information they are learning about their peers (ELA 2, 6, 7, 9).
5. Work cooperatively with their peers and teacher in evaluating the lesson (ELA 4, 6, 12; SOCS-C 2, 5).

Materials

- See the particular activity. Most of these activities require no materials. Those that do will show materials used in italics.

Procedures

Introduce students to the idea that in order to build a classroom community, it is important for them to learn one another's names as well as other information about their peers (or you can ask students: "How can we begin to get to know one another?"). Then choose one or more of the activities below. You might want to do a different activity each day during the first week of school.

Activities*

Activity 1: "My Name Is . . ."
Have each student walk around the room and "write" their name in someone else's palm using their finger and saying their name at the same time. Have them mention a positive

---

*The first five activities are adapted from T. Benzwie. (1987). *A Moving Experience: Dance for Lovers of Children and the Child Within* (pp. 43–48). Tucson, AZ: Zephyr Press.

quality to their name, something they like about themselves. Continue until everyone has "met" everyone else.

Activity 2: Circle Chant

Everyone gets into a circle on their knees shoulder to shoulder. They take turns standing in the middle of the circle. Very slowly and together, the circle group sways back and forth on their knees. As they go forward, they softly chant the name of the person standing in the middle. They repeat it as often as you think appropriate.

Activity 3: The Name Scream

Have students form a wide circle. Then have each student take a turn walking around the room using the entire space, at first whispering their name (and, if you like, their address). Then have them say it louder and louder as they continue to move all around the room doing whatever they choose with their arms, legs, head, and shoulders, perhaps moving them in rhythm with their name until they are finally screaming their name as loud as they can. They finish by "screaming" their name silently with a final pose. (You can expect a great deal of laughter, especially with older students due to embarrassment as well as fun. It tends to subside once students begin to feel more comfortable and lose their shyness. The large circle of students can support the "dancer" by joining in the chanting of the performer's name.)

Activity 4: Name with Gesture

Everyone stands in a circle. The first person says their name along with a *spontaneous* gesture showing how they are feeling at that very moment. This is followed by the whole group immediately mirroring back the person's gesture and name. (Encourage students to do whatever comes naturally during their turn and not try to think of a gesture in advance. If necessary, they can even use a gesture of "I don't know.")

Activity 5: Name a Favorite Animal

Have students say their name and an animal they like or relate to. Then have them act out that animal. (Variations: They say their name and then accompany it with an adjective with the same first letter—for example, "I'm Barbara; I'm Beautiful Barbara." Or they say their name and what they would like to have, what they would like to be, something they like in nature, or other characteristic or preference.)

Activity 6: Globe Toss

Using a *plastic balloon globe of the world,* have students toss the globe to one another. Whoever catches it states their name and, if they know their ancestry, mentions one of the countries connected to their family history, and, if possible, points to it on the globe.

Activity 7: Yarn Toss

Using a *ball of yarn,* have students sit in a circle. Explain that they will need to unravel enough yarn so that the ball reaches the person they choose to throw it to. As each person catches the ball of yarn, they say their name and what they hope to learn or do in the class this year (or anything you choose to ask them to share). Once everyone has received the "ball," they will see in front of them a criss-crossing of yarn. Ask them what that might symbolize (e.g., "We are all connected," or "The lessons we will be learning demonstrate how different subjects are connected or are interdisciplinary in nature," or "We need to cooperate to make learning successful"). Then have them throw the yarn ball in reverse order until the last person gets to hold the complete ball of yarn as at the beginning of the activity.

Assessment

- Participation in the activities (Objectives 1–5)
- Completion of the activities in a cooperative manner (Objectives 1–5)

- Participation in a debriefing session with peers and teacher (Objective 5)
- (Optional) A short written reaction to the activity(ies) and what they learned about their peers and themselves (Objective 5)

Extension

Consider doing "Introduction" activities that are created by the students themselves.

Lesson 2: Using the Jigsaw Cooperative Learning Strategy with Multicultural Content

Grade Levels: 2–12
Content: Social Studies, Language Arts
Principles: 2, 3

Earlier in this chapter (Principle 2), you will find an extensive discussion as well as the syntax for Eliot Aronson's jigsaw strategy for bringing diverse students together and enabling them to take responsibility for their own learning. Lesson 2 demonstrates one of many applications of this strategy.

Objectives

Students will be able to

1. Contribute constructively to their "expert group" and their "teaching group" (ELA 4, 6, 9, 12; SOCS-USH 10 [5–12]; SOCS-USH 3 [K–4]).
2. Demonstrate knowledge of the news item related to diversity that they had to master as well as the items they learned about from experts in their teaching groups (ELA 2, 6, 12; SOCS-USH 3 [K–4]; SOCS-USH 10 [5–12]).
3. Work cooperatively with peers in both their expert group and teaching group (SOCS-C 5).
4. Evaluate news items as well as the cooperative methods they employed to learn about them.

Materials

- Four or five current news clippings related to diversity in either local, national, or international spheres (because the jigsaw approach may be used in helping students study and learn practically *any* kind of material, the materials will vary depending on the content *you* want students to learn as they apply the strategy)

Procedures

1. Please see the syntax for the jigsaw approach under Principle 2 (pp. 49–50). Follow the steps using four or five (depending on size of your class and each expert group) news clippings related to diversity. Try to organize groups that are diverse in their make-up.
2. After each expert group has mastered the content in their news article, have them decide how they will teach this content when they meet in their teaching group.
3. After all expert groups are prepared to teach the main ideas they have mastered and discussed, place them in their teaching group.
4. Allow at least three to five minutes for each expert to teach their peers about their news item. Suggest that people take notes (or have each expert group prepare an outline to be distributed to students in their teaching group).

5. (Optional) Have students regroup into their expert groups and review *all* news items together.
6. (Optional) Debrief with whole class by discussing these questions (or have them fill in a self-evaluation questionnaire): (a) How would you evaluate your role in both groups? (b) How would you evaluate your peers' performances? (c) What, if anything, would you do—or have others do—to improve this teaching/learning strategy?

Assessment

- A quiz on main ideas contained in each of the news items (Objective 2)
- An essay asking students to compare and contrast the content of the articles in terms of location, effects on their own or others' lives, or any other basis of comparison (Objective 2)
- Observation of students' ability to work cooperatively in their groups (Objectives 1, 3)
- A class discussion of the relevance of the news items to diversity and their connections to the students' lives or to education or other subject (Objectives 2, 4)
- Self-evaluation and evaluation by teacher as to their ability to work cooperatively with peers (Objective 3)

Extension

As mentioned earlier, there are many contexts in which the jigsaw approach can be applied. In language arts, for example, different vocabulary lists can be distributed to each expert group or different short stories or biographies of about four or five authors. In mathematics, each expert group might be responsible for a different theorem or mathematics puzzle or equation.

Lesson 3: Choreographing Dances to Express Diversity and Community

Grade Levels: K–12
Content: Social Studies, Language Arts, Movement/Dance
Principles: 2, 3, 4

The Liz Lerman Dance Exchange is a New York–based cross-generational company and learning institution headed by MacArthur "Genius Grant"–winner Liz Lerman. She has worked with and included in her dances community members of all ages, from young children to senior adults. She often works in communities gathering stories and then choreographing dances based on those stories. Ms. Lerman believes that the arts can bring people together on common ground, and that dance, in particular, can give people a way to understand each other's differences. In one community in Vermont, for example, she choreographed a dance related to the issue of civil unions, and in Florida, she focused on the role of weekly card games (Lerman, 2005). The following lesson is based on her concept and includes the five steps in her "Critical Response Process" for critiquing an artist's dance in a nonintimidating way (Lerman, 2008).

Note: This lesson, if carried out in one day, would preclude students doing research. Instead, they might simply identify a topic related to diversity issues studied in class and improvise a dance or movement reflecting that topic or an issue of their choosing. If you decide to have them do research, a second or third session would be required.

Objectives

Students will be able to

1. In groups or pairs do research in their community and select an interesting story they have discovered around which to choreograph a dance (or select a classroom issue related to diversity) (ELA 5–12; SOCS-USH 1, 2, 3 [K–4]).
2. Describe in writing or orally the story they will be choreographing (ELA 4, 5, 6, 12).

3. Choreograph a dance reflecting their interpretation of the story they gathered from their community research (or from the classroom community or subject matter) (ELA 3, 7; NA-D 2–7).
4. Perform their dance for the class (or for members of the greater community) (NA-D 4, 5, 7).
5. (Optional) Do research on the art of choreographing and Liz Lerman's approach to using dance to build community and constructive human interaction (ELA 8, 11; SOCS-C 2, 5).
6. Apply Lerman's Critical Response Process in their role as both viewer and choreographer/artist (ELA 6, 7).
7. Work cooperatively with a partner or group (ELA 11; SOCS-C 2–5).

Materials

- Props for their dance
- List of steps in Lerman's Critical Response Process (given below)
- (If available) A local choreographer as guest speaker or books such as Carla De Sola's *Learning through Dance* (1974), which specifies warm-up exercises, suggestions for music, improvisations, props, and positions related to six themes: communication, freedom, love, life, peace, and happiness

Procedures

1. Discuss the Objectives and Materials with the students.
2. Ask students if they would like to create dances related to classroom diversity issues or related to stories they will be discovering after doing research in the community.
3. Brainstorm some of the issues they might focus on from the larger community or from their classroom community.
4. Divide students into groups or pairs and give them the option of doing research in community or focusing on a classroom diversity topic.
5. Have students meet and discuss their choice of topic and how they will go about doing their research. (If you decide to do this lesson in one session, they would then immediately work together on choreographing their dance. Give them a space in which to practice and then have the groups perform their dances followed by Lerman's Critical Response Process. However, if you decide to have students go out into the community, discuss with them where they might go and when.)
6. Have students meet again after they have done community research. They should decide on the story they want to tell through dance and jot down notes on their story. Together, they should also make decisions on the following: what they'll wear, props they'll need, music they want to use, where they want to perform the dance (e.g., indoors or outdoors, on grassy surface or on floor, other).
7. Provide a place for each group to practice their dance (or have them meet on their own outside of class).
8. Have students perform their dance in front of peers (and others, if possible).
9. Following each dance, engage in the five steps of Lerman's Critical Response Process:

   Step 1: Look at the work. What aspects of the dance make you curious? What do you like about the work? Give positive reinforcement.
   Step 2: The choreographers then ask the audience open-ended questions, such as "What questions do you have for us?" or "Why do you think we used this as a prop?" or "What story do you think we were trying to tell?"
   Step 3: Observers ask the artists neutral questions in order to let artists see their own work in a new way.
   Step 4: Audience members ask artists: "I have an opinion. Do you want to hear it?"
   Step 5: Audience members ask artists what they will be working on in the future or what they like about their dance and the process they engaged in (Lerman, 2008).

Assessment

- Students' research gathered from the community or classroom (Objectives 1, 2, 3)
- Self-evaluation of their role in doing research and preparing the dance (Objectives 1, 2, 3)
- Their participation in applying the Critical Response Process (Objective 6)
- Written response to the question: What is your reaction to the process and the product related to choreographing dances to express diversity and community? (Objectives 1–4, 6, 7)
- Class discussion and debriefing session as to their overall success in fulfilling all objectives (Objectives 1–4, 6, 7)

Lesson 4: Using Puppets to Resolve Classroom Conflict*

Grade Levels: K–8
Content: Conflict Resolution, Language Arts, Social Studies
Principle: 3

Role-playing is a useful method for exploring conflict, trying out different solutions, and gaining insights. Teachers can present real-life problems in skit form to which students can respond, or students themselves can make puppets and role-play actual situations that are confronting them in their classroom, from simple situations such as one student accusing another of taking his or her pencil to more complex situations in which students have acted on prejudiced attitudes that are hurtful to their peers and that destroy the cooperative relationships the teacher has tried to establish. Using puppetry in this way encourages students to think about a problem while they are not in the heat of the argument and also provides an opportunity for hearing a variety of responses to conflict.

Note: Teachers need to recognize that there are cultural differences in how conflicts are viewed and settled. With that in mind, you may find that in a diverse classroom there may not be complete consensus on how to best settle a conflict.

The lesson plan below demonstrates how puppets can be used to resolve conflict. *Note:* The same kind of role-playing can be carried out *without* puppets.

Objectives

Students will be able to

1. Participate cooperatively in discussions in which they analyze the causes of a conflict and then generate appropriate solutions (ELA 4, 5, 7, 9, 11, 12).
2. Actively listen to ideas of others and reflect on them (ELA 2, 3).
3. Create role-plays in which they represent a classroom (or other) conflict and demonstrate their way of resolving the conflict (ELA 5, 6, 11; SOCS-C 5).
4. Write about or discuss their role-playing experience expressing their views about the usefulness of the role-playing technique *and* their views about the appropriate solution to the conflict (ELA 2, 3, 4, 5, 6, 7, 12).
5. (Optional) Compare their experiences in conflict resolution to historical instances in which conflicts were settled peacefully (SOCS-USH 3 [K–4]; USH 1–10 [5–12]).

Materials

- Sock puppets (or paper bag puppets or simply paint eyes and mouth on fingers; you may also find finger puppets in toy stores or perhaps make some out of felt and other materials)

*Adapted from E. Forsythe. (1977). "Puppetry and Conflict." In S. Judson (Ed.), *A Manual on Nonviolence and Children* (pp. 41–42). Philadelphia: Philadelphia Yearly Meeting of the Religious Society of Friends—Peace Committee.

Procedures

(When a conflict arises in the classroom, consider following these procedures *on the spot*, or, if you would rather, you can adapt these procedures and make this a lesson in "how to use puppets to explore conflicts.")

1. The teacher has two sock puppets, one in each hand, and assumes the roles of the two students (or points of view) that have been in conflict that day or moment.
2. After making clear the opposing views, one puppet turns to audience and asks, "What should we do?"
3. The class can then address the question in one of many ways. For example, the teacher can divide the class into groups to discuss the problem; students can pair up with the person next to them and discuss the problem; or the whole class can brainstorm together and clarify the problem, describe what happened, and then define each side's views.
4. Once the small groups or whole class have discussed these questions, they should create solutions to the problem. Each group can then act out their solution using puppets.
5. Following the role-play of a solution by each group, the teacher can ask, "Do you think that this solution would work? Why or why not?" Then after all of the role-plays have been presented, ask which one(s) would work best and ask for specific reasons. Students should try to identify *something* positive about each solution so that their peers don't feel as if their solution is being rejected entirely.

Assessment

- Degree of participation in creating and performing a solution to a problem by role-playing with (or without) puppets (Objectives 1–3)
- Contribution to a discussion of the various solutions to the conflict (Objective 4)
- Written response to the following questions: What do you think about the use of role-playing with puppets to solve conflicts? What is your view of the solution that the class has agreed on? (Objective 4)
- Demonstration of cooperative behavior during the entire lesson (Objectives 1, 2, 3, 4)
- (Optional) Completion of an assignment in which they compare their approach for conflict resolution to a historical instance in which a conflict was settled peacefully (Objective 5)

Extension

Have groups of students do research on methods for settling conflicts peacefully. Each group could present their findings to the whole class or demonstrate one of the methods they have discussed.

Lesson 5: Affirmation Activity*

Grade Levels: K–8
Content: Social Studies, Language Arts
Principles: 3, 4

Feeling affirmed is a first step in conflict resolution, since having a sense of self-esteem makes it easier for students to see the good in others, especially those with whom they may be in conflict. Affirmation activities can help students keep an open mind to new information and alternatives to conflict situations. (Affirming someone means acknowledging and appreciating the good qualities and abilities in him or her.)

*Adapted from S. Judson (Ed.). (1977). *A Manual on Non-violence and Children* (pp. 5–10). Philadelphia: Philadelphia Yearly Meeting of the Religious Society of Friends—Peace Committee.

People who work consistently to make positive changes in a community tend to have three characteristics in common: optimism, competence, and high self-esteem. Affirmation activities alone may not be enough to nurture these three characteristics in young people, but they can play a role in raising their awareness about the value of affirming one another and themselves.

Objectives

Students will be able to

1. Listen to and respond to ideas related to affirmation and its opposite, put-downs (ELA 5, 6, 12).
2. Participate in an affirmation activity ("Affirmation Silhouettes") (SOCS-USH 1, 3 [K–4]; ELA 2, 4, 9, 11).
3. Contribute to postdiscussion about the value of the affirmation activity (ELA 3, 7, 11).

Materials

- Flip chart
- Butcher paper or newsprint
- Magic markers or crayons
- Index cards and pens or pencils
- Paste or stick pins

Procedures

1. Share with students all of the information given in the introduction to this lesson. Before explaining these ideas, consider asking the class what they think *affirmation* means.
2. Explain the opposite of affirmation, that is, the power and persuasiveness of put-downs and how important it is to counter them with affirmations ("put-ups").
3. Ask students to brainstorm all of the put-downs and put-ups they can think of in, say, three minutes. Record their responses on a flip chart or on the board, listing "put-ups" on one side of a two-column chart and "put-downs" on the other.
4. Convey to students that it's clear they have heard a lot of put-downs, that put-downs hurt people and stop us from learning and thinking and acting like a community, and that we need to consciously fight put-downs by directly affirming one another. Explain that they will now do an affirming activity, "Affirmation Silhouettes."

   - Each person has a piece of butcher paper or newsprint about a foot taller than she or he is tall. Pair the students up and have them take turns tracing each other's full length on the paper with magic markers. (Optional: they can decorate the silhouettes as time allows.)
   - Have each person stand in front of their silhouette and say something positive about him- or herself. This affirmation is then followed by every child saying something positive to that person. Write each affirmation on an index card, and, after each child has been affirmed by classmates, place the silhouettes on the bulletin board. Paste or pin the index cards, with the affirmations of each child, onto their silhouette. *Note:* For participants who may have a difficult time thinking of anything to say, it may be helpful to ask them specific questions, such as, "Is there something you like to do together?" "What's something you've seen this person do well?" Give them time to think.

5. Hold a debriefing discussion with the students about their views on the value of the affirmation activity. Ask students if they have ideas for affirmation activities that the class might carry out in the future.

Assessment

- Each student's participation in the discussion of the ideas related to affirmation and its opposite, put-downs (Objectives 1, 2, 3)
- Student's construction of their own silhouette (Objective 2)
- Students' affirming remarks on index cards for their peers' silhouette (Objective 2)
- Participation in debriefing session evaluating the affirming activity (Objective 3)

Lesson 6: Portfolios as a Way to Assess, Enhance, and Expand the Classroom Community

Grade Levels: 2–12
Content: Interdisciplinary
Principles: 1, 2, 3, 4

A portfolio, which is a compilation of a student's work, is an excellent example of an authentic assessment tool, since the work filed in the portfolio is directly related to what the student was taught in the classroom (Adams and Hamm, 1992). The number of items, the nature of the device they are stored in, and the purposes to which they are put may vary greatly, but portfolios in general can enhance student learning and expand the classroom community beyond the student and his or her peers to include parents and other professionals.

There is extensive literature on portfolio development and rationales for their use (Barrett, 2000; Danielson and Abrutyn, 1997; Wiggins, 1998), but for the purposes of this lesson, only the first step, how to introduce portfolios to your students, is described in this lesson.

Objectives

Students will be able to

1. Answer several questions related to the ways in which portfolios can enhance their learning and self-knowledge (ELA 3, 6, 7).
2. Discuss and record ideas about the process for building and using portfolios (ELA 5, 7, 12).
3. Create a cover for their portfolio (ELA 6, 12; NA-VA 1–6).
4. Begin organizing items for their portfolio. *Note:* Depending on the items the students choose for their portfolios, their items can reflect standards from many disciplines, beyond those shown here. (NA-VA 3; ELA 3, 7).

Materials

- A binder (or, if you prefer, a manila folder for each student)
- Crayons or magic markers
- Blackboard
- Poster with questions and answers related to portfolios

Procedures

1. Write the definition of *portfolio* on the board (see definition above).
2. Ask students to think of as many questions about portfolios as they can. As they raise their hands or call out questions, write them on the board. When you think there are enough good questions, say that you happen to have a poster with some of those very questions on it along with answers.
3. Hang the poster (see Figure 3.3) on the board and begin a discussion of its contents, adding answers to the other questions that they may have asked earlier. Emphasize

Figure 3.3   Poster

Questions and Answers about Portfolios

PORTFOLIOS: Collecting, Reflecting, Selecting, Projecting (or Directing), Presenting

1. *What is a portfolio?*

   A portfolio is a compilation of your work that demonstrates your growth over time.

2. *What do I put in my portfolio?*

   There are many examples of the types of work that you can place in your portfolio. Initially, COLLECT *all* of your work in your portfolio. (These assignments will have already been graded and then returned to you.) Then a week before the end of each grading quarter REFLECT on each of the items, that is, review and evaluate the artifacts you have saved and identify those that demonstrate certain criteria.

   • Which ones am I most *proud* of?
   • Which ones are my *favorite*?
   • Which ones were most *difficult* for me (and why)?
   • Which ones did I *learn the most* from?

   Through such reflection you will be able to evaluate your growth over time as well as the gaps in your learning.

   Now SELECT *two* items per criterion and place them back into your portfolio. (The items not selected may go into another file or your teacher will suggest where to save them.)

   (PROJECTING, or DIRECTING, refers to the fact that portfolios can help you identify what you need to do in the future to improve learning. You will be able to set learning goals based on your self-evaluation. Eventually you will engage in PRESENTING or sharing your portfolio with others. [See 4 below.] The feedback you receive from others will support your lifelong learning.) (Danielson and Abrutyn, 1997)

3. *What do I do after I have selected my eight item*s? (More are possible, and you and your teacher may come up with other criteria.)

   Number the items and fill in the *Contents Page* that you will use as your first page. (At this point your teacher will give you a copy of the Contents Page [see Figure 3.4] and will review it *after* the poster discussion.)

   Reflect again on the eight items, and then write one paragraph for each of the items—for example, (a) Why did I choose

these two items as those I'm most proud of? (b) Why are these two my favorite? (c) Why did I consider these two as most difficult for me? (d) Why were these two the most useful to me in terms of new learning? Label the paragraphs with the item number. Then file the narratives with the items to which they refer.

4. *How can my portfolio enhance my self-knowledge and that of my peers and expand the classroom community?* (PROJECTING and PRESENTING)

   The process of collecting, reflecting, and selecting described above will hopefully help you identify how you learn most effectively and what you might need to do in order to enjoy learning and successfully complete assignments. By sharing your portfolio with others, you will be able to further such self-knowledge while at the same time expanding the classroom community:

   • S-S (Student with Student): In groups or with a partner, you can review your portfolios and compare the contents. Discuss your choices of items. In this way, you may learn from your peers.
   • S-T (Student with Teacher): With your teacher you can discuss your choices, and in this way help your teacher get to know you better and the way you learn.
   • S-T-P (Student with Teacher with Parent): Your parents or guardians can learn more about you and the way you think within—as well as outside of—the classroom. They can also learn about ways they might help you.
   • T-T (Teacher with Teacher): Teachers can use a student's portfolio as a vehicle for professional development. When teachers share their creative assignments, projects, and tests, they are being helpful to their colleagues; and, in turn, they, too, will be able to learn from their peers.

5. *What questions do I still have about portfolios?*

   Now you and your teacher can address the questions listed earlier on the board.

6. *How do I fill in the Contents Page?*

   Review the parts of the Contents Page. Then you will be able to create a *cover* for your portfolio.

Figure 3.4   Contents of My Portfolio

Item Number (Entry Number)	Date of Item	Title of Item (Brief Description)	Comments—Self-Evaluation or Other (i.e. "a favorite of mine")	My Initials

the little slogan that appears at the top of the poster and ask students to remember it as they begin to establish portfolios. (You might also give students a handout with the same information that appears on the poster.)

4. After discussing the data on the poster, give students a copy of the contents page for their portfolio and discuss its components (see Figure 3.4).

5. Give students time now to make a cover for their portfolio using crayons or magic markers.

Assessment

- Participation in the initial discussion of portfolios (Objectives 1, 2)
- A response paper in which students express in their own words the purposes of, and process for, developing a portfolio (Objective 2)
- Their creation of a portfolio cover (Objective 3)

Extension

Electronic portfolios are an alternative to paper-based storage formats and combine the use of electronic technologies to create and publish portfolios that can use a variety of differing media types (i.e., audio, video, graphics, electronic text). See Helen Barrett's website (www .electronicportfolios.org) for more information about implementing electronic portfolios in the classroom. Like the more traditional formats, electronic portfolios also showcase learners' achievements but in addition demonstrate their growing capabilities in using technology to support lifelong learning.

Sample Unit 1: Representing Our Diverse Community in a Calendar*

Grade Levels: 1–12
Content: Interdisciplinary
Time: Approximately 3–4 weeks
Principles: 1, 2, 3, 4

*Adapted from a 2005 project created by the River Charter School in Greenfield, Massachusetts.

Teams of students can easily complete the interdisciplinary activities involved in researching and constructing a calendar that contains information about the diverse population in their community. In the process students will gain and spread knowledge as they establish meaningful relationships with members of the community.

Objectives

Students will be able to

1. Prepare questionnaires and carry out interviews with their research group (SOCS-USH 1–4 [K–4]; SOCS-USH 10 [5–12]; ELA 1, 2, 5–12).
2. Share stories of 12 local immigrants or representatives of the different cultures within their community (to be included in the calendars) (ELA 4, 5, 6).
3. Prepare a calendar that includes photographs of the interviewees along with brief biographies (ELA 6, 12).
4. Distribute and share the calendars beyond the classroom (if you decide to sell the calendars, the proceeds can go toward the printing costs, then toward purchasing multicultural books for the classroom or library) (MAT-N/O 1–3; ELA 4, 6).
5. Build tolerant and welcoming attitudes within the community (SOCS-C 5; ELA 7, 9, 11).
6. Debrief after the project is completed.

Materials

- Notebooks
- (Optional) Cassettes or other types of recorders
- Cameras (if photos are not already available)
- Calendar format
- Copying machines or other tools to facilitate the reproduction of the calendars

Procedures

Over the course of three weeks:

1. Initiate a discussion about neighborhoods, the different kinds of stores and houses of worship in their community, and the people from different cultures they have met. List some of the students' responses on the board.
2. If there are English language learners (ELLs) in the class, ask them where they came from and then list all of those countries on the board.
3. Discuss the difficulties people sometimes have when adapting to a new country, such as learning a new language, getting to know people outside of their cultural group, and other challenges.
4. Brainstorm ways that people can get to know diverse members of the community who live and work among them. Share the idea of interviewing immigrants or others from different cultures and constructing a calendar with summaries of those interviews.
5. Pair English speakers with ELLs and have them discuss whom they will interview, possibly someone from one of their families. Approximately 12 pairs of students will be working on the project.
6. Discuss how they will then approach or contact their potential interviewees and go through the process of introducing themselves, explaining the purpose of their project, asking permission to photograph them (or borrow photographs), and so on.
7. Schedule work sessions during which students meet to compare progress and help one another research and prepare biographies (i.e., discuss what resources they will need and where they will be able to find them). For example, are there churches, social centers, or neighborhoods where immigrants gather and where students could go to meet them? Then establish times and dates for interviews.

8. Discuss any costs involved, and if it is determined that students will need to pay for reproducing the calendars, assign a team to find out those costs. Then decide what price to put on the calendars so that members of the community can contribute—through purchase of calendars—to those printing costs.

9. On completion of brief biographies, work with someone from the school or community familiar with how to lay out a calendar.

10. Get the calendars printed and discuss how to go about distributing or selling them.

11. Hold a debriefing session at which students evaluate their efforts.

12. Invite parents, community members, interviewees and their families and other classes to a meeting—with refreshments—to launch the calendar and explain its purpose.

13. Reassemble the class a few weeks after initial sales of the calendar to discuss the responses to their project.

Assessment

- Cooperation in the research groups (Objective 1)
- The calendar produced by the teams of students (and individual contributions comprising interviews, stories, and the photos they took or gathered) (Objectives 1, 2, 3)
- Participation in a community meeting made up of the interviewees, their classmates, parents, and others from the community at which they discuss the purpose of their project (Objectives 4, 5)
- Contributions to a meeting at which students discuss responses, and those of others, to the project (Objective 6)

Extension

Adapt this unit to your particular needs or resources (e.g., possibly produce a newspaper instead of a calendar).

Sample Unit 2: Writing and Performing a Play about U.S. (or Their Community's) Multicultural History

Grade Levels: 3–12
Content: Interdisciplinary
Time: Approximately 4 weeks
Principles: 1, 2, 3, 4, 5

Students in small groups can contribute a scene or vignette to a larger thematic production without the need for a lot of preparation time. The first decision the class needs to make concerns what they want to portray in a theater piece related to diversity? That is, do they want to do research on their own community's multicultural history or U.S. history? Secondly, how do they want to structure the play?

The process delineated in this lesson is only one of the many ways a class can work cooperatively to write a play. The format demonstrated is an "I was there" approach to community history. The size of each scene-writing group will depend on the total number of vignettes the class decides they want to present.

Objectives

Students will be able to

1. Do research on events that took place—well known or not—in their community's history. That is, students can identify important events related to family members whose

stories represent interesting episodes within their *community*'s diverse history. On the other hand, they could focus on an event in U.S. history (SOCS-USH 1–4 [K–4]; USH 1–10 [5–12]; ELA 1–12). (This research could be part of a separate unit in which you apply the seven steps of the group investigation model described in Figure 3.2 earlier. The construction and performance of a play could then follow as a miniunit that expands on the research project.)

2. Assist their study group in preparing an "I was there" vignette using the steps in Figure 3.5 and the concept map comprising Figure 3.6 (SOCS-USH 1–4 [K–4]; ELA 2, 6, 12).
3. Participate in the presentation of the vignette they helped to prepare (NA-T 1–8).
4. Evaluate the project and their role in it (ELA 4, 5, 11).

Materials

- Notepaper and pencils
- Appropriate props and costumes
- Figures 3.5 and 3.6: Steps for creating "I was there" vignettes and the concept map

Procedures

You might want to refer to Figure 3.2 for the steps in the group investigation model. The GIM can be applied to a study of the historic diversity within the students' community (two weeks), followed by a miniunit in which students prepare a play (two weeks).

1. Review with the class the events that students discovered when they did research on diversity in their community's history. The students will likely have gathered extensive notes, completed papers, and maybe even prepared a bulletin board display.
2. Together decide which three or four events they want to depict using the "I was there" format (see Figure 3.5). (Among these events might be a scene in which one of the students' families is shown arriving in the United States for the first time or a scene in which students depict one of their families celebrating a cultural holiday. These kinds of vignettes might accompany the better-known events related to their community's diverse history.)
3. List the chosen scenes on the board and then decide on the composition of the student play-writing groups. You may want to choose groups based on mutual interests

Figure 3.5   Steps for Creating "I Was There" Vignettes

Many decades ago there was a popular television program called "You Are There," in which the viewer was able to watch a historical episode reenacted. The object was to make the viewer a virtual eyewitness who could view the event and listen to a simulated conversation between historical figures who had had an impact on history.

Students can become the reenactors of historical scenes that reflect the diversity—past and present—of their community by

1. Researching and identifying the famous (or not so famous) people they want to portray
2. Creating a script
3. Deciding what role each person in group should play
4. Deciding who the narrator(s) of the vignettes should be and what they should say
5. Establishing the props or costumes that are required

---

or you may want to organize heterogeneous groups with a cross section of ability and gender within each group. (See Principle 2 in this chapter.)

4. Give each person a copy of a concept map (see Figure 3.6) that they can fill in individually and then bring to their group for discussion.
5. Groups meet to develop and plan their vignette. Through consensus they decide on the final version for the concept map and share it with the teacher.
6. Once approved, students gather the necessary resources, practice their scene, and then present it to their peers.
7. After appropriate changes are made for each scene, students can decide on a title for their play, when they want to perform the play for the public, how to advertise the play and what to include in the printed program, and what refreshments, if any, should be available. Assign roles—or ask for volunteers—to complete all of these tasks once everyone has contributed their ideas and decisions have been made.
8. Rehearse the vignettes or play.
9. Perform the play. (You may want to videotape it.)

Assessment

- The written notes or report reflecting student's research on the diverse history of their community (Objective 1)
- Participation in the preparation and performance of their group's vignette within the larger play (Objectives 1, 2, 3)
- A self-evaluation assessing the quality of their participation and the value of the experience of writing and performing a play (Objective 4)

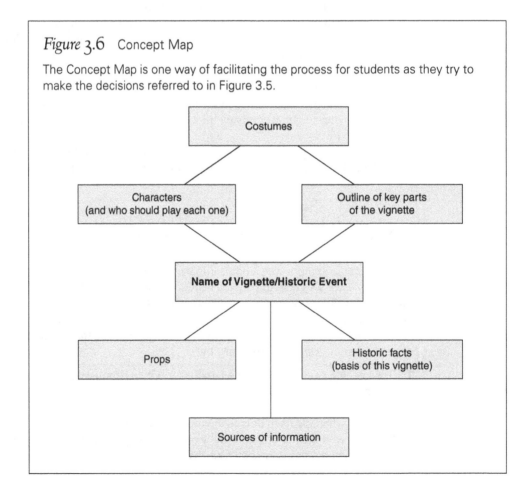

Figure 3.6   Concept Map

The Concept Map is one way of facilitating the process for students as they try to make the decisions referred to in Figure 3.5.

Costumes

Characters
(and who should play each one)

Outline of key parts
of the vignette

Name of Vignette/Historic Event

Props

Historic facts
(basis of this vignette)

Sources of information

Extension

These historical vignettes could be produced in the form of a book created by students with their parents, or they could produce a booklet about their own family's history. Their parents could illustrate the book and the students could write the simple text. They could write the book in their native language or English. McCaleb (1994) describes in detail the project she facilitated in which the children of immigrants and their families told their stories reflecting themes like "Families Building Together" and "Families as Problem Solvers through Struggle and Change." Writes Caleb, "Encouraging students and their families to write stories about themselves gives them the opportunity to become the main characters of their own stories. . . . The powerful experience of becoming an author is in strong contrast to their experience as ethnic or linguistic minority persons in the United States and always being forced by the dominant culture to listen and learn about someone else's story" (McCaleb, 1994, pp. 115, 126).

Summary Chart of Principles and Their Applications

Principle	Applications
1. Students of all backgrounds and income levels are more likely to have success in school when classroom community building involves strong parent–teacher communication and partnership.	1. View each student's native language and culture as a positive foundation and resource on which to build knowledge as well as facility in English. With that attitude in mind, teachers can demonstrate respect for parental involvement by providing translation for all parents who request or need it when parent conferences are scheduled. 2. Schools can create parent resource centers where materials—and refreshments—are made available to parents. 3. Visit the homes of students as a way of reaching out to parents. 4. Invite parents into classroom as tutors, presenters of information, chaperones, snack-time monitors, storytellers, or simply observers. 5. Involve parents in a school project that taps into the parents' experiences and cultural practices.
2. When students from different backgrounds, cultures, and ability levels engage in cooperative small-group learning, in which they are able to observe that their peers often make useful contributions to the group, such interactions can lead to prejudice reduction.	1. Students can learn to work in cooperative heterogeneous groups on common goals or projects, thereby taking responsibility for their own learning. The jigsaw approach and the group investigation model are two of the many cooperative learning strategies described in the literature. 2. Before implementing cooperative strategies, take time to explain to students the purpose and values of cooperative learning and the nature of their roles within the group. 3. Students can rotate through a number of different roles within the group process, thereby putting into practice democratic decision making and critical thinking skills.

(continued)

3. Building the classroom-as-community involves teaching about and providing opportunities for positive interactions among members of the class *and* within the larger community.	1. Teachers can foster a sense of community within the class by modeling certain behaviors, including speaking in a natural way and without bias and valuing and responding to students' needs and interests. 2. Teach students about ways they can resolve conflicts peacefully in the classroom. 3. Cooperative learning opportunities can improve learning for diverse students. 4. Service learning projects tied to academic content can connect students to their local community in ways that benefit them both. 5. Internships and field research are other ways that students can connect with their community outside the school.
4. Differentiated instruction enables teachers to tailor their instruction to the needs of individual students with attention to auditory, visual, and kinetic differences, differences in ability, and differences in student interests. Such instruction uses both cooperative and independent study strategies.	1. Provide opportunities in the classroom for students to work on tasks independently as well as in groups. 2. Allow students to make choices among possible topics or tasks involved in a course of study. 3. Assist students in reflecting on their own needs and preferences as well as assessing the areas in which they need improvement.
5. "The school must itself be a community life in all which that implies...." (Dewey, 1966, p. 358)	1. John Dewey's communal vision of education challenged the factory model of education. 2. James Comer's School Development Program radically restructures the school as a community.
6. Other models exist that promote student-school-community relationships that are mutually beneficial.	1. The Community Learning Center (CLC) redefines school as a community learning center in which pedagogy is a two-way street. The school remains open after hours and on weekends to accommodate that purpose. 2. The Community as School (CAS) model—as its name implies—views the entire community as the main resource for learning; students travel to areas of the community where they engage in learning for one day or longer, perhaps returning to the formal classroom occasionally.

 LINKS: Recording in Your Journal

The following questions may be useful as you reflect on the goals of building the classroom as community and establishing school-family-community relationships that can enhance student learning and growth. These questions will also assist you in reflecting on the research, principles, lessons, and strategies related to these goals.

1. What does the concept of community mean to you? Think about communities of which you have been a part. What, if anything, did they have in common? How would you de-

scribe your role in those communities? What makes a meaningful community different from one based simply on the close proximity of people to one another?

2. Have you ever completed a service-learning project, that is, performed community service either as part of a school-related assignment or on your own? If so, what value did it have for you *and* the people who benefited from that service? Find out about other examples of community service from your peers. (Perhaps you would want to work with your peers in designing community service projects appropriate for implementation by elementary, middle school, and high school students.)

3. This chapter contained suggestions for involving parents and community in children's education. A contemporary approach for accomplishing this was described by a third-grade teacher who created a blog so she could involve busy parents online. The blog turned into a "chatty community" (Sacchetti, 2006, B9), according to Melanie Sullivan, who said, "Parents just want to know what's going on. The more they know, . . . the less they get upset" (Sacchetti, 2006, p. B9). Can you think of any other innovative ways of involving parents and the community in the schools? You might first want to review all of the suggestions for involving parents and the community in the schools presented in this chapter. (This author would like to note that one ingredient for nurturing constructive parental involvement of any kind is the inclusion of food sharing during meetings. Refreshments help to open people's hearts and minds as well as being avenues for communication.) Finally, investigate the many blogs and wikis (editable websites) that enable teachers to communicate with one another and students to collaborate (Ferriter, 2009, pp. 34–38).

4. Two ideas described in this chapter—cooperative learning and portfolio development—offer students the opportunity to take responsibility for their own learning *and* share responsibility for learning with their peers. Again, reflect on your own experiences, if any, with these community-building approaches. How was your experience similar to the descriptions in this chapter? How could you adapt one of the lessons or units in this chapter so that it would be appropriate for use in *your* subject area or grade level?

5. Classroom management is intrinsically connected to curriculum content and method. That is, if students are excited by what and how they are learning, there will likely be less misbehaving and conflict. However, even in the most stimulating classrooms conflicts arise that need to be resolved. Reflect first on your experience with resolving conflict and on the causes of those conflicts. What methods have proven effective for resolving them and why did they work? Have you ever observed situations in which students play a role in conflict resolution? What are your views concerning the lessons and strategies presented in this chapter that address this important aspect of establishing the classroom as community?

6. "Community is the entire orchestra playing in harmony, with each musician contributing his or her best to the piece" (Fisher, 1995). What other metaphors or images can help you to envision community in the classroom and the kinds of learning and caring that play a role in the building of that community?

References

Adams, D. M., and M. E. Hamm. (1992). "Portfolio Assessment and Social Studies: Collecting, Selecting, and Reflecting on What Is Significant." *Social Education* 56(2). Washington, DC: National Council for the Social Studies.

Aronson, E. (1978). *The Jigsaw Classroom.* Beverly Hills, CA: Sage Publications.

Balkcom, S. (June 1992). "Cooperative Learning." *Education Research Consumer Guide.* Washington, DC: Office of Research, Office of Educational Research and Improvement of the U.S. Department of Education.

Barrett, H. (April 2000). "Create Your Own Electronic Portfolio." *Learning and Leading with Technology, 27*(7), pp. 14–21.

Bazron, B., D. Osher, and S. Fleischman. (September 2005). "Creating Culturally Responsive Schools." *Educational Leadership, 63*(1), pp. 83–84.

Berkowitz, M. W., and M. C. Bier. (September 2005). "Character Education: Parents as Partners," *Educational Leadership, 63*(1), pp. 64–69.

Bickmore, K. (Summer 2001). "Student Conflict Resolution, Power 'Sharing' in Schools, and Citizenship Education." *Curriculum Inquiry, 31*(2), pp. 137–162.

Boaler, J. (February 2006). "Promoting Respectful Learning." *Educational Leadership, 63*(5), pp. 74–78.

Bradley, A., and J. D. Anderson-Nickel. (April/May 2006). "Contributors to Sage Advice." *Edutopia, 2*(3), p. 16.

Briscoe, R. V., A. Smith, and G. McClain. (2003). "Implementing Culturally Competent Research Practices." *Focal Point, 17*(1), pp. 10–16.

Bryk, A. S., and M. E. Driscoll. (1988). *The High School as Community: Conceptual Influences and Consequences for Students and Teachers.* Madison, WI: National Center for Effective Secondary Schools.

Comer, J. (2004). *Leave No Child Behind: Preparing Today's Youth for Tomorrow's World.* New Haven, CT: Yale University Press.

Cushman, K. (November 2005). "It Takes a Village: Bringing School Into the Community and Community Into the School." *Edutopia, 2*(2), pp. 47–49.

Cushman, K., A. Steinberg, and R. Riordan. (2005). *Schooling for the Real World.* San Francisco: Jossey-Bass.

Damon, W. (Spring 2005). "Good? Bad? Or None of the Above?" *Education Next, A Journal of Opinion and Research, 5*(2), pp. 21–27.

Daniels, H. (2002). *Literature Circles: Voice and Choice in the Student-Centered Classroom.* York, ME: Stenhouse Publishers.

Danielson, C,. and L. Abrutyn. (1997). *An Introduction to Using Portfolios in the Classroom.* Alexandria, VA: Association for Supervision and Curriculum Development.

DeSola, C. (1974). *Learning through Dance.* New York: Paulist Press.

Dewey, J. (1966). *Democracy and Education.* New York: Free Press. (Original work published 1916)

Driscoll, M. E. (1995). "Thinking Like a Fish, The Implications of the Image of School Community for Connections between Parents and Schools," in P. W. Cookson, Jr. and B. Schneider (Eds.), *Transforming Schools* (pp. 209–236). New York: Garland Publishing.

Epstein, J. L. (1987). "Parent Involvement: What Research Says to Administrators." *Education and Urban Society, 19*(2), pp. 119–136.

Ferriter, B. (February 2009). "Learning with Blogs and Wikis." *Educational Leadership 66*(5), pp. 34–38.

Fisher, B. (1995). *Thinking and Learning Together: Curriculum and Community in a Primary Classroom.* Portsmouth, NH: Heinemann.

Furger, R. (March 2006). "Secret Weapon Discovered!" *Conflict Resolution Curriculum for High School.* Chapel Hill: The Mediation Network of North Carolina.

Gilbert, S. (March 27, 2001). "No One Left to Hate: Averting Columbines." *New York Times.* Retrieved from www.nytimes.com/2001/3/27/health/27CONV.html

Grant, R. A., and S. D. Wong. (2004). "Forging Multilingual Communities: School-Based Strategies." *Multicultural Perspectives, 6*(3), pp. 17–23.

Henderson, A. T., and K. L. Mapp. (2002). *A New Wave of Evidence: The Impact of School, Family, and Community Connection on Student Achievement.* Austin, TX: Southwest Educational Development Laboratory.

Johnson, D. W., R. Johnson, and E. Johnson Holubec. (1988). *Cooperation in the Classroom.* Edina, MN: Interaction Book Company.

Johnson, D. W., and R. T. Johnson. (Winter 1996). "Conflict Resolution and Peer Mediation Programs in Elementary and Secondary Schools: A Review of the Research." *Review of Educational Research, 66*(4), pp. 459–506.

Karasik, R. J. (April 2006). "Successful Service Learning." *NEA Higher Education Advocate, 23*(4), pp. 5–8.

Lerman, L. (2005). "Making Rules, Breaking Rules, The Artist in the 21st Century." Chautauqua Lecture Series.

Lerman, L. (2008). "Toward a Process for Critical Response." Available at www.communityarts.net

Levy, S. (1996). *Starting from Scratch: One Classroom Builds Its Own Curriculum.* Portsmouth, NH: Heinemann.

McCaleb, S. P. (1994). *Building Communities of Learners: A Collaboration among Teachers, Students, Families and Community.* New York: St. Martin's Press.

Millis, B. J. (December 2003). "Understanding Cooperative Learning." *Thriving in Academe, 21*(2), pp. 5–8.

Nair, P. (July/August 2006). "Getting Beyond the School as Temple." *Edutopia, 2*(5), pp. 28–31.

Pearlman, B. (June 2006). "New Skills for a New Century." *Edutopia, 2*(4), pp. 51–53.

Read, C. (September 13, 2005). *Best Teacher Essay.* Unpublished paper, Massachusetts College of Liberal Arts.

Rowan, B. (1990). "Commitment and Control: Alternative Strategies for the Organizational Design of Schools." *Review of Research in Education, 16*(1), pp. 353–392.

Sacchetti, M. (September 7, 2006). "Teachers Take Bulletin Boards Online." *The Boston Globe.*

Schniedewind, N., and E. Davidson. (1998). *Open Minds to Equality.* Boston: Allyn and Bacon.

Sharan, S., P. Kussell, R. Hertz-Lazarowitz, Y. Bejarano, S. Raviv, and Y. Sharan. (1984). *Cooperative Learning in the Classroom: Research in Desegregated Schools.* Mahwah, NJ: Erlbaum.

Slavin, R. (1983). *Cooperative Learning.* New York: Longman.

Smith, F. (February 2006). "Learning by Giving." *Edutopia, 2*(1), pp. 55–57.

Stein, R., and S. Hurd. (2000). *Using Student Teams in the Classroom: A Faculty Guide.* Boston: Anker.

Strauss, V. (March 21, 2006). "Putting Parents in Their Place: Outside Class." *Washington Post,* p. A08.

Teach for America. (2004). *Diversity, Community and Achievement.* Summer Institute.

Thelen, H. A. (1954). *Dynamics of Groups at Work.* Chicago: University of Chicago Press.

Tomlinson, C. A. (1999). *The Differentiated Classroom: Responding to the Needs of All Learners.* Alexandria, VA: Association for Supervision and Curriculum Development.

Wiggins, G. (1998). *Educative Assessment: Designing Assessments to Inform and Improve Student Performance.* San Francisco: Jossey-Bass.

Recommended Resources

Bickart, T., J. R. Jablon, and D. T. Dodge. (2005). "Building a Classroom Community," in *Building the Primary Classroom*. Retrieved from www.teachingstrategies.com/content/pagetocs/BPC_Ch2.pdf

Daylanghout, R., J. Rappaport, and D. Simmons. (2002). "Integrating Community into the Classroom." *Urban Education*, 37(3), pp. 323–349.

Fiore, D. J. (2002). *School Community Relations*. Larchmont, NY: Eye on Education.

Gibson, M. A., P. Gándara, and J. Peterson Koyama (Eds.). (2004). *School Connections: U.S. Mexican Youth, Peers, and School Achievement*. New York: Teachers College Press.

Glasgow, N. A. (1996). *Taking the Classroom into the Community: A Guidebook*. New York: Corwin Press.

Henton, M. (1996). *Adventure in the Classroom: Using Adventure to Strengthen Learning and Build a Community of Life-Long Learners*. Dubuque, IA: Kendall-Hunt.

Jay, G. (July/Aug 2000). "The Community in the Classroom." *Academe*, 86(4), pp. 33–37.

Smoke, T. (Ed.) (1998). *Adult ESL: Politics, Pedagogy, and Participation in Classroom and Community Programs*. Mahwah, NJ: Lawrence Erlbaum.

Solomon, M., M. Watson, V. Battistich, E. Schaps, and K. Delucchi. (1996). "Creating Classrooms That Students Experience as Communities." *American Journal of Community Psychology*, 24(6), pp. 719–748.

Tashlik, P., and C. Tomaszewski. (2006). *Serving the Community: Guidelines for Setting Up a Service-Learning Program*. New York: Teachers College Press.

Thomas, D., W. Enloe, and R. Newell (Eds.). (2005). *The Coolest School in America: How Small Learning Communities Are Changing Everything*. Lanham, MD: Rowman & Littlefield.

Websites

www.edutopia.org/1476 and www.glef.org
George Lucas Educational Foundation is publisher of the journal *Edutopia* that provides Web links to parental involvement resources.

www.electronicportfolios.org
Dr. Helen Barrett's "Electronic Portfolios and Digital Storytelling for Lifeling and Lifewide Learning."

www.naf.org
National Academy Foundation, school-to-work curriculum

www.ncrl.org
North Central Regional Education Laboratory

www.pwcs.edu/curriculumsol/groupinves.htm
Group Investigation Strategies

www.servicelearning.org
National Service Learning Clearinghouse

www.service-learningpartnership.org
National Service Learning Partnership

www.toolbox.danceexchange.org
Liz Lerman's techniques for choreography and community building

Chapter Four

Strategies and Lessons for Increasing Knowledge about Diversity

Cathy Marden, CATA 2007–2008 program year

"We ought to think that we are one of the leaves of a tree, and the tree is humanity. We cannot live without the others, without the tree."

Pablo Casals, cellist (1877–1973)

The purpose of this chapter is to help teachers increase their students' knowledge about diverse peoples within the American mosaic of microcultures based on race, religion, ethnicity, class, gender, language, and exceptionality. The goal, however, is not to provide a compendium of facts about each microculture. That would require a much lengthier text. Rather, the purpose here is to provide lessons, research, and teaching principles broad enough to apply to a study of any or all of these groups. To assist in that process, this chapter includes Bloom's taxonomy of skills in three domains, an invaluable tool for implementing and designing creative and challenging learning experiences as well as providing students with skills for learning.

Chapter 4 also reveals ways that students can establish direct and indirect connections with members of diverse groups within their school and community. The two units of instruction at the end of the chapter incorporate interdisciplinary instructional activities that can actively engage students in the field as they increase their knowledge about the richness and power of difference and the variety of affirming and negative responses it engenders.

Imagine being in the audience at the United Nations as Eleanor Roosevelt delivers these remarks. What other ideas would you add to this vision of human rights?

Where, after all, do universal human rights begin? In small places, close to home—so close and so small that they cannot be seen on any map of the world. Yet they are the world of the individual person: the neighborhood he lives in; the school or college he attends; the factory, farm, or office where he works. Such are the places where every man, woman, and child seeks equal justice, equal opportunity, equal dignity without discrimination. Unless these rights have meaning there, they have little meaning anywhere. Without concerted citizen action to uphold them close to home, we shall look in vain for progress in the larger world.

—Eleanor Roosevelt, Remarks at the United Nations, March 27, 1958

 **What the Research Says**

ONE Television as Source of Multicultural Education

> Throughout their lives, our students will experience thousands upon thousands of hours of television . . . [with one thing remaining a] constant: this programming will continue to be culture-bound and, as such, will present mixed and often confusing messages about race, ethnicity and social class. (Pohan and Mathison, 2007, p. 20)

According to Pohan and Mathison's study of preservice teachers' evaluations of children's television programming, the media perpetuates generalizations and stereotypes about both dominant and nondominant groups in the United States and is "providing far more multicultural education than our public school system" (Pohan and Mathison, 2007, p. 19).

Future teachers and their students need to become aware of the socially constructed nature of television programming and its potential for distorting reality. For example, the media often portrays people as members of particular social, ethnic, or other categories, which leads to stereotypical thinking that ignores what is unique about each individual. And there is another potential cause of distortion: Because some minorities are more visible in the media than others and have disproportionate numbers in the lower class due to economic, political, and social factors beyond their control, teachers and students alike may sometimes generalize about them as a group. Interestingly, the cultural and racial history of European Americans, the dominant group, does not often receive attention in the media, though understanding the history of *all* Americans is crucial for educators working to create an inclusive, pluralistic society.

The research reveals that media distortion of reality about the diverse groups within our society can also be the result of their *omission* from the media. For example, Chon Noriega and Alison Hoffman, in a study for the Chicano Studies Research Center of the University of California, Los Angeles, found a drop in Hispanic and other minority lead characters on programs on the six major networks, even when the setting was in an ethnically diverse city. While Los Angeles County's population is nearly 45 percent Hispanic, Hispanics accounted for only 14 percent of the characters seen on the eight 2004 prime-time series set in Los Angeles, and all of those characters were in one series, the ABC sitcom "George Lopez." There were no Asian American regular characters, the study found, although that ethnic group makes up 12 percent of Los Angeles County's population (Associated Press, 2004).

The National Council for the Social Studies (NCSS) points out in its position statement for multiculturalism that in order to build a successful and inclusive nation-state, "the hopes, dreams and experiences of the many groups within it must be reflected in the structure and institutions of society" (Adler, 2003, p. 111). The media is, of course, one of our country's major institutions, but for many reasons—among them the bias that exists within society—it certainly does not always reflect the "dreams and experiences" of certain groups.

One person who has tried to remedy this situation by including children from often ignored groups is Marc Brown, creator of the series "Postcards from Buster," a series about an animated rabbit known primarily as a close friend of Arthur, the world's most famous aardvark. The series is aimed at young elementary schoolchildren who can watch Buster travel to 24 different states with his father and then send video postcards home. In one episode, Buster visited a Mormon family in Utah. He has dropped in on fundamentalist Christians and Muslims as well as American Indians and Hmong. He has shown the lives of children who have only one parent and those who live with grandparents.

However, the PBS network decided not to distribute to its 350 PBS stations an episode that included lesbian mothers. The decision by PBS appeared to be influenced by a statement from Education Secretary Margaret Spellings indicating that many parents would not want their children exposed to a lesbian lifestyle (Salamon, 2005, p. C4), despite the fact that the federal grant with which the series was developed specified, "Diversity will be incorporated into the fabric of the series to help children understand and respect differences and learn to live in a multicultural society" (Salamon, 2005, p. C4). (WGBH-TV of Boston, the show's producer, did broadcast the episode and offered it to other PBS stations.)

Because of the significant role played by the media in indirectly teaching about diversity, Pohan and Mathison suggest ways that future teachers and their students can start to both recognize the multicultural teaching power of the media and increase their *critical literacy* as consumers of the media, referring to an increased awareness of the sociocultural constructs that drive the words and images they encounter on television and in other media. Their program for preparing future teachers with critical television viewing habits includes the following elements:

1. Conveying to parents or caregivers the importance of monitoring the viewing habits of their children
2. Helping their students evaluate the content of various programs and then leading debriefing sessions
3. Designing meaningful assignments aimed at developing media and critical literacy skills among students

4. Recognizing the instructional potential of television, that is, its multicultural teaching power
5. Building awareness of the role television plays in the lives of their students and using this opportunity to teach about diversity and social justice (Pohan and Mathison, 2007, p. 23)

Reflective question: What observations have you personally made about the multicultural content of television programming? What do *you* believe is the responsibility of the media to honor diversity and tolerance?

TWO Blurring of Identities

The ethnic, social, and religious identities of students are becoming less defined as a result of intermarriage, assimilation, and other factors.

Some students who are asked to check off the appropriate boxes that appear on some questionnaires asking for race, religion, or nationality are faced with a dilemma. There are more and more children from mixed race, mixed religion families and those with multiple ethnicities as well. For example, there are children from Asia, Africa, and South America who have been adopted by white families. The result is that it's not so easy to attach labels that have been and continue to be employed for a variety of reasons and that are also included as criteria for identifying school populations, a requirement of the No Child Left Behind Act.

In a fascinating article for the *New York Times Magazine*, Jack Hitt (2005) writes about another phenomenon that is blurring the definitions of race and ethnicity. He describes how more and more people—in this case, among Native Americans and those interested by indigenous cultures—are claiming to have discovered tribal ancestries and so are carrying out what sociologists call "ethnic shopping," or changing out of the identities they were born into and donning new ones in which they feel more at home. He notes also that today's scattered, more mobile generations "have less access to such stable memories of ethnic identity" (such as neighborhoods populated by a single immigrant or ethnic group), which may account for the current practice of laying claim "through participation in ethnic festivals or religious conversion to an identity that better suits the itch of our increasingly intermarried, interracial, intertribal America" (Hitt, 2005, p. 41).

Reflective question: Have you seen evidence in your community of the blurring of identities? If so, what, if any, have been the observable results?

THREE Culturally Relevant Laws and Decisions

Congress and the courts have issued culturally relevant laws and decisions respectively that have led to the increase—or erosion—of equal educational opportunities.

While the Supreme Court has not consistently decided in favor of minority rights, there is no question that the Court's decisions (some of which are listed in Table 4.1) over the last 50 years or so have played a major role in advancing educational equity for underserved groups. However, there are areas where some of that progress has been eroded. For example, in the area of civil rights, the judiciary, according to legal researcher Michael LaMorte, can no longer be relied on to assist in furthering desegregation measures. He refers to the findings of Frankenberg and colleagues in *A Multiracial Society with Segregated Schools, Are We Losing the Dream?* (Frankenberg, Lee, and Orfield, 2003) and concludes that "desegregation gains made since *Brown* [*v. Board of Education* (1954)] are increasingly being lost" (La Morte, 2008, p. 330). Why has there been a move toward resegregation? And why has there been

Table 4.1   A Sample of Culturally Relevant Laws and Court Decisions

Issue	Name of Law/Court Case	Provision of the Law/Decision
Microcultures	The Civil Rights Act of 1964	Forbids discrimination on the grounds of race, religion, or national origin by any institution receiving federal funds. The law also extends this protection to include members of language minority groups under the national origin provision.
Language	Title VII of the Elementary and Secondary Education Act (ESEA), also known as the Bilingual Education Act	Initially passed in 1968, this provision marked the first time the federal government got involved in assisting in the education of English language learners. While the law brought public attention to the needs of English learners, its intent was not clearly explained in terms of appropriate methods for accomplishing the goals of learning English.
	Lau v. Nichols (1974)	Affirmed the right of non-English-speaking students to an education equal to that of their English-speaking peers by providing access to the curriculum via primary language instruction. (As in the *Brown* case, the remedies proposed for addressing the respective issues have been controversial, and there are an increasing number of skeptics.) (Gandara et al., 2004, pp. 27–46)
Religion	*Ecklund v. Byron Union School District (No. 05–1539)* (U.S. Court of Appeals for the 9th circuit in San Francisco)	Held that the Islam unit activities in a world history class in California were not "overt religious exercises" in violation of the establishment clause.
	Zelman v. Simmons-Harris (2002)	Upheld the State of Ohio's private school voucher program for Cleveland's students, which included the participation of religious schools.
	Lee v. Weisman (1992)	Ruled that prayers mandated or organized by school officials at graduation exercises were unconstitutional based on the establishment clause of the First Amendment's freedom of religion provision ("Congress shall make no law respecting an establishment of religion")
Disability	IDEA: Individuals with Disabilities Education Act (1975)	Federal legislation that requires a free and appropriate public education for children regardless of the degree or type of their disabilities.
	Zobrest v. Catalina Foothills School District (1993)	Allowed the provision of a sign language interpreter at public expense for a deaf student in a religious school.
Gender	*David Parker, et al., v. William Hurley, et al.* (2007) (U.S. District Court and Massachusetts Court)	Decided that the constitutional right of parents to raise their children does not include the right to restrict what a public school may teach them. In this case, the federal judge threw out a lawsuit filed by parents who objected to discussions of gay families in their children's classrooms.

(continued)

Table 4.1   *Continued*

Issue	Name of Law/Court Case	Provision of the Law/Decision
Gender	Title IX of the 1972 Education Amendments Act	States that no students in the United States can be denied benefits of education programs receiving federal financial assistance on the basis of their sex.
Race	*Brown v. Board of Education of Topeka* (1954)	*Brown* I: Ruled that de jure (by law) racial segregation in public schools was unconstitutional and that "separate educational facilities are inherently unequal." *Brown* II: Ruled that the effort to desegregate public schools proceed "with all deliberate speed."
	Parents Involved in Community Schools v. Seattle School District and *Meredith v. Jefferson County Board of Education* (2007)	Supreme Court struck down two school districts' race-conscious student assignment plans as a violation of the 14th Amendment Equal Protection Clause. The majority said that the districts did not meet their burden of showing that their interest in maintaining racial diversity justifies using racial classifications in making school assignments. (However, the majority also endorsed the compelling educational benefits of integrated schools.)
	Gutter v. Bollinger (2003)	Upheld the consideration of race in principle and approved the system used by Michigan's law school to achieve a "critical mass" of underrepresented minorities.

so little resistance to that movement? These are questions you may want to find answers to through additional research.

Reflective question: Several of the culturally relevant laws and decisions in Table 4.1 bring to mind the controversial issue of the extent to which the 14th Amendment's "equal treatment under the law" provisions should be enforced, particularly when school systems want to support diversity. How important should diversity of all kinds be within the school environment?

Principles and Applications for
Increasing Knowledge about Diversity

Principle ONE

 A major goal of culturally responsive teaching and content is to humanize students by addressing real-life issues.

Among the real-life issues that many students grapple with are poverty, substance and other abuse, bullying, racial and ethnic differences, discipline (in home and school), physical appearance, and disabilities.

Classroom Applications and Strategies

These real-life issues can be addressed through the use of methods and content that not only help students solve problems but also increase their empathy toward others.

First and foremost, the authors of the handbook "Curriculum Infusion of Real Life Issues" (Glick, Joleaud, and Messerer, 2006) believe that teachers need not separate these issues from the standard curriculum; instead, they recommend that they be geared to subject areas. They point out that many of the objectives delineated in state standards include or imply skills stressed in addressing real-life issues, including decision-making and problem-solving skills, critical thinking, prejudice reduction, and role-playing.

The goal of the Network for Dissemination of Curriculum Infusion (NDCI) at Northeastern Illinois University is to prepare future and in-service teachers to integrate real-life issues into classes across the K–12 curriculum. To begin the process, they recommend that teachers take the following steps:

1. *Assessment: Assess the Class's Diversity.*   Identify real-life issues in their school and community, such as the impact of social injustice on diverse populations or the social and environmental influences affecting real-life issues. Some ways of identifying issues include conversations with students and observations of their interactions, discussions with parents, and contacts with personnel in community organizations, agencies, health departments, and others involved in providing services in problem areas. Preservice teachers can begin the identification process by assessing the strengths of the community they are or will be teaching in so they can become actively involved in solving the community's problems.

Teachers should also perform self-assessment of their own attitudes and particular connections to and experiences with these issues (Glick et al., 2006, p. 4).

2. *The Seamless Fit.*   Endeavor to achieve the normal curriculum goals set forth by the school and state with components of instruction woven in and adjusted to include relevant information regarding a specific real-life issue (Glick et al., 2006, p. 5).

3. *Evidence-Based Strategies.*   Engage students in the following five strategies that can enable them to prevent problems and positively resolve real-life issues:

- Involving students in community prevention of social injustice
- Promoting prosocial norms
- Correcting misperceptions of norms
- Increasing perceptions of personal risk
- Developing or enhancing life skills (e.g., antibullying curricula also encourage students to care for others)

See also the Real Life Issues Curriculum Infusion website at www.neiu.edu/K12pac for further explanations and lesson plans.

Principle TWO

 Simple ideas for promoting equity and celebrating diversity can be applied not only in the classroom but on a personal enrichment level, in the workplace, and within the community (Teaching Tolerance, 2000).

Classroom Applications and Strategies

Ideas for Personal Enrichment

1. Imagine what your life might be like if you were a person of another race, gender, or sexual orientation. How might today have been different?

2. Test for hidden biases that you may have and read about what you can do to address them (www.tolerance.org/hidden_bias/index.html).
3. Shop at ethnic grocery stores and specialty markets. Get to know the owners. Ask about the foods and their family histories.

Ideas for Your Home

1. Bookmark equity and diversity websites on your home computer.
2. Read books with multicultural and tolerance themes (to your children).
3. Invite someone of a different background to join you (and your family) for a meal or holiday.

Ideas for Your School

1. Invite bilingual students to give morning greetings and announcements on the PA system in their home languages.
2. Ensure that schools comply with the McKinney Act, the federal law mandating educational services for homeless children.
3. Gather art supplies and have students do a mural about the cultural composition and heritage of your community.

Ideas for the Workplace beyond School

1. Partner with a local business and encourage employees to serve as tutors or mentors.
2. Encourage businesses to add social justice funds to 401(k) investment options.
3. Suggest to a business leader to take on sponsorship of a community-wide "I Have a Dream" essay contest.

Ideas for the Community

1. Write a letter to the editor if your local newspaper ignores any segment of the community or stories about cooperation and tolerance.
2. Establish an ecumenical alliance. Bring people of diverse faiths together for retreats, workshops, or potluck dinners. Be welcoming to agnostics and atheists as well.
3. Start a "language bank" of volunteer interpreters for all languages used in your community (Teaching Tolerance, 2000).

Principle THREE

Honesty is a key element in addressing the needs of all children no matter what their identity.

Classroom Applications and Strategies

Honesty is the variable that can lead to teaching that is truly culturally responsive. For example, if you don't know something about a child's culture—or anything else—be honest. Ask them for information (without crossing inappropriate lines) and tell them to correct you if you say something that is inaccurate. The students can be the best source for teachers who recognize the importance of discovering the physical, mental, emotional, spiritual, and financial needs of each student; their socioeconomic class; and the students' knowledge of the school's hidden rules and role models.

Besides the students themselves as a source, teachers can, of course, learn more about each student by talking with parents, other teachers, and the student's friends and peers. Armed with knowledge of each student, teachers are better able to seek appropriate support systems available to them.

Principle FOUR

 Concerned teachers can play a major role in counteracting homophobia or hetero-sexism (a term referring also to any form of prejudice against nonheterosexual behavior) in their schools and community. There are positive steps teachers can take to change these discriminatory attitudes and behaviors.

In a report from the Governor's Commission on Gay and Lesbian Youth (1993), research revealed the following problems facing gay and lesbian youth:

- High drop-out rate
- Poor school performance
- Alienation from school activities
- Fear of rejection
- Suicide attempts

The study also revealed that more than half of students surveyed at one high school "would be afraid or upset if people thought they were gay, lesbian or bisexual" (Governor's Commission on Gay and Lesbian Youth, 1993, p. 20). The study found hostility towards gays and lesbians among staff and fear among teachers of openly supporting gay and lesbian students.

As a result of this study, many schools have developed programs and curricula to counteract the problems just cited. Nevertheless, homophobia persists across the country and failure to act on the problem allows it to continue.

Classroom Applications and Strategies

Teachers can educate themselves by practicing the following suggestions (Governor's Commission on Gay and Lesbian Youth, 1993):

- Attending workshops on homophobia.
- Reading about and viewing films that address gay/lesbian/bisexual/transgender (GLBT) issues.
- Being open about your identity (if you are GLBT). The more visible GLBT individuals are, the more the stereotypes and myths are contradicted.
- Being an ally for GLBT colleagues and students (if you are heterosexual).
- Recognizing your own attitude and how it affects your language, behavior, and friendships (i.e., do you have stereotypic expectations or beliefs about GLBT people or those who "look" gay or lesbian?).
- Encouraging your local, regional, and national professional organizations to include sexual orientation in their antidiscrimination policy statements if they don't already do so.

Schools can address homophobic behavior among students and faculty by

- Establishing guidelines for name-calling, harassment, and teasing that treat homophobic behavior as seriously as racial or sexual incidents and then acting on them by letting faculty and students know that homophobic jokes or innuendoes are unacceptable.
- Adding books about homosexuality and homophobia to class, school, and professional libraries so students and faculty have easy access to them.
- Inviting GLBT speakers to address staff, students, and parents.
- Sponsoring a support group for GLBT students.
- Providing in-service for all staff about the needs of GLBT students, about homophobia, and about GLBT curriculum development.

Principle FIVE

 To benefit from culturally diverse education, students need their teachers' help to get past their fears.

"No matter how skillful and sensitive we are, tense moments in the democratic classroom will inevitably surface" (Frederick, 2000). There are classroom-tested strategies that can lead to "mastering the dreaded diversity discussion" (Frederick, 1995) within a safe, cooperative, yet challenging environment.

Peter Frederick, professor of history at Wabash College in Crawfordsville, Indiana, has written extensively about his personal experiences helping students overcome their fears and prejudices as they participate in multicultural conversations. He points out that the "teaching styles (holistic, cooperative, connected, caring, interactive) that facilitate the learning of most students of color, women, and other non-traditional students are also those that help all students learn" (Frederick, 1995, p. 85). His strategies, which are appropriate for students of all ages, from upper elementary to college, appear in the following section.

Classroom Applications and Strategies

• *Establish guidelines for safe discussions.*   Together with students, agree on a series of guidelines for acceptable classroom behavior. For example, agree that the only "political correctness" appropriate for the course is the search for truth and the commitment to engage the goals of the course and each other with openness, honesty, and mutual respect (Frederick, 2000, pp. 6–7).

• *Get the emotional issues out early.*   Because students come to diversity courses and topics with fears, it is important to anticipate the "hot button" issues such as sexual orientation, interethnic rivalries, or fear of using the wrong group labels (Frederick, 2000, p. 7). Get these concerns out on the table. For example, you can have students explain how they define themselves. Or start with a reading that raises the controversial issues. This information can proceed according to these steps: think, write, pair, share (large group).

Teachers can also diffuse tension by confronting their own feelings about diversity and talking about them, thus showing that it is all right to be confused and uncertain. If teachers can acknowledge their own fears yet still move ahead and risk having the conflict they fear, they empower students to find their own courage (Frederick, 1995, p. 90).

• *Use student stories.*   Have students tell a story about their names; or about a racial, gender, ethnic, class, or ability moment that had a powerful impact on them; or a moment when they either felt they mattered or felt victimized. In debriefing the stories, focus on common themes, patterns, and issues (Frederick, 2000, p. 7).

• *Use powerful, evocative quotations and visuals.*   Well-chosen quotations enable students to focus on a single image or paragraph that lend themselves to different interpretations. Frederick suggests looking for such quotes in multicultural biographies and essays such as W. E. B. Du Bois's *Souls of Black Folk* or Ruben Navarrette Jr.'s *A Darker Shade of Crimson,* an account of a Chicano's years at Harvard. Teachers should consider consulting books about whites as well in order to underline the point that European Americans, like other groups, are also a culture, with enormous diversity within it (Frederick, 1995, p. 89).

• *Use the mirror technique.*   There is one rule that seems to work for teachers when they hear an especially sexist, racist, homophobic, or inappropriate remark in class. Frederick suggests that when that happens you take a deep breath, turn to the person who made the remark, and slowly mirror or repeat back the words. "End your repeated statement with an invitational inflection supported by a hand gesture or other nonverbal cue that makes it clear the person has another opportunity to speak" (Frederick, 1995, p. 91). Often this leads the student who made the offensive remark to rephrase or reconsider it. However, if the student maintains their position you might say, "That comment offends me; I'd like you to think about it." So often the apparently insensitive students are masking fears and pain. Giving them a chance to open up as well as listen to others can often lead to their examining their beliefs and sometimes changing them.

Principle SIX

Culturally relevant lessons and strategies enable students to learn and then apply higher-order thinking skills that encourage critical thinking.

Bloom's taxonomy provides a hierarchy of skills in three domains: cognitive, affective, and psychomotor. Within each domain are skills listed from simple to more challenging. Figure 4.1 is an abbreviated chart containing those domains and skills. Because this hierarchy challenges students to think on higher levels beyond simple recall, the chart could be humorously labeled the HOTS (Higher-Order Thinking Skills), an acronym that might be useful in helping them remember to think critically. When teachers integrate the taxonomy of objectives in Figure 4.1 into their diversity curricula, students benefit. Their knowledge of diversity is increased, their attitudes about diversity (i.e., tolerance, open-mindedness, curiosity, cooperation) become more positive, and they are able to practice and reinforce their psychomotor

Figure 4.1   Bloom's Taxonomy of Objectives in Three Domains

Cognitive Domain

1. *Knowledge*
   - List
   - Identify
   - Define
2. *Comprehension*
   - Compare/contrast
   - Explain
   - Provide an example
3. *Application*
   - Apply the idea to
   - Develop
4. *Analysis*
   - Classify
   - Compare/contrast
5. *Synthesis*
   - Draw conclusion
   - Predict
6. *Evaluation*
   - Agree/disagree and explain why
   - Select

Affective Domain

1. *Receiving*
   Demonstrates attention
2. *Responding*
   Responds in acceptable way
3. *Valuing*
   Shows preference and defends position

4. *Organizing*
   - Sees relationships
   - Develops a value system
5. *Characterizing by a value*
   Acts in ways consistent with values (demonstrates)

Psychomotor Domain

1. *Perception* (attending)
   Recognizes cues and relates them to action
2. *Set*
   Displays mental, physical, and emotional readiness to perform
3. *Guided response*
   Imitates a response
4. *Mechanism*
   Performs task habitually
5. *Complex or overt response*
   Performs with confidence and proficiency
6. *Adaptation*
   Adapts skills to fit situation
7. *Origination*
   Creates new performance

skills (i.e., reading, writing, speaking, organizing, constructing) in conjunction with diversity curricula as well as in all of their other studies.

Strategies and Lessons for
Increasing Knowledge about Diversity

Lesson 1: Multicultural Bingo*

Grade Levels: 5–12
Content: Social Studies, Language Arts
Principles: 1, 2, 5

Bingo is a familiar game involving a grid filled with numbered squares. In this lesson, however, the squares contain questions related to students' knowledge and experiences with diversity. Students not only discover some interesting facts but they also get to know more about their classmates.

Objectives

Students will be able to

1. Share their experiences of diversity with their peers (ELA 4, 9, 11; SOCS-C 2, 5).
2. Interact with their peers around questions related to personal connections to diversity via the Multicultural Bingo game (ELA 4, 7, 9; SOCS-C 2; SOCS-USH [5–12] 1–10).
3. Discover facts about different cultures and express their learning in a debriefing session following the game playing (ELA 4, 8, 9; SOCS-USH [K–4] 3, 4).

Materials

- Pen or pencil
- Sheet with a grid made up of five squares across and five squares down containing questions related to diverse groups, with each square also containing a line on which students can place their names (see Figure 4.2)

Procedures

1. Introduce the lesson by asking if they know how to play bingo. Then explain that the goal of Multicultural Bingo is to get people to meet each other by getting as many signatures as possible from those who can answer "Yes"—with an explanation—to the questions on the grid.
2. List the following instructions on the board or print them on the back of the sheet with the grid. Give students the grid sheet.
   a. Students put their own name in the center (square 13).
   b. Each student seeks other students who can answer one of the questions affirmatively. Write down a brief answer in the square where someone answered affirmatively. Then ask that person to sign his or her name in the square with the answer.

*Adapted from Diversity Awareness through Resources in Education (1991), University of California at Berkeley; The Stanley Foundation (1989), Las Palomas de Taos, New Mexico; and L. R. Kohls and J. M. Knight. (1994). *Developing Intercultural Awareness.* Yarmouth, ME: Intercultural Press, pp. 29–31.

Figure 4.2   Multicultural Bingo Grid

1 Have you had your name mispronounced? _____	**2** Do you know what *Nisei* means? _____	**3** Are you from a mixed-heritage background? _____	**4** Can you define *Mahatma*? _____	**5** Do you under-stand the symbol of "One Thousand Cranes"? _____
6 Have you had to overcome physical barriers in life? _____	**7** Have you experienced being stereotyped? _____	**8** Can you identify Ramadan? _____	**9** Do you know who Harvey Milk was? _____	**10** Do you know what the upside down pink triangle symbolizes? _____
11 Do you know what Yom Kippur is? _____	**12** Do you know what Kwanzaa refers to? _____	**13** Are you studying diversity? Yes, my name is _____	**14** Do you know what Cinco de Mayo is? _____	**15** What is the significance of the Pipe? _____
16 Do you know what "comparable worth" means? _____	**17** Do you know what Juneteenth means? _____	**18** Have you eaten Thai food in the last three months? _____	**19** Do you know the original meaning of the swastika? _____	**20** Do you know what St. Patrick did for Ireland? _____
21 Do you have a friend from a different culture? _____	**22** Do you know what *mainstreaming* means? _____	**23** Do you know who Thurgood Marshall was? _____	**24** Do you know who Susan B. Anthony was? _____	**25** Do you know the significance of the "Red Envelope"? _____

Explanation of the Answers

1. (depends on personal answer)
2. The term *Nisei* refers to the first generation born in America to people who emigrated from Japan.
3. (depends on personal answer)
4. *Mahatma* means Great Soul. Mohandas Gandhi, born in India in 1869, was one of India's greatest leaders and was known as Mahatma. He led a campaign of peaceful civil disobedience that eventually won India's independence from Great Britain.

5. "One Thousand Cranes" is the symbol for worldwide peace. In 1955 a 13-year-old Japanese girl died of "atomic bomb disease," a radiation-induced leukemia. During her illness, Sadako Sasaki buoyed her spirits by folding paper cranes. Japanese legend says that cranes live a thousand years and that the person who folds a thousand paper cranes will be granted a wish. Sadako wished for recovery from her fatal disease. Before she died, she had folded 644 paper cranes. Classmates

(continued)

Figure 4.2   *Continued*

completed her task so that she was buried with a thousand cranes. Children around the world remember this young girl by folding cranes in her honor.

6. (depends on personal answer)
7. (depends on personal answer)
8. Ramadan is observed by Muslims to demonstrate their commitment to God and to purify their souls. They fast during the day for 30 days. The date is in accordance with the Islamic Calendar.
9. Harvey Milk was a city councilor in San Francisco who was gay and outspoken on gay issues. He was murdered by a colleague.
10. The upside down pink triangle symbolizes pride and support for the Gay and Lesbian community. During World War II, this symbol was used by the Nazis to label gay and lesbian prisoners in concentration camps for torture and extermination.
11. Yom Kippur is the Jewish Day of Atonement. It is the most solemn holiday in the Jewish year and is the culmination of ten days of repentance. It is a day of fasting.
12. *Kwanzaa* is a Swahili word for "first." This African American celebration begins on December 26 and ends on New Year's Day. The festival was started in 1966 in California by black nationalist Maulana Ron Karenga. Rooted in traditional harvest celebrations in Africa, Kwanzaa is an alternative to the commercial celebration of Christmas in the United States. The focus is on African and African American history and culture as well as on seven principles: unity, self-determination, collective work and responsibility, cooperative economics, purpose, creativity, and faith.
13. (your name)
14. Cinco de Mayo is a Mexican holiday that commemorates the defeat of French colonial forces at the historic city of Puebla. It is a Mexican Independence Day.

15. The Pipe is a symbol of great reverence by the Lakotas and many other Native American tribes. The belief is that through the elements of Fire, Land, and Air (all represented in the Pipe and its smoking), they are able to communicate with the spirits and make their hearts known.
16. "Comparable worth" means equal compensation for jobs of comparable but different skills, efforts, and working conditions. The concept came out of the women's movement.
17. Juneteenth is the anniversary of the day when the slaves in Texas were freed. It wasn't until June 19, 1865 that the slaves there were freed, since the Emancipation Proclamation (January 1, 1863) had little impact on Texas.
18. (depends on personal answer)
19. The original meaning of the swastika is an Indo-European Roman symbol for peace, knowledge, and fertility.
20. St. Patrick was a Roman slave brought to Ireland on a slave ship at age 16 in the middle of the fifth century. He brought Christianity to the people of Ireland.
21. (depends on personal answer)
22. *Mainstreaming* refers to inclusion of students with disabilities into the regular classroom.
23. Thurgood Marshall was the lawyer for the NAACP (National Association for the Advancement of Colored People) who argued and won the *Brown v. Board of Education* case in which segregation was outlawed. He went on to become the first African American Supreme Court justice.
24. Susan B. Anthony helped to organize the Seneca Falls Convention where the Declaration of Sentiments was written demanding equal rights for women (1848).
25. The "Red Envelope" signifies good luck in Chinese culture. Most often envelopes are given at the beginning of the Chinese New Year.

c. Each person can sign another's grid only *once*.
d. All bingos win (horizontal or vertical).
e. (Optional) Have students continue the game until everyone has achieved bingo.

3. At the end of the game, debrief with such questions as

- Which questions were easiest to answer? Most difficult? Why?
- What information did you find to be interesting or new?
- Were there any questions that made you want to do further research? Explain.

Assessment

- Students' participation in the Multicultural Bingo game (Objectives 1–3)
- Students' participation in the debriefing discussion (Objective 3)
- (Optional) Written answers to the debriefing questions (Objective 3)

Extension

You can fill in an empty grid with your own list of questions. For example, if you want to emphasize knowledge about a particular culture or about global connections, create appropriate questions, such as

- Have you ever bought an album of World Music?
- Have you ever traveled outside of this country?

If you want a human rights emphasis you can fill in the grid with such questions as

- What is a human right?
- Name an organization that fights for human rights.
- Name a singer who sings about rights (Flowers, 1998, pp. 47–48).

Lesson 2: Respecting Oneself and Others: Making a Patchwork Quilt*

Grade Levels: K–5
Content: Language Arts, Social Studies, Art
Principles: 1, 3, 6

Differences among students—whether based on race, religion, ethnicity, language, gender, class, or ability—don't need to create obstacles in building relationships. The character trait of respect for self and others can be learned through activities like the following one in which students begin first by identifying what they respect about themselves. Respecting oneself is the basis for being open to respecting diverse others.

Objectives

Students will be able to

1. Develop respect for self and others (SOCS-C 2, 5).
2. Participate in activities (quilt-making) that nurture the trait of respect (NA-VA 1, 2, 3, 4, 5, 6).
3. Behave with respect towards others during and after the lesson (SOCS-C 2, 5; ELA 2, 6, 10, 11).

Materials

- 6" × 6" squares of colored paper or squares cut from wallpaper sample books
- Magazines from which pictures can be clipped
- Art supplies (i.e., tissue paper, glitter, sequins, markers, fabric, and other items)
- Posterboard or white mural paper

---

*Adapted from "Field-Tested Resources in Character Education." (1998). St. Louis, MO: Cooperating School Districts of Greater St. Louis, pp. 47–50. (Inspired by Cathy Ely, Meramec Elementary School, School District of Clayton.)

Procedures

1. Ask students if they have ever seen a patchwork quilt. (Perhaps have pictures of such quilts to show them). Discuss the way that many smaller—and different—pieces add to the uniqueness of the larger quilt.
2. Explain that they will create a paper quilt from squares that represent the individuality of each student. Together these squares will represent the uniqueness of the class as a whole.
3. Give each student a quilt square measuring 6" × 6".
4. Instruct them to each write his or her name on the square and decorate it to illustrate a quality, talent, or experience they respect in themselves. They can draw it, cut out a picture depicting that aspect of themselves, or use a photograph. To add to color and dimension, encourage students to then decorate the squares with some of the art supplies you have provided. (You can alternate the students' squares with colored squares that may or may not have some kind of abstract decoration.)
5. Glue the squares together on posterboard or white mural paper. Hang on a wall in or outside of the classroom or on the door of the room.
6. Have the class—that same day or the next day—describe and discuss their unique squares and what they have learned about others from this activity.

Assessment

- The students' square for the quilt (Objectives 1, 2)
- Cooperation and respect for others' work demonstrated during the end-of-activity discussion (Objectives 1, 2, 3)

Note: There are unlimited contexts in which you can integrate quilt-making. For example, students might be inspired by the work of African American artist Aminah Brenda Lynn Robinson (*Aminah* is an African term meaning "trust"), who celebrates her identity and that of her neighborhood in Columbus, Ohio. In her art, she portrays the people and energy of her community in all their diversity and color, using a variety of materials and techniques that reflect her subjects and the respect she has for them. The accompanying figure is a copy of a piece done with paint and dyes on rag cloth, called "Quilters Catching Up on Gossip."

Source: Aminah Brenda Lynn Robinson, American, b. 1940, *Quilters Catching Up on Gossip*, 2000, paint and dyes on rag cloth, 30 in. x 48–1/4 in., private collection © Aminah Brenda Lynn Robinson. Reprinted by permission of Columbus Museum of Art.

Extension

The following activities are ways to extend the focus on, and development of, the trait of respect:

- Have students act as reporters for a week, and whenever they observe an example of respect in the class and school, they should write a little story about it. Put these stories together in a "newspaper." Make copies that students can take home for their parents.
- Have students hold a family meeting in their own homes at which they discuss how they will try to show respect to each family member and how they would like to be respected in turn.
- Have students explore and report on indicators of respect for different groups and individuals in their community. For example, are streets and sidewalks wheelchair accessible? What special accommodations are there for senior citizens? Are there welcoming committees for new people moving into the community? Student investigations may result in suggestions that can be sent to community newspapers, city officials, and other appropriate places.

Lesson 3: A Sports Story Raises Diversity Issues

Grade Levels: 7–12
Content: Language Arts, Social Studies, Physical Education
Principles: 1, 5

Diversity—or lack of it—within the sports arena has often been a source of controversy. Symbolic of that controversy, for example, was the history-making decision by Commissioner of Baseball "Happy" (Albert Benjamin) Chandler to integrate baseball in 1947. He supported Brooklyn Dodgers' general manager Branch Rickey in his choice of hiring Jackie Robinson, thus making Robinson the first African American in the Major Leagues. (Some say that Chandler's decision cost him a second term as Commissioner.)

In the excerpt in Figure 4.3, from an article by Bill Plaschke, a somewhat different scenario is portrayed that raises a number of diversity-related questions.

Objectives

Students will be able to

1. Do research on one issue raised by the article excerpt (ELA 1, 8; SOCS-USH 10; SOCS-C 2).
2. Write an editorial expressing an opinion on the issue (ELA 3, 4, 6, 7).
3. Share their perspectives during a discussion of the issues raised in the article excerpt (ELA 4, 5, 6).

Materials

- The essay excerpt
- Pen and paper or personal computer

Procedures

1. Give students a copy of the article excerpt. Have them read it on their own or as a class.
2. Ask students if they see any relationships between the article content and their experiences at school or in other situations they have observed.

Figure 4.3   Excerpt from "Welcome Wagon," by Bill Plaschke

(This excerpt is from an article about David Meriwether, who became the first white basketball player in Crenshaw High School's 30-year history.)

He just knew there would be stomping.

He just knew there would be chants. . . .

When he was introduced as a junior guard for the Crenshaw High basketball team . . . more than 1,000 students pointed.

While cheering and whooping and high-fiving. . . .

And, yes, by the time he walked into the blue-and-gold embrace of teammates, there were chants:

"Milk! Milk! Milk! Milk!". . .

Meet David Meriwether, the first white male basketball player in the 30-year history of Crenshaw High.

The students have, and they overwhelmingly accept him. . . .

"This is cool," Meriwether said Monday, bouncing off the shoulders of buddies, posing for giggling girls, looking at home in a place as foreign to most whites as Mars. . . .

You can literally count the number [of whites] at Crenshaw High [a high school of about 2,760 students] on one hand. . . .

His teammates protected him from the thugs, who would shove him and square to fight before he was ushered away.

"When I was first told he was coming, I thought, 'It's not true,'" said E. J. Harris, Crenshaw's star guard. . . . "I figured, he has to be pretty strong." . . .

Crenshaw has a notable program for gifted students, for students who want to become teachers, for those who want to sing in an internationally acclaimed choir.

Crenshaw also gives basketball players a chance to learn under a coach, Willie West, who is considered one of the finest in the country. . . . But many eligible kids are steered elsewhere. . . .

"Some people are just afraid," said West. . . . "It's too bad. It's not fair, but that's the way it is."

For some, it's the poor reputation of the surrounding neighborhood. For others, it's the foreignness of an enrollment that is about 81% African American and 18% Latino.

For West, the scene is always the same.

"The dad and the son will come here and get all excited about it," West said. "Then the mom will show up and say, 'No way.'"

It's happened so often that when Meriwether's father approached West . . . with the idea of his son transferring from Fairfax, West did all but wave him off. . . .

West obviously didn't know Meriwether's father. . . .

"My son told me he wanted to play basketball and eventually coach," the senior Meriwether said. "When I heard that, I thought, 'He needs to go to a school that helps you become a teacher, and to learn from the [best] . . . of high school basketball coaches.'"

[The young] Meriwether qualified for the teacher training program so he was able to transfer.

"I didn't even think about the race thing," said the senior Meriwether. . . . "To me, it didn't matter."

Even after he impressed West on a summer-league team, the younger Meriwether had to audition with about 70 other students. . . . His defense and raw skills were good enough to warrant a uniform. . . .

Yvonne Garrison, assistant principal, said, "It's good for him, and others like him, to realize what we have here. And it's good for everyone here to get to know him." . . .

"In class, they will ask me what my life is like, what I talk about at home, what I think about blacks," Meriwether said. "Actually, it's kind of neat, being on the other side of things. I'm learning a lot."

And the chant continues. Everyone who sees him in the halls, in the cafeteria, at local hangouts where he is becoming one of a suddenly expanding group.

"Yo, Milk! Milk!"

Source: Plaschke, B. (November 10, 1998). "Welcome Wagon." *Los Angeles Times.* Available online at http://articles.latimes.com/1998/nov/10/sports/sp-41227. Used with permission of the Los Angeles Times.

3. Ask them what diversity issues the article excerpt raises. You can mention the following issues if students don't:

- De facto segregated school environments
- The unusual situation of one white basketball player on an all-black team in a largely African American school and the possible outcomes of such a situation
- Curriculum that implicitly leads to stereotyping and perhaps increased racial tensions

4. (Optional) Read aloud two or three editorials from the local paper and discuss the format. These editorials can serve as models for the students as they complete the next step.
5. After briefly discussing some of these issues, list them on the board and ask students to write an editorial—a subjective essay—in which they take a position on one of the issues in item 3 or a related issue.
6. (Optional) Collect the editorials and make a booklet of them to share with others.

Assessment

- Completion of an editorial taking a position on one of the diversity-related issues listed on the board or a related issue (Objectives 1, 2)
- Participation in the discussion of the issues raised by the article excerpt (Objective 3)

Extension

1. Either before or after this lesson, invite the editorial writer from a local newspaper to visit the class and discuss the editorial writer's role and how he or she prepares for writing an editorial.
2. Have students do research reports on historically significant events or people related to the intersection of sports and diversity.

Lesson 4: Don't Laugh at Me, Walk in My Shoes

Grade Levels: 4–12
Content: Interdisciplinary
Principles: 1, 2, 4, 5

The wish expressed in the title of this lesson (song) is one that many students can identify with. Whatever is different about someone can become the catalyst for other students to tease them, laugh at them, express slurs, and in some cases, physically abuse them. This lesson is intended to help students recognize the importance of respecting differences and being responsible for one another by letting them have the experience of walking in the shoes of those who may differ from them in some way.

Objectives

Students will be able to

1. Read and understand the feelings expressed in the song "Don't Laugh at Me," shown in Figure 4.4 (ELA 1; NA-M 6).
2. Respond to the content of the song during a discussion (or in writing) (ELA 2, 3, 4).
3. Discuss their personal experiences of being different—a minority—in a particular situation or their observations of others in such a situation (ELA 2, 4; SOCS-C 2).
4. Write a poem or story in which they express what it would be like to "walk in someone else's shoes" (who the "someone else" is can be decided by student or teacher) (ELA 4, 6).

Materials

- Words to song "Don't Laugh at Me" (see Figure 4.4) (CD or video available for ordering online at OperationRespect.com)
- Scarves or bandanas
- Stories and poems or songs about people with disabilities (librarians can be helpful here)

Figure 4.4   Don't Laugh at Me

I'm a little boy with glasses
The one they call a geek
A little girl who never smiles
Cuz I got braces on my teeth
And I know how it feels
To cry myself to sleep

I am that kid on every playground
Who's always chosen last
A single teenage mother
Trying to overcome her past
You don't have to be my friend
If it's too much to ask

Don't laugh at me
Don't call me names
Don't get your pleasure from my pain
In God's eyes we're all the same
Someday we'll all have perfect wings
Don't laugh at me

I'm a cripple on the corner
You pass me in the street
I wouldn't be out here begging
If I had enough to eat

And don't think I don't notice
That our eyes never meet

I lost my wife and little boy when
Someone crossed that yellow line
The day we laid 'em in the ground
Was the day I lost my mind
Right now I'm down to holding
This little cardboard sign

Don't laugh at me
Don't call me names
Don't get your pleasure from my pain
In God's eyes we're all the same
Someday we'll all have perfect wings
Don't laugh at me

I'm fat, I'm thin, I'm short, I'm tall
I'm deaf, I'm blind, hey, aren't we all

Don't laugh at me
Don't call me names
Don't get your pleasure from my pain
In God's eyes we're all the same
Someday we'll all have perfect wings
Don't laugh at me

Source: Seskin, S., and A. Shamblin. Don't Laugh at Me © 1997 Sony/ATV Music Publishing LLC, David Aaron Music and Publisher(s) Unknown. All rights on behalf of Sony/ATV Music Publishing LLC and David Aaron Music. Administered by Sony/ATV Music Publishing LLC, 8 Music Square West, Nashville, TN, 37203. All rights reserved. Used by permission.

Procedures

1. Begin by reading the introduction to this lesson and then asking if there's anyone in the class who would share their personal experiences with—or observation of—a situation in which someone who was different (not necessarily someone with disabilities) was the source of hurtful laughter.
2. Give students a copy of the lyrics to "Don't Laugh at Me." Read it together at least two times.
3. Discuss the song. Going verse by verse, ask students to try to imagine what it would be like to be that person (girl with braces, a beggar, and so on). Can they imagine themselves walking in the shoes of these people? Do they consider the lyrics useful? Is there anything about the song they'd change? Why? What would they have done differently? Are there some students with differences not mentioned in the song who suffer from verbal attacks, such as gay and lesbian youth?
4. If there are students with disabilities in the school who would be willing to discuss their disabilities with the class as well as their experiences dealing with people who have been either compassionate or offensive in some way, invite them to participate in this lesson.
5. Have a selection of stories, poems, and songs available for students to read following this lesson. (The librarian may be helpful in selecting these for the class.)

6. For homework, ask students to read about someone like Helen Keller (or others who may be represented by the materials available in class). Ask them to write a story, song, or poem from the perspective of someone with a disability or who is different in some way from the majority, expressing the feelings and experiences they have undergone.

Assessment

- Participation in the discussion of the song and their own experiences with difference (Objectives 1–3)
- Completion of a poem or story in which they "walk in someone else's shoes" (Objective 4)

Extension

- Have students pair up and do a "Blind Walk" in which they take turns in the roles of sightless student and guide. One partner's eyes are covered by a bandana or scarf while the other student issues commands such as "We'll walk down the hallway." The guide then assists the "sightless" student using verbal directions and cues about their surroundings. After everyone has experienced both roles, the students return to the classroom and write journal reactions responding to questions about their reactions. How did it feel to be "blind"? How did it affect your other senses? Did your guide's touch convey caring and patience? What do you imagine would be your most difficult challenge if you were blind?
- Have students do research on their school district's inclusion policies.
- Find copies of songs or poems that portray people who have been discriminated against because of their differences, such as the following examples:
  - "Welcome, Welcome Emigrante," by Buffy Sainte-Marie (available at www.you tube.com)
  - "Deportee" ("Plane Wreck at Los Gatos"), by Woody Guthrie (available at www .youtube.com)
  - "Hello In There," by John Prine (available at www.lyricsdownload.com)
  - "My Moccasins Have Not Walked," by Duke Redbird (available at www.inquiry unlimited.org/lit/poetry/ghistpoems1.html)

Lesson 5: Taking Inventory: What Do Toys and Games Teach Us About Diversity?

Grade Levels: 3–12
Content: Social Studies, Language Arts, Mathematics
Principles: 2, 4, 6

Just as television advertisements and programming indirectly influence attitudes about race, ethnicity, gender, class, and ability, games and toys also convey messages through the illustrations and explanations provided in their packaging. This lesson gives students the opportunity to do some original research by taking an inventory of the toys and games in their own homes and in local stores as well as in their school.

Objectives

Students will be able to

1. Complete a chart on which they have collected data about the illustrations and explanations toy and game makers place on the packaging of their items (ELA 1, 4, 8).

2. Describe the packaging on toys and games in their homes and in stores in terms of depictions of race, ethnicity, gender, class, and ability (ELA 3, 6).

3. Respond orally to relevant questions about the kinds of messages these pictures and words convey (ELA 4, 7; MAT—CONN 3; SOCS-C 2).

4. Share their observations with other classes as well as their parents and seek responses from their audience (ELA 4, 5).

Materials

- Toys and games in the school, home, and local stores in town
- Chart on which to take inventory (see Figure 4.5)
- Pen or pencil

Procedures

1. Introduce the inventory activity by asking students if they can describe from memory any illustrations on the packaging of any toy or game they have in their homes. Explain that part of the reason companies choose to depict particular people, situations, and verbal messages on their packaging is to attract attention and appeal to buyers. Mention that the choices of illustrations made by these companies sometimes convey discriminatory or prejudicial messages.

2. Show the students the inventory sheet and explain that they will have the opportunity to take an inventory of games and toys they find in their homes, at school and,

Figure 4.5   Inventory of Messages and Pictures on Packaging of Various Toys and Games

Name of Toy or Game	Race/Ethnicity	Gender	Ability	Class	Other

if possible, at local toy stores. Explain that they can record on the inventory sheet brief descriptions of the pictures or messages on the packaging in terms of how race, ethnicity, gender, class, and ability are depicted or are absent. Suggest that they make predictions about what pictures or messages they will find during their research.

3. After students do their inventory (they may work individually, in pairs, or in teams of three or four), they should share their findings and respond in a discussion to some of these questions:

- Was the outcome of your inventory what you would have predicted? Why or why not?
- Which toys or games portrayed only boys or only girls? Why is that the case? Were the illustrations or messages stereotypical? If so, what does this packaging indirectly teach the buyer about these groups?
- Did any of the packaging depict children with disabilities? If so, how were they portrayed? If not, why do you think these children—or other minority children—were not shown?
- Do you think any packaging should be changed? If so, how would you change it?
- Did you observe any connection between the price of certain items and the illustrations or messages on the packaging?
- What percent of the packaging indicated an awareness of differences among children?

4. Place the inventory items on a larger version of the inventory sheet (e.g., posterboard); in other words, "pool" the students' data in one place so they can share their findings with other classes and their parents and engage them in conversations in which they solicit others' perspectives on the influence of toy or game packaging.

5. Ask students to record in journals the feedback they receive from parents or other respondents.

Assessment

- Students' completion of inventory sheet (Objective 1)
- Participation in follow-up discussion (Objectives 2–4)
- Sharing of data with other classes and their parents and recording feedback in journals (Objectives 3, 4)

Sample Unit 1: A Heritage, USA (or Heritage, My Community) Luncheon

Grade Levels: 2–12
Content: Interdisciplinary
Principles: 1, 2, 5, 6

It may be most appropriate for students to begin increasing their knowledge about diversity by doing research on their own cultural backgrounds and history and then sharing their findings.

This instructional unit includes opportunities for learners to investigate their heritage by employing and practicing communication, study, and social skills such as reading, interviewing, organizing, note-taking, summarizing, and giving presentations.

The time needed to complete this unit depends on the number of activities that the teacher decides to implement. (See the group investigation model and other descriptions of cooperative learning formats in Chapter 3 for ideas on how to organize students into committees for some of the activities.) The nature of the methods students use to express their learning will depend on their age and experience. For example, younger students might report on their heritage through the use of pictures, family photographs, and oral storytelling, while older students might explore, for example, the roles of men and women within their family's culture or construct timelines on which they place historical events alongside major events in their family's history.

Objectives

Students will be able to

1. Do research on their own cultural backgrounds and family roots (ELA 8, SOCS-USH 3).
2. Compare and contrast their family's history and culture to those of others in their class (ELA 7, 9, 12; SOCS-USH 3)
3. Participate in research and other activities involved in presenting a Heritage, USA, luncheon for parents (ELA 6, 9; NA-M 8; SOCS-USH 3).
4. Express their learning about diversity in a variety of formats (NA-VA 3, 4, 6; ELA 6).
5. Evaluate themselves in terms of the preceding objectives (ELA 3).

Materials

- Library and Internet access
- Paper (lined and colored) and pencils and pens
- Crayons and other color implements
- Map of the world
- (Optional) Recording devices
- Photos
- Recipes
- Yarn

Procedures

1. Introduce the unit with a discussion in which *heritage* is defined and the concept of culture is discussed. For example, you can explain that what constitutes a cultural group may be based on a common geographical location, common attitudes, practices, rules, customs, and structures. You can further explain that the customs considered common by one culture may not appear so to someone from another culture. This does not make a custom wrong or strange, just simply different. For example, Nigerian children are taught to respect their elders by not looking at them directly, while the opposite is true for students in the United States. You could also note that the United States is a nation of immigrants and was built by people of all races and ethnicities, which somewhat complicates the idea of a national heritage.
2. Brainstorm with students some of the ways they can gather information about their family's culture. (You may want to share your own personal experience with this kind of research.) The following list shows some questions you can write on the board for students to use during their interviews with relatives and during their research. (Students can record their answers in writing, or they can record the interviews electronically.) Students should choose only *one* of the countries or cultures from which their family originally comes. (They may opt to explore more than one but for the purposes of this unit, a choice of one would be appropriate.)

   - When did the first members of our family come to America? From where? Why?
   - Where did they settle first?
   - What did they do?
   - Did they experience any problems?
   - Is there a genealogy on record?
   - What are some customs our family still practices from this country?

   Students may pursue these questions and conduct interviews *before* planning for the Heritage luncheon. Or you may want to go right on with a discussion related to planning the luncheon.

3. Along with the questions that students can ask their relatives, they can ask one relative for help identifying and preparing a recipe from their heritage that they can bring to a luncheon in their classroom celebrating Heritage, USA (or the heritage of their local community).

4. Form committees to complete *some* of these activities:

   • Make placemats in the form of flags representing the cultures in the classroom.
   • Prepare a bulletin board made up of family photographs gathered by students with labels underneath each one.
   • Prepare a booklet of the recipes that will be represented at the luncheon along with the country of origin and the name of the student who contributed it. This booklet could be given as a gift to parents. Students could also illustrate the recipe by drawing the dish. (The table should be set up with 3 × 5 cards in front of each dish indicating its name, country of origin, and name of student.)
   • Prepare a booklet of folksongs, one from each student's culture and in the language of that culture. Students can teach peers the songs or the music teacher can get involved in locating songs and teaching the chorus of each to students so that they can sing them for or with parents at the luncheon.
   • Delegate responsibilities for bringing in items like plastic forks, spoons, plates, napkins, cups, and other items needed for the luncheon. Decide who sets up tables, cleans up, greets parents and visitors, and so on.
   • Send home a letter informing parents or guardians about the project and asking them to assist their child in preparing a special dish for the luncheon. Include in the letter—or in a follow-up letter—an invitation to the luncheon. See Figure 4.6 for a sample letter.
   • Place a wall-size world map on the bulletin board. Students' names should be listed to the left of the map and then a pin attached to yarn can be extended from each name to the countries from which their ancestors (or *they*) came.
   • Consider having students prepare a Heritage, USA, mural to which they all contribute a scene of their own creation.

   (The possibilities for this luncheon are unlimited and teachers and students should tailor the Heritage, USA, project or luncheon to fit their situation in terms of time available for the unit, size of class, and the nature of the committees working on the project.)

Figure 4.6   Letter to Parents

Dear Parents or Guardians,

The class is involved in learning about diverse cultures, their own and others, and this study involves you and your kitchen! Can you help your child choose and prepare an authentic dish from one of the cultures represented in your family? The steps you can share are: shopping, preparing, reading about the foods, cleaning up, and then bringing the dish to school on _____ at _____ and then enjoying the luncheon that will complete the class's "Heritage, USA" journey.

Thank you so much for your assistance. I look forward to seeing you. Bon appetit! Please contact me at _____ if you have any questions.

Sincerely,

_____

5. At the luncheon all of the above projects, activities, and creations should be shared and implemented by student committees. Consider inviting members of the news media to do an article about the luncheon and the Heritage, USA (or Heritage, My Community) project. You may also want to invite the building administrator or other school and community officials.

Assessment

- Participation in research of their family's heritage *and* in the activities related to preparing for and presenting the Heritage, USA, luncheon (see the rubric in Figure 4.7 that may be used as an assessment tool) (Objectives 1–5)
- Self-evaluation of their contribution to the project (Objective 6)

Extension

When doing cultural studies, Herrell and Jordan (2004) suggest having high school students read a book in which a culture is explored and then having students relate their own family's culture to that author's experience. They describe one teacher's use of *Plain and Simple: A Woman's Journey to the Amish* by Sue Bender (1989), "because the book tells about one woman's visit to another culture and how the things she learns about another culture causes her to reflect on her own" (Herrell and Jordan, 2004, p. 107).

Sample Unit 2: Monuments and Multiculturalism: A Walk around Town

Grade Levels: 6–12
Content: Interdisciplinary
Principles: 2, 6

Since 1884, the Statue of Liberty, a gift from France to the United States as an expression of friendship, has been standing in New York Harbor welcoming immigrants from all over the world. Lady Liberty symbolizes the gateway to a land that offers freedom and opportunity for a

Figure 4.7   Assessing Participation in Heritage, USA, Project

Nature of Participation	Quality of Participation		
	High	Moderate	Low
Written data from interview/research on their heritage	_____	_____	_____
Contribution of recipe and actual dish	_____	_____	_____
Worked on the following:	_____	_____	_____
Map	_____	_____	_____
Booklet of recipes and labels	_____	_____	_____
Booklet of folksongs	_____	_____	_____
Placemats	_____	_____	_____
Mural	_____	_____	_____
Implements for the luncheon	_____	_____	_____
Participation in the luncheon	_____	_____	_____
Presentations at the luncheon	_____	_____	_____

better life to those who come here. Monuments like the statue remind us and teach us about important ideas, like freedom, and they often honor people who have made significant contributions to the country or the world. Think of the Lincoln Memorial and the Jefferson Memorial. Buildings and museums honor people, too, such as the National Holocaust Memorial Museum and the Smithsonian Museums in Washington, D.C. In this author's community, there is a clinic named for Austen Riggs, a noted doctor who furthered research on treatment of individuals with emotional and other disabilities, and there are certainly many buildings, museums, or monuments representing people from diverse backgrounds within the students' community. (*Note:* Streets are often named for important people, including the early settlers in an area. In this author's region, many streets and natural sites have Native American names. Students should note such signs as well.)

Objectives

Students will be able to

1. Discover monuments and buildings in their own community that represent important ideas, people, or events related to the diverse nature of the United States and their local area (ELA 8; SOCS-USH [5–12] 1–10; NA-VA 2, 6).
2. Complete a poem or other response (e.g., project) related to these monuments, markers, and buildings, and the ideas, people, or events that they signify (ELA 6, 8, 12; SOCS-USH 1–10; NA-VA 5).
3. Discuss their learning and present their projects in class (ELA 4, 5; SOCS-USH 3).
4. Visit New York City or Washington, D.C., or a more regional location such as the capital of their state, and view first-hand some of the monuments and buildings related to diversity (SOCS-USH 1–10).

Materials

- Notebooks, pen, pencil
- Sketchpads

Procedures

1. Begin by talking about how certain buildings, monuments, streets, or areas got their names. Lead up to the idea that sometimes they are named for certain people, ideas, or events. Discuss some local examples. (Maybe their school is named for a historical figure). Then discuss how these historic markers, monuments, and buildings often convey the diverse cultural origins of their area. Briefly have them identify some of the names, events, or ideas linked to local monuments and buildings with which they are familiar. Get students thinking with these questions:
   - Are there historic markers that you might read by taking a walk around your town or city?
   - Is there a map in your library or school that shows the location of monuments in your town or city?
   - Are there buildings such as the local hospital or a senior center in your community named for certain people? If so, who were these people and why were they honored?
   - Are there parks in your community—or other areas—where you might find statues of important people?
2. Divide students into teams and assign a weeklong scavenger hunt for these markers, monuments, and buildings. Encourage them to first stop by the school library, public library, or local historical society for maps and other information. Encourage them to explore their own neighborhoods as well as the center of town. If possible, they should try to go by public transport or drive with their parents to parts of the city or town not accessible by foot.

3. Have them sketch the monuments or other structures or bring cameras with them on their walk, and remind them to read and copy excerpts from all of the signs on or around the monuments. For example, on the Statue of Liberty's pedestal is a plaque inscribed with a poem, "The New Colossus" by Emma Lazarus, that conveys the significance of the statue, as shown by the following excerpt from the poem:

> Give me your tired, your poor,
> Your huddled masses yearning to breathe free,
> The wretched refuse of your teeming shore.
> Send these, the homeless, tempest-tossed, to me.
> I lift my lamp beside the Golden Door!

4. A meeting of the class should be held after the weeklong scavenger hunt at which students briefly share their findings. Each team of students should try to report on the same number of monuments as the number of students on their team. It doesn't matter if *some* of the buildings or monuments presented by a team at the culmination of the unit are the same as those studied by other teams.

5. Give students time to do additional research on the buildings they have discovered. They should, if possible, note the relevance of the name of the building, date of its establishment, its former and current uses, significance of its particular location, its design or style, and so on.

6. Teams of students should meet and decide how they will share their findings, whether by a display of photos, drawings, or reports on their diverse findings or by preparing a booklet entitled "Monuments and Multiculturalism: A Walk Around Our Town," or by other creative ways of sharing their findings. Students might also write poems that describe the monuments that most impressed them.

7. Have teams of students give presentations using formats they chose and prepared.

Assessment

- Students' written and oral reports, sketches and photos, poems, or other responses related to the monuments, markers, and buildings in the community (Objectives 1, 2)
- Discussion and presentation of their activities in class (Objective 3)

Extension

1. Have the students construct a three-dimensional "life-size" or scale replica of a local statue or other monument or the Statue of Liberty itself. This can be done with styrofoam, corrugated boxes, silver paint, or other materials.

2. Archeological Dig: While the preceding activities deal with historic places and sites above ground, the following activity gets students involved in exploring underground for information about local diversity.

   Archeology can reveal the story of people and places in ways that traditional research cannot. For example, by literally digging for evidence of the town of New Philadelphia, Illinois, founded by a freed slave in the 1800s, students—working with anthropologists, archeologists, and representatives from the U.S. Army Corps of Engineers—unearthed 3,000 artifacts that helped to shed light on a town that was a "rare example of biracial cooperation before the Civil War" (Mackenzie, 2005, p. 26). The students catalogued their finds at the Illinois State Museum in Springfield where they cleaned the objects, placed them in plastic bags, and entered them into logbooks.

   Contact local historians or archeologists at a local college or university who might be able to assist students in organizing an archeological dig. Short of that, these experts could serve as guest speakers describing their own work in the field and educating students about the nature of archeology and how it can help to expand knowledge of local history.

Summary Chart of Principles and Their Applications

Principle	Applications
1. A major goal of culturally responsive teaching and content is to humanize students by addressing real-life issues.	1. Integrate these real-life issues within the standard curriculum along with skills such as decision making, prejudice reduction, and role-playing. 2. Identify real-life issues in your own school and community (e.g., drugs, prejudice, gangs, bullying). 3. Assess the impact of social injustice on diverse populations in the community and assess your own attitudes and connections to local real-life issues. 4. Engage students in strategies that enable them to prevent problems and resolve real-life issues in their school and community.
2. Simple ideas for promoting equity and celebrating diversity can be applied not only in the classroom but on a personal enrichment level, in the workplace, and within the community.	1. Ideas for self: • Imagine your life if you were a person of a different color, sexual orientation, or microculture. • Test yourself for hidden biases. 2. Ideas for home: • Bookmark equity and diversity websites on your home computer. • Invite someone of a different background to join your family for a meal or other occasion. 3. Ideas for school: • Invite bilingual students to give morning greetings on the PA system in their home language. • Ensure that schools comply with McKinney Act, which mandates educational services for homeless children. 4. Ideas for workplace: • Partner with a local school and engage employees to serve as tutors. • Encourage businesses to add social justice funds to 401(k) investment options. 5. Ideas for community: • Write a letter to the editor if the local newspaper ignores a segment of the community or stories about tolerance. • Establish an ecumenical alliance.
3. Honesty is a key element in addressing the needs of all children no matter what their identity.	1. Students are among the best sources of information. Ask them about their culture if you don't know something about it. 2. Tell them to correct you if you say something that is inaccurate. 3. Talk with parents, other teachers, and the student's friends and peers to find out about each of your students.
4. Concerned teachers and schools can play a major role in counteracting homophobia or heterosexism in their schools and community. (Homophobia is one of the most persistent prejudices.)	1. Teachers can educate themselves by taking several different steps to counteract homophobia. 2. Schools can address homophobic behavior among students and faculty by carrying out six different activities. (See Principle 4 in body of chapter.)
5. To benefit from culturally diverse education, students need their teachers' help to get past their fears.	1. Establish guidelines for safe discussions. 2. Get the emotional issues out early. 3. Use students' stories. 4. Use powerful, evocative quotations and visuals. 5. There are ways to deal with students who make intolerant remarks.

6. Culturally relevant lessons and strategies enable students to learn and then apply higher-order thinking skills that encourage critical thinking.

Bloom's taxonomy of objectives in three domains specifies a hierarchy of thinking skills, attitudes, and psychomotor skills from simple to complex that can assist teachers in designing diversity curricula.

 LINKS: Recording in Your Journal

Perhaps the best way to begin increasing your knowledge about diversity and how to teach students about this complex topic is by making a list of questions about this subject that interest you most. In addition to the five suggestions for reflecting on Chapter 4 mentioned below, you might begin by doing just that: listing those questions that are compelling to you. Then review this chapter—and the other chapters—to see if you can locate some answers. Your questions can serve as a guide for further research using sources listed at the end of each chapter, as well as other references you may locate.

1. At what point in your life did you become aware that the United States is made up of people of diverse races, religions, ethnicities, classes, genders, languages, and exceptionalities? (*Exceptionality* refers to students needing special attention because of mental, physical, or emotional disabilities; it also can refer to those with advanced abilities.) Can you recall those discoveries, your reactions to them, and how those experiences have influenced your current attitudes about diversity? Likewise, when did you become aware of your own multi-identities and the effects they had on others?

2. One of this chapter's main ideas is that acting to end intolerance and generate intercultural awareness and understanding is not simply the responsibility of teachers and schools, but of a broader spectrum including parents, students, the community, and those in the workplace. Can you think of some creative ways of communicating this idea to those along that spectrum? Is this idea worthy of an ad campaign? Do such ad campaigns achieve results? Try to find out about previous efforts that have been made. You might try to find out how effective was the "World of Difference" campaign, for example, launched in 1985 by a coalition made up of the Anti-Defamation League of B'nai B'rith, WCUB-TV (Channel 5) in Boston, Shawmut Bank of Boston, the Greater Boston Civil Rights Coalition, and the Facing History and Ourselves organization, with consultation by Dr. James Banks of the University of Washington. This campaign targeted the entire spectrum and made free educational materials available to all. More information can be found at the Anti-Defamation League website (www.adl.org).

3. Have you ever participated in discussions about diversity during which students expressed intolerant remarks? How did the teacher deal with the situation? How would *you* deal with such a situation? (Think about that question in terms of your role as a student in that class *and* as a teacher of a class.)

4. There are an infinite number of strategies and lessons that can address diversity and help to humanize students, as shown by the examples included in this chapter. Clearly the author of this text and authors of other texts containing ideas for teaching about multicultural topics believe that these lessons can, indeed, lead to an increase in tolerance and concern for social justice among their students. But are these beliefs overly optimistic? Are there always going to be students who are too set in their biased beliefs to be influenced by their teachers' efforts? What does current research say about the success of diversity curricula? Reflect on these questions in writing; then hold a conversation with your peers.

5. Review the following sections of this chapter: "What the Research Says" and the "Principles." Did any of the ideas contained in those sections change the way you thought about your role as a teacher dealing with diversity topics? If, so, explain.

References

Adler, S. (March 2003). "A Response to David Warren Saxe." *Social Education, 67*(2), pp. 111.

Anti-Defamation League of B'nai B'rith, et al. (1986). *A World of Difference Teacher/Student Study Guide.* Boston: Anti-Defamation League of B'nai B'rith and Facing History and Ourselves National Foundation.

Associated Press. (December 14, 2004). "Study: TV Series Slight Hispanic Characters." Available at www.msnbc.msn.com/id/6715092.

Bender, S. (1989). *Plain and Simple: A Women's Journey to the Amish.* New York: HarperCollins.

Columbus Museum of Art. (2002). *Symphonic Poem: The Art of Aminah Brenda Robinson.* Columbus, OH: Harry N. Abrams.

Flowers, N. (1998). *Human Rights Here and Now.* Chicago: Human Rights Educator's Network, pp. 47–48.

Frankenberg, E., C. Lee, and G. Orfield (2003). *A Multiracial Society with Segregated Schools, Are We Losing the Dream?* Cambridge, MA: Harvard Civil Rights Project.

Frederick, P. (1995). "Walking on Eggs: Mastering the Dreaded Diversity Discussion." *College Teaching, 43*(3), pp. 83–92.

Frederick, P. (2000). "Appropriate to Teaching Diversity." *Thriving in Academe, 17*(4), pp. 6–7.

Gandara, P., R. Moran, and E. Garcia. (2004). "Legacy of Brown: Lau and Language Policy in the United States." *Review of Research in Education, 28*, pp. 27–46.

Glick, R., B. Joleaud, and J. Messerer. (November 2006). *Handbook: Curriculum Infusion of Real Life Issues.* Chicago: Northeastern Illinois University.

Governor's Commission on Gay and Lesbian Youth. (1993). *Making Schools Safe for Gay and Lesbian Youth. Education Report.* Boston: Department of Education.

Herrell, A., and M. Jordan. (2004). *Fifty Strategies for Teaching English Language Learners.* Columbus, OH: Pearson.

Hitt, J. (August 21, 2005). "The Newest Indians." *New York Times Magazine*, pp. 36–41.

LaMorte, M. W. (2008). *School Law: Cases and Concepts.* Boston: Allyn & Bacon.

Mackenzie, D. (January, 2005). "Ahead of Its Time?" *Smithsonian Magazine*, pp. 26, 28.

"Man arrested after dispute at school over lesson on gays." (April 29, 2005). *Berkshire Eagle*, p. A1.

Pohan, C. A., and C. Mathison. (2007). "Television: Providing Powerful Multicultural Lessons Inside and Outside of School." *Multicultural Perspectives, 9*(1), pp. 19–25.

Salamon, J. (January 29, 2005). "PBS embroiled in gay flap." *Berkshire Eagle*, p. C4.

Teaching Tolerance. (2000). *101 Tools for Tolerance: Simple Ideas for Promoting Equity and Celebrating Diversity.* Montgomery, AL: Southern Poverty Law Center.

Walsh, C. E. (Ed.). (1996). *Education Reform and Social Change, Multicultural Voices, Struggles and Visions.* Mahwah, NJ: Lawrence Erlbaum.

The World Book Encyclopedia. (1988). "Statue of Liberty." Chicago: World Book.

Recommended Resources

Baron-Cohen, S. (1995). *Mindblindness: An Essay on Autism and Theory of Mind.* Cambridge, MA: MIT Press.

Brown, W., and A. Ling (Eds.). (1991). *Imagining America: Stories from the Promised Land.* New York: Persea Books.

Chang, J. (2005). *Can't Stop Won't Stop: A History of the Hip Hop Generation.* New York: St. Martin's Press.

Cole, M., and The Distributed Literary Consortium (2006). *The Fifth Dimension: An After-School Program Built On Diversity.* New York: Russell Sage Foundation.

Flores-Gonzalez, N. (2002). *School Kids, Street Kids: Identity Development in Latino Students.* New York and London: Teachers College Press.

Hines, S. M. (2005). *Multicultural Science Education.* New York: Lang.

Powell, R. R., S. Zehm, and J. Garcia. (1996). *Field Experience: Strategies for Exploring Diversity in Schools.* Engelwood Cliffs, NJ: Merrill Prentice Hall.

Robins, K. N., et al. (2006). *Culturally Proficient Instruction.* Thousand Oaks, CA: Corwin Press.

Sadker, D., and E. S. Silber (Eds.). (2006). *Gender in the Classroom: Foundations, Skills, Methods and Strategies Across the Curriculum.* Mahwah, NJ: Lawrence Erlbaum.

Shapiro, J. P. (1994). *No Pity: People with Disabilities Forging a New Civil Rights Movement.* New York: Random House.

Shreve, S. R., and P. Shreve. (2000). *Tales Out of School: Contemporary Writers on Their Student Years.* Boston: Beacon Press.

Singleton, G. E., and C. Lenton. (2006). *Courageous Conversations about Race*. Thousand Oaks, CA: Corwin Press.

Takaki, R. (1993). *A Different Mirror: A History of Multicultural America*. New York: Little, Brown.

Understanding Islam and the Muslims. (1989). Washington DC: The Embassy of Saudi Arabia.

vanDriel, B. (Ed.). (2004). *Confronting Islamophobia in Educational Practice*. New York: Trentham Books.

World Diversity Calendar. (2008). Grantham, PA: Orison Publishers. Available at www.WorldDiversityCalendar.com

Videos

"Don't Laugh at Me". [Audio CD by Peter Yarrow and Video] (2000). www.operationrespect.org

Gay Youth. Wolfe Video. (408) 268-6782

It's Elementary, Talking about Gay Issues in School. Women's Educational Media, 2180 Bryant St., Suite 203, San Francisco, CA 94110. wemdhc@aol.com

The Multicultural Collection (2007). *America: A Cultural Mosaic*. New York: Modern.

A collection of 75 videos for multi-ages. Provides an overview of cultures in the United States today.

Off-Track: Classroom Privilege for All, by M. Fine, B. T. Anand, C. P. Jordan, and D. Sherman.

Available from NECA/Teaching for Change, P.O. Box 73038, Washington, DC 20056. www.teachingforchange.org and Teachers College Press, 1234 Amsterdam Avenue, New York, NY 10027. www.teacherscollegepress.com

Websites

www.adl.org or antidefamationleague.us

The Anti-Defamation League is an advocacy group whose aim is to "secure justice and fair treatment to all citizens"; has links to many other sites with extensive sources related to diversity and prejudice

www.chavezfoundation.org

Service learning resource guides for K–12 classrooms

www.crf-usa.org

The Constitutional Rights Foundation dedicated to educating young people about the importance of civic participation in a democratic society

www.inquiryunlimited.org/lit/poetry

Poetry related to geography and U.S. history

www.myceconline.org/phpBB2

Ideas for adapting teaching for special-needs students under the general discussion thread "Lesson Swap and Share" at the Council for Exceptional Children website

www.nylc.org

National Youth Leadership Council: Service Learning Diversity/Equity Project

www.operationrespect.org

Words to song: "Don't Laugh at Me"

www.racematters.org

Sites that assist educators interested in providing materials about diversity and how to build socially responsible attitudes and skills

www.teachingtolerance.org/magazine

The website of the Southern Poverty Law Center

Youtube.com

Buffy Sainte-Marie on "Rainbow Quest with Pete Seeger"

Bob Dylan and Joan Baez, "Deportee"

Chapter Five

Strategies and Lessons for Reducing Prejudice

Carol Ray, CATA 2007–2008 program year

America, on the whole, has been a staunch defender of the right to be the same or different, although it has fallen short in many of its practices.

Gordon Allport, 1958

Group prejudices . . . take root early and go deep.

Alice Miel and Edwin Kiester, Jr., 1967

Americans cannot afford to shut themselves off from human differences, for these differences are precisely what the chief problems of our time are about.

Alice Miel and Edwin Kiester, Jr., 1967

*T*he purpose of this chapter is to address the pressing concerns articulated in the opening quotes. Many people have spent years trying to address those concerns and, in doing so, have added to our understanding of the causes of prejudice. For example, Professor Edward O. Wilson's research at Harvard led him to conclude: "Our species retains hereditary traits that add greatly to our destructive impact. . . . Cooperation beyond the family and tribal levels comes hard" (Wilson, 1993, pp. 24, 26). Wilson's research and that of others in the sciences, as well as in fields such as philosophy and theology, have helped to explain why there is no corner of the world free from group scorn (Allport, 1958, 4), and why, in spite of intellectual and technical progress, humanity is still caught up in the idol worship of blood ties, property, and institutions (Fromm, 1961).

Aristotle himself believed that people do not naturally or spontaneously grow up to be morally excellent or practically wise. They become so, if at all, as the result of a lifelong personal and community effort (Wynne and Ryan, 1993).

On the other hand, some psychologists have shown that prejudice of any kind is neither innate nor hereditary (Allport, 1958), but rather learned as a result of environmental influences, including parents, friends, school, books, and other media. The late Harvard psychologist Gordon Allport believed that the school, in particular, can play a significant role in helping America achieve a desirable "unity in diversity" (Allport, 1958, p. 480). He wrote, "As in the home, the atmosphere that surrounds the child at school is exceedingly important. . . . If . . . the school system is democratic, if the teacher and child are each respected units, the lesson of respect for the person will easily register. [However] as in the society at large, the *structure* of the pedagogical system will blanket, and may negate, the specific intercultural lessons taught" (p. 473).

Keeping in mind this warning about potentially harmful models of school governance and the limitations of curriculum aimed at reducing prejudice, you will, nevertheless, discover that the lessons and strategies in this chapter offer simple and effective ways of counteracting and preventing bias among your students, the major purpose of this chapter. In addition, the references to current research, along with several teaching principles related to prejudice reduction, will provide helpful background knowledge to assist you in implementing the lessons and instructional units contained in Chapter 5.

Do you think that a film such as Crash *has the power to change prejudiced attitudes? Why or why not?*

The film *Crash* begins with "out-of-focus lights, moving in the dark, as if a stunned post-collision consciousness were slowly coming back into focus. . . . The movie then goes back to the previous afternoon. . . . Two young African-Americans . . . argue merrily on the street. Anthony is convinced that everything in his life . . . is part of a white plot to humiliate blacks. His friend [Peter] tries to tease him out of it. The real joke, however, is that Anthony, who rants that whites assume all young black men are thugs, actually is [one]" and the two jump a prosperous white couple at gunpoint and take off in their car (Denby, 2005, pp. 110–111).

Crash (2005) explores how people from various ethnic and racial groups bring their own biases into each new "crash" or rough contact with folks from different groups, whether blacks, Latinos, Middle Easterners, Asians, or whites. Filmmaker Paul Haggis's characters are shown indulging in what he calls a kind of "well-argued racism" that holds a challenging mirror up to the audience (Halbfinger, 2005, p. E7).

The film touched a nerve among its viewers with its vignettes on intolerance and led to a surprise Oscar for "Best Picture" at the 2006 Academy Awards. One of the lessons it aimed to convey was that prejudice does, indeed, mean

"prejudge," and that we must always be on guard against jumping to conclusions before we know all the facts about people we encounter.

Reviewer David Denby wrote that "*Crash* is the first movie I know of to acknowledge not only that the intolerant are also human, but further, that something like white fear of black street crime, or black fear of white cops, isn't always irrational" (Denby, 2005, p. 111). In this film, no one is entirely innocent or entirely guilty. (The truth is that stereotypes are not always wrong. They often originate from a kernel of truth. The problem is that they prevent us from getting to the richer reality that lies beyond them.)

Filmmaker Haggis perhaps expressed it best: "It's not the big bad wolf you have to be afraid of. It's too easy to point the finger at some redneck and say there's the problem. The problems . . . are within us" (Halbfinger, 2005, p. E7).

What the Research Says

ONE Prejudice among Young People

The Anti-Defamation League, an organization that monitors the influence of extremist groups, noted that a 2001 report by the U.S. Department of Justice found that 33 percent of known "hate crime" offenders were under the age of 18 (Cavanagh, 2005, p. 12).

According to Randy Blazak, an associate professor at Portland State University in Portland, Oregon, who has studied the influence of extremist organizations, "extremists have modified their message to teenagers in recent years from outright advocacy of racism to a more subtle emphasis on the loss of ethnic identity in an increasingly diverse American society" (Cavanagh, 2005, p. 11).

Mark Potok, the director of The Intelligence Project of the Southern Poverty Law Center, a nonprofit organization in Montgomery, Alabama, that also monitors extremist groups, noted the profile of many teenagers who seek out such organizations: a troubled family, isolation from peers, and a sense that their community is being destroyed in the face of demographic changes (Cavanagh, 2005, p. 12).

Dr. Timothy Jay, psychology professor at the Massachusetts College of Liberal Arts, addresses the use of language that underlies prejudice, that is, ethnic and racial slurs uttered by young people. He notes that psychologists and those in the legal profession have not determined just exactly what impact these words have on others or if such language constitutes illegal behavior or not, although most schools prohibit the use of discriminatory speech. Writes Jay,

> At one extreme words like "nigger" are sometimes used between members of the same race without any harm intended. Whether this use is benign and should be ignored is debatable. (However, teachers do have the right to forbid the use of words like "nigger" in their classrooms regardless of the intent of the students who use these slurs, i.e., "we do not use this kind of language in this class. Please express yourself without using these terms in the future.") (1996, Ch. 42)

Jay makes several recommendations to teachers for preventing discriminatory verbal behavior and believes teachers can train students at the earliest possible age to respect differences:

- Teachers may want to take class time to discuss "words that hurt and why."
- Teachers may establish rules and policies that ban the use of extreme forms of ethnic slurs.

- Ethnic slurs should be eliminated from the speech of all official representatives of the school, including athletes, coaches, band members, and others.
- Teachers need to comprehend the meaning of terms that groups use against each other in anger. (Do not pretend to know the meanings of words that you do not. Ask a student in private to define the word you do not understand.)
- Teachers should be aware of the stereotypes and bigoted attitudes in their school (Jay, 1996).

Along the same lines, teachers can advise students on how *they* can respond when they hear prejudiced remarks or ethnic jokes that are clearly in bad taste. One way of responding is by simply saying "I find that remark (joke) offensive." It is important to point out that while responding in this way may cause the responder anxiety, in the long run he or she will feel proud to have stood up and not allow blind prejudice to continue. Students can learn that they have the power to make a difference and that apathy, in some ways, is as dangerous as hate.

Reflective question: What kind of antiprejudice policy would you design for your classroom?

TWO Prejudice Explained in a Simple Formula

Gordon Allport, in his definitive study, *The Nature of Prejudice* (1958), described hundreds of studies on the causes of prejudice and ways of reducing it. He identified the role of frustration as lying at the heart of the problem of prejudice (Allport, 1958, p. 329). There are, he writes, four possible ways people respond to frustration: to try to surmount the obstacle in one's path, to blame oneself for the frustrating experience, to blame no one, or to seek outside agencies to blame. This last type of reaction involves placing blame on other objects, specifically on available out-groups. (Allport, 1958, 330). This theory of prejudice is referred to as the scapegoat theory and can be illustrated graphically as follows:

$$F \to A \to D$$

Frustration $\to$ Aggression $\to$ Displacement

(Allport, 1958, p. 331)

The theory assumes three stages:

1. Frustration generates aggression.
2. Aggression becomes displaced upon relatively defenseless "scapegoats."
3. This displaced hostility is rationalized and justified by blaming, projecting, stereotyping. (Allport, 1958, p. 331)

Stereotyping is defined as labeling a whole group without sufficient knowledge or by what one knows about only a few members of that group.

If one applies this theory to both past (the Nazi Holocaust) and current (anti-Arab prejudice) situations, its veracity becomes clear, though, of course, there may also be other variables responsible for the resulting prejudice and aggressive behavior exhibited towards the out-group or minority group.

Allport's simple but profound formula for explaining the cause of prejudice is only one of the many insights revealed by the extensive studies contained in his classic work.

Reflective question: Have you personally observed in action Allport's equation explaining the cause of prejudice?

THREE   Race as a Sociocultural Construct

Biological evidence leads to the conclusion that race categories are sociocultural constructs (Cohen, 1968; Olson, 2001; Rodriguez, 2002; Smith, 2005). Members of the human race—whatever their color—belong to one species. This means that we all have a common ancestor, according to Robert Cohen, in the simply written book *The Color of Man* (1968). Perhaps millions of years ago, a complicated series of gene changes, or mutations, in a prehuman species, produced the first human being (Cohen, 1968, pp. 39, 42).

According to Ritchie Witzig, the divisions of Homo sapiens into race taxons started in the eighteenth century, when the sciences of genetics and evolutionary biology were not yet invented. "These disciplines have since shown that human race taxonomy has no scientific basis. Race categories [though still widely used] are social constructs, that is, concepts created from prevailing social perceptions without scientific evidence" (Witzig, 2006).* Categories of people based on color were likely constructed by humans for political, social, economic, legal, physical, and cultural reasons, and—as past and current history reveals—used as a basis for perpetuating prejudice, in part because color differences are easiest to identify. Genetically, however, humans are racial hybrids, as bloodlines have crossed and mingled at points all over the globe. So, indeed, all people are related.

The sources of the various shades of color were determined by geography and climate, and, in particular, the sun. Science tells us that color depends on the amount of melanin—or black pigment—in the skin and eyes and hair. Dark skin and dark eyes give better protection from strong sunlight than light skin and eyes (Cohen, 1968).

Another pigment, yellow-orange carotene, also plays a part in skin color, as does the thickness of one's skin. Blood types—A, B, AB, and O being the major ones—can be found in all people regardless of color.

While humans belong to the same species, writes Cohen, we still have many differences. Those characteristics we are born with are called "inherited traits" and those we learn are "acquired traits" (Cohen, 1968, p. 42). Inherited traits include everything from our sex to the shape of our noses and skin color. Acquired traits include such things as language and customs. Psychologists have shown that prejudice of any kind—including color prejudice—is not innate or inherited.

Steve Olson also debunks the idea that racial classifications used by different societies have a genetic basis, even though there are some genetically based physical differences (i.e., in skin color) broadly associated with membership in different groups of people popularly classified as belonging to different races (Olson, 2001).

Richard Rodriguez uses the "browning of America" as a metaphor for the mixing of the races and argues that the United States has been brown from its inception, beginning the moment the African and European met with the Indian (Rodriguez, 2002). He refers to American racial "impurity" and "hybridity" and celebrates that phenomenon. He argues that our historical and contemporary conceptualization of race is rudimentary and psychologically and culturally damaging. Rodriguez, himself of Mexican, Indian, and white Catholic descent, believes that while the United States often represents itself as a melting pot, founded on principles of equality and freedom, the citizens of this country too often are responsible for efforts to continue to divide and categorize.

High school teachers like Nathaniel Smith (2005) have taken the difficult step of introducing students to the slippery concept of race, beginning with the "curriculum premise that individuals can discover and address their own racism more effectively when they understand that all race categories are political lines drawn in the sands of cultural and genetic diffusion and evolution" (Smith, 2005, p. 33). Smith made use of the knowledge that exists about the biology of race, the students' family histories, and primary source materials. The result was a

---

*Despite the previous discussion of race as a social construct, this author refers in some places to "different races" based on the historical reality that society has done so.

revision of students' consciousness about race, encouraging them to raise questions and, in some cases, affirm antiracist attitudes.

Teachers need to recognize that some students might experience discomfort in confronting the topic of race. As students mature, they may indirectly get the message that comments dealing with race are rude or socially unacceptable. However, Brooks and Thompson (September 2005), both associated with Hofstra University, believe that "when we discourage students from engaging in public conversations about race and social justice, we lose an important component of education" (Brooks and Thompson, 2005, p. 48). They argue that early on, students need to make sense of their world, and teachers need to help them clarify misconceptions related to race—as in one child's view that coffee can make a person's skin darker—by sharing scientific data. For example, a simple and direct lesson involving foods and skin color can help students learn that some foods *can* affect the color of one's skin, as in the case of sweet potatoes, carrots, peaches, and apricots. If eaten in excess, these foods can, in fact, make a fair-skinned baby's skin more orange because of their high beta-carotene content. The excess beta-carotene that the body doesn't convert into Vitamin A does, in fact, get deposited in the skin (Brooks and Thompson, 2005, p. 48).

Reflective question: After reflecting on the way that scientific knowledge—particularly in the area of biology—can help to eradicate prejudices, share some of the data above with someone for whom the information might be new.

FOUR Literature as a Tool for Prejudice Reduction

Reading friendship stories can change children's attitudes toward stigmatized groups (Cameron et al., 2006). A study out of the United Kingdom and published in the journal *Child Development* (2006) found that children between the ages of 5 and 11 who read books that show children of varied genders and ethnicities being friends have more favorable views of an otherwise stigmatized group (Cameron et al., 2006).

Psychological research shows that from a very young age children express prejudice and favoritism for their own ethnic, racial, and gender groups. On the other hand, research has also shown that this tendency can be ameliorated. Researchers from the University of Kent in Canterbury and the University of Sussex in Brighton investigated whether making children aware of friendships between their group and a stigmatized group could make children feel more favorable towards the stigmatized group—in this case, refugees. The researchers used fictional stories that featured English children and refugee children. The students participated in reading groups once a week for six weeks for about 20 minutes.

Compared to a control group that did not read any stories, the children who read the stories believed refugees held more positive and fewer negative attributes, and they were also more likely to say they would like to play with refugees. "Overall," said lead author Lindsey Cameron, "these findings suggest that reading about friendships between different groups could be a possible prejudice-reduction tool for use with students as young as 5" (Cameron et al., 2006, p. 1208).

The Southern Poverty Law Center has made available free of charge a book with 12 tales intended to teach tolerance (Sapp, 2006). *Rhinos and Raspberries: Tolerance Tales for the Early Grades* contains tales from around the world. Each of the stories is accompanied by a character education and community building lesson, as well as focused discussion questions and writing themes to aid children in receiving the messages of peace and justice in each tale. For more information about this free resource, go to www.tolerance .org/teach/resources.

Reflective question: Can you recall any stories that you read—or that were read to you—that had messages of tolerance or appreciation for differences? If so, do you think they influenced your attitudes?

Principles and Applications for Reducing Prejudice

Principle ONE

Teaching at every level must reflect that Americans—no matter what their differences—are full and equal citizens, possessing the same rights and privileges.

Classroom Applications and Strategies

There are a number of useful strategies for helping teachers to model for their students behaviors and attitudes respecting cultural differences. When there is bigoted talk among students, simple reprimands may do more harm than good by, for example, causing students to cover up rather than change their attitudes. To turn such classroom incidents to full advantage, there needs to be a coherent policy for dealing with them.

• Teachers can emphasize what is common to all humans: birth, marriage, death, family, making a living, providing basic necessities, though these commonalities may be handled differently by different people for physical, economic, or other reasons (Miel and Kiester, 1967, p. 61).

• Teachers can demonstrate how traditions, language, and religion often cut across racial lines.

• Lessons can help students recognize that the predominantly white society surrounding them is very different from the rest of the globe, where the overwhelming majority of the population is nonwhite.

• Teachers should avoid presenting customs of unfamiliar groups as quaint or fantastic, but rather as making sense within the context of their particular cultures.

• Stereotypes should be explored and then exploded. For example, in studying Africa as the origin of African Americans, emphasis can be placed on the continent's variety of countries and peoples and on its many living styles, both rural and urban.

• Slavery should not be presented as a phenomenon peculiar to African Americans in the United States, but as an institution with a long history involving many races, nationalities, and civilizations. In any given class, a large number of children are likely to be descended from people in bondage: from serfs in medieval Europe or Czarist Russia, from Jews who were slaves in Egypt, or from indentured servants in colonial America, who, while not the same as slaves, did work for nothing and could earn freedom.

• Stereotypes can be combated—and an awareness fostered that diverse Americans are equal citizens—by bringing students into contact with people from different racial groups either within the school or by inviting them to school or through films and other media. In this way students will see that members of different racial groups are not all the same but can differ in terms of socioeconomic backgrounds or may have different national origins.

• Students, no matter what their age, can deal with large issues on their own terms. They can discuss violence, school desegregation struggles, demands for equal rights, and other charged issues, especially since they have likely already been exposed to these matters from television, the Internet, and other sources. With a teacher's guidance, these issues can be clarified and researched so as to illuminate facts.

Principle TWO

One of the goals of a social studies program should be to convey to students many important points about socioeconomic differences.

Teachers can help students recognize that all persons do not share equally in material things, but that all, nonetheless, are full and equal members of society, and that the work of some is no less worthy for being less highly rewarded than that of others (Miel and Kiester, 1967, p. 62).

Classroom Applications and Strategies

• Help students realize that members of minority groups are found at various socioeconomic levels, but that discrimination often deprives some of them from access to opportunities.

• The current nature of poverty and unemployment should be addressed using film, literature, photographs, current articles, and the Internet, so that students can learn about the socioeconomic differences among groups. Historic aspects of poverty should also be presented, including the Depression, sweatshops, and other such examples from America's past. Touch on other nations as well, where such conditions as sweatshops may still exist.

• Show how our society has developed programs that value the individual regardless of occupation or income, with institutions like Social Security, Medicare, food stamps, and other programs. Generally speaking, it is important for students to recognize that democracy seeks to provide adequate schooling, housing, food, and care for everyone, though these basic rights are not consistently pursued and are often not viewed as priorities by all national, state, and local officials.

Principle THREE

Helping students to personalize prejudice is one way of helping them to connect with this subject. This can be done within traditional humanities disciplines like history as well as in mathematics classes.

Classroom Applications and Strategies

• Mathematics, once considered immune to real-world issues, is now being employed in the work for equity (Gutstein and Peterson, 2005). Called social justice math, it was the focus of a first-ever conference on math education and social justice that met on the Brooklyn campus of Long Island University in the spring of 2007 (Murrey and Sapp, 2008, p. 52). The conference paired two key objectives: (1) increasing success in math for students of color and those disadvantaged by poverty and (2) identifying socioeconomic issues in the students' neighborhoods that can be better understood through a mathematical lens (Murrey and Sapp, 2008, p. 52).

  • Janet Wayne, a teacher in an eleventh-grade classroom in Los Angeles, taught a statistics unit based on domestic abuse. "Students learned about math concepts like averages, percents, graphs of all kinds, mean and median" (Murrey and Sapp, 2008, p. 55).
  • A school in the Williamsburg neighborhood of Brooklyn, El Puente Academy for Peace and Justice, actively responded to a proposal by borough officials to build a large incinerator that would spew toxins into this already chemically toxic community. They joined other environmental activists and used their mathematical skills to help build a case against the incinerator. Based on the students' mathematical findings, the city officials reversed their vote. Calling themselves the Toxic Avengers, these students learned that mathematics, indeed, has important real-life applications (Murrey and Sapp, 2008, p. 53).

Supporters of this pairing of mathematics and social justice are aware of arguments against this approach, the main two criticisms being that it waters down the discipline and "inserts a political left-wing perspective." Jonathan Osler, founder of radicalmath.org, responds to these arguments by stressing that "teaching math is what is most important to us, and having social justice connections isn't at the expense of vigorous mathematics" (Murrey and Sapp, 2008, p. 54). Most supporters believe students need to learn how to use mathematics so they can be informed participants in a democratic society.

• Students can be introduced to methods for exploring their own personal experiences with prejudice through the use of questionnaires, an example of which is included in the unit on prejudice in this chapter. Before administering the questionnaire or broaching the subject of the students' personal experiences with prejudice, you might consider revealing your own experiences in what Robert Coles (1993) calls "the confessional tradition," putting one's cards on the table by telling a story or two and explaining oneself as a means of helping others pay attention and earning their trust. Coles, former professor of psychiatry and medical humanities at Harvard University, discovered this useful approach when he volunteered to teach in a Boston high school. Students were less fearful and more willing to honestly share their observations and their stories when he revealed discoveries he had made about himself and his attitudes. Writes Coles, "We don't need an orgy of overwrought psychology in our classrooms, but the blunt candor of the personal story, the proverbial cry of the heart, the soul bared to young souls embattled and in jeopardy can sometimes break the ice of class and race [and the gap between teacher and student]" (Coles, 1993, p. A52).

• Connecting certain holiday traditions to the topic of prejudice is another way to personalize the subject. For example, Thanksgiving presents a teachable moment for integrating lessons that give students an opportunity to walk in the shoes of Native Americans, as in the following activities:

  • *Critique books.*   Compare books that depict Native Americans accurately with books that depict stereotypes.
  • *Consider multiple viewpoints.*   Tell the Thanksgiving story from the perspective of Native Americans as well as of the European immigrants. Students need to learn both sides if they are to become critical thinkers and not repeat or continue the injustices of the past and present.
  • *Critique Thanksgiving TV specials.*   Include parents in the discussion and suggest ways they can talk with their children about which images are fair and which are unfair.

• In the context of the study of history, "Teachers have found that the process of discussing their community's or school's racial past can itself markedly lessen racial prejudice," as James Loewen stated in his bestseller, *Lies My Teacher Told Me* (1995). An instructor of race relations at the University of Vermont, he noted in his research that as students share what adults have told them about local history, stories of racist actions emerge freely because they are not about or by the speaker. Often, he says, revealing the town's past can become a force for liberation (Loewen, 2008, p. 27).

Principle FOUR

Making use of news media can enlarge students' awareness of local, national, and international examples of prejudice and its causes.

Classroom Applications and Strategies

Current news sources should be consulted on a daily basis so that students can follow crises that have their origins in cultural prejudices both worldwide and in their own backyards.

• Use television or computers in the classroom as well as library sources to gather data on the facts and origins of these cultural conflicts.

• Discuss with students the possibilities of taking an active role in helping end a crisis the class is following. Students can learn about the power of writing to congressmen and senators, of organizing and creating posters to educate others about the situation, of writing letters to the editor, or of other activities in which they can help to lessen the suffering prejudice has caused.

Principle FIVE

Choosing appropriate literature for teaching about other cultures—both within and beyond the United States—must be done with attention to criteria that can help prevent passing on inaccurate or stereotypical ideas. These criteria are also relevant to teaching about any group within the society who may be subject to stereotyping.

Classroom Applications and Strategies

• Ten guidelines for selecting bias-free texts and storybooks were identified by the Council on Interracial Books for Children (Derman-Sparks, 1989):

1. Checking illustrations for stereotypes or tokenism
2. Checking the story line
3. Looking at the lifestyles described and watching out for the "cute-natives-in-costumes" syndrome, for example
4. Weighing relationships between people
5. Noting the heroes
6. Considering the effect on a child's self-image
7. Considering the backgrounds of the author and illustrator
8. Examining the author's perspective
9. Watching for loaded words
10. Checking the copyright date

• There is an emerging canon of transgender-inclusive young adult (YA) literature that is integrating controversial subjects and allowing topics once considered inappropriate for teen readers to become legitimate areas for exploration and debate. According to Elsworth Rockefeller, a young adult services librarian in New Jersey, transgender fiction is making a stumbling debut as part of this canon. "While some of the first attempts offer readers thought-provoking topics and well-developed characters, at least as many include offensive language and trite characters, and most—even some of the best—don't move beyond problem-novel formulas" (Rockefeller, 2007, p. 526). This new genre should, he notes, deepen its focus and go beyond gender, a point to be considered when choosing appropriate literature related to diversity.

Principle SIX

Including material concerning any aspect of religion in the public school curriculum requires careful planning (if legal problems are to be avoided).

Supreme Court decisions on prayer and Bible reading in the classroom have vigorously upheld the principle of separation of church and state that the Founding Fathers wrote into the Bill of Rights. Educators—and religious leaders, too—are still sharply divided on what other classroom activities might violate this principle. Methods of introducing religious subject matter need to be judicious (Miel and Kiester, 1967, p. 64).

It should be possible, however, to make religious differences between people a topic for fruitful discussion in school. What is perhaps needed most is a clear school board policy regarding how such matters may be taken up in class. Also needed may be approval by the community and cooperation by parents in curriculum that exposes children to information about other faiths.

Classroom Applications and Strategies

• A reasonable working rule is that religious indoctrination and devotional exercises—even nonsectarian ones—do not belong in the public school. Objective study *about* religion, however, is an important part of human life, culture, and history, and has a place there. Similar criteria would seem to apply to holiday activities (Miel and Kiester, 1967, p. 64).

• Find out what children already know and believe about religious differences and build on that knowledge. Seek to discover where their confusion lies.

• Teach comparative religion, even at early ages. For example, as children grow in understanding, go beyond Christianity and Judaism to include Islam, Hinduism, Buddhism, Confucianism, and more. Help students to understand the common elements of various faiths, as well as the nature of the differences between them (see, for example, Activity 3 in Sample Unit 1 later in this chapter). Point out that religions of the West profess one God, but explain other ideas (such as polytheism, animism, ancestor worship) and even religions without a God, such as Buddhism, as well as agnosticism, humanism, and atheism. In higher grades, try to address what is basically spiritual and religious in man (Miel and Kiester, 1967, p. 65).

• Through pictures and first-hand contact, help children understand that religion does not correspond to race or appearance. For example, show photographs of a Chinese Protestant or a blond Jew, a black Catholic or a white Buddhist.

• Find out what guidelines exist in your school system for approaching such issues as textbook content, values education, creation science, and religious holidays so that the constitutional guarantee of religious liberty is respected. Clarify the distinction between legal and religious holidays in this country. Discuss the problems involved in trying to be fair to minority groups of various kinds and sizes in the community.

• Enlist the help of parents and religious leaders in determining what can be effectively taught at school about religious differences and in what ways. Let parents assist in arranging field trips and obtaining materials.

Several organizations can provide materials and assistance for establishing guidelines for including religion in the public school curriculum and for defining what is appropriate in terms of including religious holidays in the schools. Among these organizations are the National Council for the Social Studies, the National Education Association, the American Federation of Teachers, and the Association for Supervision and Curriculum Development, as well as the National Conference of Christians and Jews, now known as the National Conference for Community and Justice, and the Anti-Defamation League.

What is important to keep in mind, no matter the challenges of integrating the discussion of religion into the curriculum, is that religion has played a significant role in world and U.S. history and *can* be taught within appropriate historical and cultural contexts (Haynes and Kniker, 1990, p. 305). One of the underlying goals of teaching should be promoting understanding and respect for religious differences free of advocacy for any one religion.

Strategies and Lessons for
Reducing Prejudice

Lesson 1: "Emmett Till": A Poem of Sorrow and Hope

Grade Levels: 2–6
Content: Language Arts, Social Studies, Art
Principles: 1, 3, 4, 5

The often brutal results of prejudice are reflected in the true story of the murder of 14-year-old Emmett Till. In 1955, he had been visiting relatives in a small Mississippi town when he was accused of giving a white woman a "wolf whistle" outside a market. Her husband and half-brother pulled Till from the house where he was staying, drove him to the banks of the Tallahatchie River, and shot him in the head. Despite eyewitness testimony, an all-white jury acquitted the two men of murder. Outrage over Till's death helped to mobilize the civil rights movement (Chideya, 2005).

Poet Marilyn Nelson's narrative poem *A Wreath for Emmett Till* (2005) (see excerpt in Figure 5.1) was her attempt to find the right words for teaching young readers about the violence and injustice of Till's murder. The intent of this lesson, which contains an excerpt of Nelson's poem, is to present ways of conveying to children not just the story of Till's murder but also why people commit acts of violence based not on reason but on irrational hate.

Objectives

Students will be able to

1. Listen to the excerpt from the poem and visualize its content (ELA 7, 9, 12).
2. Discuss questions posed by the teacher, such as, What role did prejudice play in causing such an act of violence? (ELA 5, 7, 12).
3. Imagine themselves in the same situation as Emmett Till (ELA 9; SOCS-USH 3).
4. Refer to other acts of violence based on prejudice (SOCS-USH 3).
5. Create a work of art related to Emmett Till's life (ELA 2, 9; NA-VA 1, 6).

Figure 5.1   Excerpt from *A Wreath for Emmett Till*

Emmett Till's name still catches in my throat,
like syllables waylaid in a stutterer's mouth.
A fourteen-year old stutterer, in the South
to visit relatives and to be taught
the family's ways. His mother had finally bought
that White Sox cap; she'd made him swear an oath
to be careful around white folks. She'd told him the
truth of many a Mississippi anecdote:
Some white folks have blind souls. In his suitcase
she'd packed dungarees, T-shirts, underwear,
and comic books. She'd given him a note
for the conductor, waved to his chubby face,
wondered if he'd remember to brush his hair.
Her only child. A body left to bloat.

Source: Nelson, M. (2005). *A Wreath for Emmett Till*. New York: Houghton Mifflin. Text copyright © 2005 by Marilyn Nelson. Reprinted by permission of Houghton Mifflin Harcourt Publishing Company. All rights reserved.

Materials

- Excerpt from the narrative poem A *Wreath for Emmett Till* (see Figure 5.1)
- (Optional) Other books and news sources about Emmett Till's murder

Procedures

1. Begin by asking students if they know the meaning of *prejudice*. Simple definitions you can offer include

   The feeling of one group in a society that members of another group are inferior (Brandwein et al., 1972, p. 45)

   Thinking ill of others without sufficient warrant

   Prejudging members of a different group based on what you may know—or may not know—about only a few members of that group

2. Briefly discuss any examples that the children share based on their personal experiences.

3. Before sharing with the class the facts given in the introduction to this lesson, explain that some people have gone beyond prejudiced attitudes or name-calling and have actively discriminated against certain members of a different group using violence. Ask the class if they know of any such events. (*Discrimination* is behavior resulting from prejudiced attitudes.)

4. After sharing the facts of the Emmett Till story, ask students to listen to the excerpt from A *Wreath for Emmett Till* (Nelson, 2005) and visualize its content. (You may want to define certain terms before reading the poem, such as *stutterer, oath, dungarees* [a dated term for *jeans*], or *bloat*.)

5. After reading the excerpt, ask students for their reactions. What did they "see" as you read the poem? How did they feel? Could they imagine themselves in a similar situation? In what ways are they like Emmett? How would *their* parents feel? What role did prejudice play in his death, or, to put it differently, was his murder based on anything besides prejudice? Did this poem remind them of any other similar events?

6. (Optional) Find a copy of Marilyn Nelson's book, A *Wreath for Emmett Till*, and read the entire narrative poem.

Assessment

- Participation in discussion of the poem and questions posed by teacher (Objectives 2, 3, 4)
- Drawing of an aspect of Emmett Till's life based on images in the poem (Objective 5)

Extension

- This lesson can be adapted for grades 7 to 12 with the addition of the following materials: The DVD, "The Murder of Emmett Till" (PBS, American Experience Series, 2003) which can be ordered from Amazon.com. Also go to www.pbs.org/wgbh/amex/till for related articles and photographs. The documentary, 50 minutes in length, can accompany the poem and provide important details and images. See www.facinghistory.org/resources/lesson/emmett-till for four lessons intended for grades 8 to 12 that can be used along with the documentary. Each lesson requires two or more class sessions and are entitled as follows: Confronting the Murder, Examining the Choices People Made, Connecting the Victims of Lynching to the Murder, and Choosing to Remember.
- Emmett Till's murder in 1955 caused outrage throughout the country and helped to mobilize the civil rights movement. Consider following up this lesson with a study of Martin Luther King's leadership in this movement and his message of nonviolence.

Lesson 2: Ladder of Prejudice*

Grade Levels: 5–9
Content: Social Studies, Language Arts
Principles: 1, 4

The Ladder of Prejudice provides a useful visualization of the prejudice that occurs in schools, communities, and the world. At the same time this image challenges students to consider ways they can help to change their world for the better by beginning to address acts of prejudice they see in their own backyards. Stefanie Fox, a teacher at Kingsway Middle School in Woolwich, New Jersey, uses the ladder within the context of a unit on the Holocaust to address issues of diversity, bullying, and community building (Fox, 2007, p. 12).

Objectives

Students will be able to

1. Work together in defining the terms on the ladder (SOCS-WH 8, 9; ELA 7, 8, 11).
2. Contribute examples of each of the "steps"/terms on the ladder, including those contained in newspaper articles (SOCS-USH [K–4] 2; SOCS-USH [5–12] 10; ELA 4, 7).
3. Brainstorm ideas for addressing some of the examples of prejudice (ELA 4, 5, 9, 11).

Materials

- A poster or bulletin board showing the ladder of prejudice (see Figure 5.2)
- Five strips of paper

Procedures

1. Write the following five terms on the strips of paper and post on the board: *speech, avoidance, discrimination, attack, extermination.*
2. As a whole group or in small groups define the five terms.
3. Draw a ladder on the board or cut one out ahead of time and place it on the bulletin board *without* the words.
4. Ask students to decide on the hierarchy of the terms from least to most severe. Then have them place the strips of paper on the rungs of the ladder (see Figure 5.2). (The ladder begins with speech—people talking about others and this leads to avoiding a group of people. This results in treating that group differently, making it easier to attack them physically. Extermination is the extreme outcome of this ladder of prejudice.)
5. After the terms have been discussed and placed on the ladder, have students write on Post-it notes something that has happened in the school or community that could be placed next to one of the terms on the ladder. For example, if a student overheard someone use an ethnic slur, the Post-it describing that speech could be placed next to the first rung of the ladder, *Speech.* (Fox discusses the stages of the ladder as they were experienced during the Holocaust.)
6. Continue using the ladder on a daily basis by reading and watching the news and placing the examples of prejudice they have gathered from the media on the appropriate rungs of the ladder.
7. After a few days of gathering articles, begin brainstorming ideas for addressing some of the examples of prejudice, especially those closest to their own local area.

*Adapted from S. Fox. (Fall 2007). "Ladder of Prejudice." *Teaching Tolerance* 32, p. 12.

Figure 5.2   Ladder of Prejudice

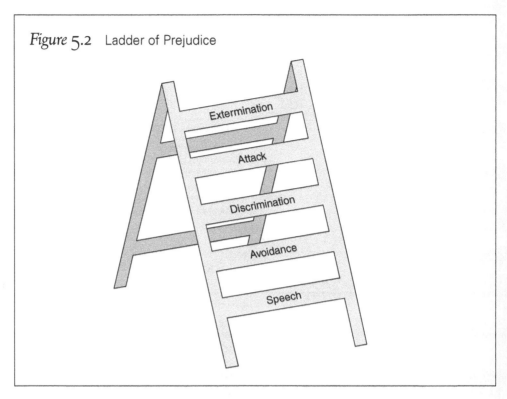

Source: Fox, S. (Fall 2007). *Teaching Tolerance* (p. 12). Montgomery, AL: Southern Poverty Law Center. Reprinted by permission of Teaching Tolerance, www.tolerance.org.

Assessment

- Contribution to the discussion of the terms on the ladder (Objective 1)
- Contribution of articles and examples of prejudice on the ladder of prejudice (Objective 2)
- Participation in the brainstorming session on ideas for addressing some of the examples of prejudice (Objective 3)

Extension

A similar version of the ladder called "Pyramid of Hate" is included in a curriculum guide to a study of the Nazi Holocaust (see Figure 5.3). You may want to have students compare and contrast the images and decide which is more effective.

Lesson 3: Unequal Resources*

Grade Levels: 3–6
Content: Social Studies, Language Arts
Principles: 1, 2

Children begin developing attitudes about various groups in society as early as ages 3 and 4, and as they get older, such attitudes become more difficult to change. That idea led Dr. Deborah A. Byrnes to develop a series of lessons for elementary students that deal with prejudiced

*Adapted from D. A. Byrnes. (1995). *"Teacher, they called me a _____!", Confronting Prejudice and Discrimination in the Classroom* (p. 49). New York: Anti-Defamation League and The Utah State Office of Education.

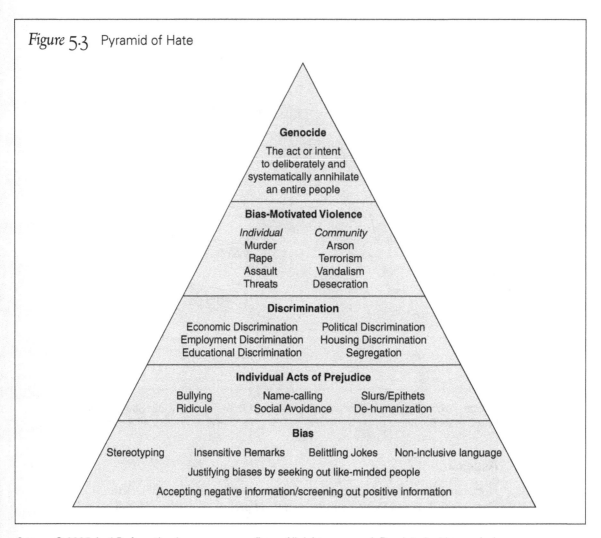

Figure 5.3   Pyramid of Hate

attitudes based on economic class differences (Byrnes, 1995). In this lesson young students learn many important points about economic difference and the effects of this difference. (See also the material under Principle 2.)

Objectives

Students will be able to

1. Participate in a hands-on activity intended to help them become aware of economic difference (SOCS-GEO 4, 5; SOCS-EC 1, 3).
2. Recognize that discrimination often deprives people of access to opportunities and resources (SOCS-EC 1, 3; SOCS-WH 9; ELA 9).
3. Develop empathy with people who are—for a variety of different reasons—dealing with disadvantaged economic circumstances (SOCS-GEO 4; SOCS-USH [K–4] 1, 3; SOCS-USH [5–12] 10).
4. Describe various programs that have been developed to address socioeconomic differences and needs (SOCS-USH [5–12] 10; SOCS-C 1, 2, 5; SOCS-EC 3, 15).
5. Write about what they learned as a result of this activity (ELA 6, 12, 5).

Materials

- Pencils, pens, felt pens, crayons
- Scissors, rulers
- Construction paper of different colors, manila paper, white poster paper
- Glitter, stencils

Procedures

1. Divide the class into five groups and say that each group is to make one poster showing what they have learned about some topic they have been studying within any of their subjects.
2. Explain that the posters will be displayed on the bulletin board when they are finished. Set a certain amount of time for them to complete their posters.
3. Tell each group they can only use the materials that are given to them.
4. Provide the groups with the following materials:

   Group 1: Pencils and a large sheet of manila paper

   Group 2: Pencils, crayons, and white poster paper

   Group 3: Pencils, crayons, felt pens, and assorted colors of poster paper

   Group 4: Pencils, crayons, felt pens, scissors, rulers, and assorted colors of poster paper

   Group 5: Pencils, crayons, felt pens, scissors, rulers, glitter, construction paper, stencils, assorted colors of poster paper, and anything else that will help this group.

5. If students complain about the differences in resources, simply say: "That's the way it is. Life isn't always fair." Say this in a matter-of-fact way and allow no changes.
6. After students have completed their posters in the allotted time you have given them, carry on a discussion that includes the following questions and any other questions you believe are appropriate:

   - How did you feel when you noticed that some people had more materials (or less) than you did?
   - In what ways did your resources affect your project?
   - How would you have felt if I had judged your final projects for a prize or a grade? Would this be fair? Why? Why not?
   - If other people were shown our posters and asked who were the most talented students in the room, whom would they say? Would these posters necessarily be a fair assessment of what all of you can do?
   - Why do you think I set up this activity this way?
   - Are there other situations you know about where people have advantages over others? Where they have more resources, money, or power? (Provide some examples to prompt the class.)
   - What role might discrimination play in economic difference?
   - Is it important to consider individual circumstances and opportunities before judging what a person may or may not be capable of doing? Why?
   - Do you know about any programs developed by private or public organizations that address socioeconomic differences and needs? (You might share with them the following: Medicare, food stamps, Social Security, hunger banks.)

Assessment

- Students' participation in the small-group hands-on activity (Objective 1)
- Participation in the follow-up discussion (Objectives 2, 3, 4)
- Written response to question: "What did you learn about economic difference as a result of this activity?" (Objective 5)

Lesson 4: Amulets of Ladakh*

Grade Levels: 2–8
Content: Social Studies, Art
Principle: 6

People within most cultures and religions actively pursue the quest for good fortune. Amulets—or symbols of good luck—play a role in this quest. Though they may differ, these symbols serve people's hopes for good health and fortune for themselves and their friends.

The population of Ladakh, one of the most remote districts of India, is approximately half Buddhist and half Muslim. Both groups share certain cultural practices. For example, Buddhist and Muslim children alike wear protective amulets to ward off evil spirits. The charms often show a traditional symbol of luck and power, such as a dragon or a deity, surrounded by a curvilinear frame. The amulets reflect the influence of Indian and Chinese art (China borders India and also has substantial numbers of Buddhists and Muslims). The parents of Ladakh, like parents everywhere, hope for good fortune for their children.

Objectives

Students will be able to

1. Recognize and appreciate the values shared universally by people in cultures and religions everywhere, such as beliefs in good luck symbols (SOCS-USH [5–12] 4; SOCS-WH 1–9).
2. Conduct a survey among family members about good and bad luck symbols (ELA 4, 6, 9, 12).
3. Discover examples of unique values or beliefs held by individual cultures and why people developed these beliefs (SOCS-WH 1–9; ELA 9).
4. Make a good luck amulet (NA-VA 1–6).

Materials

- Pencil and paper
- Clay
- Cardboard or poster paper
- (Optional) Paint and brush
- String or silken cord

Procedures

1. Discuss with the class symbols of luck (good and bad) in our own and other cultures and religions and why people develop beliefs in such objects.
2. Sketch on the board (or have students sketch) some examples of the objects which people believe will give good (or bad) luck (e.g., good luck: rabbit's foot or lucky penny; bad luck: black cat, Friday the 13th). (Collect samples of these objects if possible.)
3. Design with students a survey they can conduct among family members to discover good luck rituals and symbols that they believe in or know about. Try to trace their origins.
4. Give the children paper and pencil so they can complete one of these options: either design their own good luck symbol or make a sketch of a good luck symbol they know about.

*Adapted from M. W. Ryan. (1989). *Cultural Journeys: 84 Art and Social Science Activities from around the World* (pp. 75, 76). Holmes Beach, FL: Learning Publications.

5. After completing their sketches, tell them to take some clay and sculpt the symbol. Using the pencil, have them make a hole in the object so it can hang from a string or a silken cord and either be worn by them or hung up on the bulletin board next to a simple explanation of the symbol and its origin.

Assessment

- Participation in a discussion about the universal quest for good fortune and how amulets are believed to be helpful in such a quest (Objectives 1, 2, 3)
- Completed survey conducted among family members and with data from other sources about amulets and their origins (Objectives 2, 3)
- A work of art: an amulet fashioned from clay (Objective 4)

Lesson 5: Are Fairy Tales Sexist?

Grade Levels: 5–12
Content: Language Arts, Social Studies
Principle: 5

The messages in fairy tales and children's stories usually reflect the cultural beliefs and attitudes of the people who created those messages. So that they can discount certain attitudes while still enjoying the stories, children need to be aware that some attitudes may be biased or stereotypical.

This lesson provides students with the opportunity to investigate a number of children's books and fairy tales using a checklist that will help them discover how males and females are depicted in those tales (see Figure 5.4).

The conversation that follows their investigation should include references to the consequences of sex discrimination, such as why, for example, there has never been a female president of the United States and why there are so few women in Congress, why most fathers still don't stay home with children, and why so many people still believe that these and other culturally influenced sex differences are a natural consequence of biology. The awareness raised by such a conversation can prepare students to actively oppose gender-related constraints.

Objectives

Students will be able to

1. Read one or more fairy tales or children's books (ELA 1).
2. Complete a checklist of variables in order to identify how males and females are depicted (ELA 2, 3, 6).
3. Demonstrate awareness of sexism in children's books and fairy tales (and awareness that such readings may perpetuate stereotyping) after analyzing the results of their checklists (ELA 3, 5, 9, 11).
4. Discuss origins of gender stereotypes and biases (SOCS-USH 3; ELA 9).
5. Critique the checklist and add or change some of the variables (ELA 3, 6, 7).

Materials

- Several fairy tales and children's books selected by the teacher and school librarian with the help of students (approximately 20 stories, one or two for each pair of students to investigate)
- Checklist of variables for students to use as they seek to identify the roles and behaviors of males and females in the stories they are reading (Figure 5.4)

Figure 5.4   Checklist of Variables Associated with Gender-Related Behaviors and Attitudes Depicted in Children's Books and Fairy Tales

Behaviors and Attitudes	Male	Female	Both	N/A
1. Children depicted:	_____	_____	_____	_____
a. playing a sport	_____	_____	_____	_____
b. washing dishes, cleaning house	_____	_____	_____	_____
c. playing by themselves	_____	_____	_____	_____
d. crying	_____	_____	_____	_____
e. getting praise	_____	_____	_____	_____
f. being creative	_____	_____	_____	_____
g. getting help	_____	_____	_____	_____
h. giving help	_____	_____	_____	_____
i. involved in work	_____	_____	_____	_____
j. in leadership position	_____	_____	_____	_____
k. showing emotion	_____	_____	_____	_____
l. playing with dolls	_____	_____	_____	_____
m. being affectionate	_____	_____	_____	_____
2. The main character	_____	_____	_____	_____
3. Hero or heroine depicted?	_____	_____	_____	_____

Source: Adapted from E. T. Nickerson, et al. (1975). *Intervention Strategies for Changing Sex Role Stereotypes* (p. 39). Dubuque, IA: Kendall/Hunt Publishing.

Procedures

1. After approximately 20 stories or tales have been selected for investigation and placed in the classroom, divide the class up into pairs and give them time to examine one or two fairy tales or children's books.
2. Review the checklist of variables and how they should check one column or the other. (Optional: Have them write a few notes identifying precisely how the story depicted that variable.)
3. After pairs of students complete their reading and the checklist, discuss with the class the frequency of the stereotypes depicted and the value messages implied in those stereotypes.
4. Discuss how they might have rewritten certain tales without the stereotypes and how they might change or add to the checklist as a result.

Assessment

- Completion of one or two fairy tales or children's books (Objective 1)
- Completion of a checklist of variables related to behaviors of males and females in the books (Objective 2)
- Analysis of checklist results followed by discussion of origins of sexist attitudes and stereotypes contained in some of the books.
- Discussion of how the tales might be rewritten without the stereotypes and an explanation of their additions or changes to the checklist as a result (Objectives 3, 4, 5) (*Note:* Point out the limitations of such a checklist and the resulting conclusions; for example,

if a boy cries in a story, that doesn't necessarily imply that the story is nonsexist. Individual differences occur in gender groups. However, differences that appear with a degree of regularity should be identified and discussed.)

Sample Unit 1: Understanding Prejudice

Grade Levels: See individual activities
Content: Interdisciplinary
Time: 4 weeks
Principles: 1, 2, 3, 4

Prejudice has traditionally prevented people from living, working, and learning productively together. This problem continues despite attempts by teachers to reduce prejudice through character education curricula, community service projects, multicultural education, and the modeling of tolerant behavior in the classroom. No doubt these indirect approaches have had positive effects on the attitudes and behavior of many students. However, another approach, that is, systematic, accurate, and direct teaching about prejudice, may be the best ally of improved human relations.

In the following unit of instruction, students learn key definitions, discuss and analyze their own connection to the topic, and engage in several activities and projects that enable them to discover ideas on their own. Each activity or lesson can be implemented without any of the others, or you can choose to do as many as you want and in any order. Direct teaching may not automatically alter prejudice—few would claim that the whole problem of prejudice is simply a matter of education—but accurate information has a role to play and may help to promote in students a personal commitment to tolerance and respect for differences.

Objectives

Students will be able to

1. Explain the meaning of prejudice and its destructive aspects including stereotyping, scapegoating, and other forms of discrimination (ELA 9, 11; SOCS-C 2, 5; SOCS-USH [K–4] 1, 3, 4).
2. Examine their own (and others') attitudes and treatment of people who are different from themselves (ELA 3, 7, 9; SOCS-USH [K–4] 3, 4).
3. Complete one or more unit activities and share resulting reactions with peers (ELA 1–12; SOCS-USH [K–4] 1–4; NS 6).
4. Develop a commitment to tolerance and acceptance of diversity in our society in terms of attitudes and actions that promote fair treatment of others (ELA 9, 11; SOCS-C 2, 5; SOCS-USH [K–4] 1, 3).

Materials

- Bulletin board space
- Internet and library sources
- Questionnaire (see Figure 5.5)
- (Optional) Films: *Dumbo, Eye of the Storm, Tubby the Tuba, The Ugly Duckling, Shrek*

Procedures

See procedures that accompany each of the six activities included in this unit.

Figure 5.5   Questionnaire on Personal Connections to Prejudice

1. Have you ever been the victim of discrimination or prejudice? If so, please explain.
2. Have you ever heard anyone express a prejudiced view or seen anyone commit a prejudiced act? If so, please explain. (For example, have you ever heard someone label all the people from a certain group in the same way—that is, stereotype?)
3. Have *you* ever acted in a prejudiced way against an innocent person or group? If so, please explain.
4. Have you ever been a member of a minority group? If so, explain when. What did it feel like?
5. Do you believe there is any prejudice in your town or school? Please explain.
6. Can you list three or more historical or current events that occurred because of prejudice?

Assessment

- Participation in and completion of assigned activity(ies) (Objective 3)
- Contribution to the discussion based on responses to the questionnaire related to their own attitudes and behavior (Objective 2, 3)
- Observable cooperative behavior and respect for others throughout the unit activities (Objective 4)
- Quiz or other form of feedback on aspects of prejudice and their destructive impact (Objective 1)

Activity 1: Questionnaire on Personal Connections to Prejudice (Grades 4–12)

Procedures
1. Make copies of the questionnaire (see Figure 5.5) and have students complete it.
2. Collate answers and share results with students the next day.
3. Discuss these results and their implications with students. (Students may be willing to share their feelings and experiences without concern for anonymity.) Ask questions such as the following:
   - Why do these examples of prejudice exist?
   - How can these prejudices be proven false?
   - How can these prejudices be reduced?
4. Ask students their opinions of possible remedies for reducing prejudice.

Activity 2: Understanding Prejudice (Grades 3–8)*

Procedures
Designate the word *prejudice* as a theme for a week, and carry out some or all of the following activities:

1. Have students collect definitions of *prejudice, scapegoating,* and *stereotyping* from many sources and put them all over the bulletin board. Do the same for *tolerance* (i.e., *prejudice:* thinking ill of others without sufficient warrant or not based on actual experience; *tolerance:* the capacity for recognizing and respecting the beliefs or practices

*Adapted from D. A. Byrnes (1995). *"Teacher, they called me a _____!"* (p. 7). New York: Anti-Defamation League and The Utah State Office of Education.

Figure 5.6   The Flaws of Stereotyping

Source: Trudeau, G. (March 15, 1988). Doonesbury. © 1988 G. B. Trudeau. Reprinted by permission of Universal Press Syndicate. All rights reserved.

of others; *scapegoating*: blaming an innocent person or group for something they did not do; *stereotyping*: labeling a whole group based only on what you know about one or a few members of that group). Share the cartoon in Figure 5.6 that captures the flaws of stereotyping.

2. Have the class write an essay about an experience they had with prejudice or one they observed.

3. Have students design a bulletin board with slogans related to prejudice (e.g., "Prejudice is being down on something you're not up on," "Ecidujerp: No matter how you spell it, it doesn't make sense," or "Stereotyping is lazy thinking."

4. Have the class write stories, poems, or skits demonstrating the unfairness of prejudice.

5. Discuss with students why people have prejudices and what effects prejudice has on people. (Help students become aware that our likes and dislikes are influenced by our frame of reference, that is, by where we live, our experiences, upbringing, values, and beliefs. Share with students Allport's simple formula explaining the cause of prejudice discussed earlier in this chapter.)

6. Have students make collages in which they portray respect for differences in such matters as religion, race, class, gender, ethnicity (language), and ability.

Activity 3: We're All the Same, We're All Different (Grades 6–12)

In this activity students have the opportunity to do research on world religions. They will come to see the similarities among these religions (e.g., most have a belief about creation) as well as the differences (e.g., how beliefs about creation vary).

Procedures

1. Give the students the chart on comparative religions (Figure 5.7) and have them do research in order to fill in the answer blanks. Students can work in pairs, small groups, or individually. They can be assigned the whole chart or the religions can be divided up among the students.

2. After the chart is complete, hold a discussion in which students share their observations about the similarities and differences among the religions.

3. Mention how religious intolerance has led to violent acts in cultures all over the world, from Belfast to Bosnia, in Europe during the Nazi Holocaust, between India

Figure 5.7   Comparative Religions

Religion	Date of Origin and Location	Most Solemn Holiday	Fast Days	Creation Belief	Marriage Beliefs	Coming of Age Ceremony	Dietary Laws	Beliefs about Death
Buddhism								
Christianity								
Hinduism								
Islam (Muslims)								
Judaism								
Shintoism								
Taoism								

Note. Mention that these are not the only religions in the world. (There are tribal religions, folk religions, mixes of religions, etc.) Also mention that within each religion, like Christianity, there are major differences. Have students record the most common belief within each. Mention also the fact that some people may not believe in any organized religion or in God and that in a democracy everyone is free to believe—or not believe—as they wish. *Atheists,* for example, do not believe in the existence of a God or deity, and *agnostics* believe the existence of a God is not knowable or provable.

and Pakistan, and in so many other places. Ask students if they think knowledge about religions could help to prevent such violence. Why or why not?

Activity 4: Teaching Tolerance Using Animated Films (Grades K–5)

Procedures

1. Show one or more of the films listed in the Recommended Resources section at the end of this chapter.
2. Have students retell the story in the film in their own words.
3. Discuss the ways in which innocent people or animals in the film were hurt just because they were different. (Share the terms *prejudice, scapegoating,* and *stereotyping* as you discuss these incidents.)
4. Ask student if they identified in any way with any of the characters or if they have observed that kind of hurtful behavior in or outside of school.
5. Ask them what lesson the film teaches and how they might carry out that lesson in their own lives. (The message in all four films is basically that often differences can be good.)
6. (Optional) Have students draw a scene from the film that meant a lot to them. They might write two or three sentences explaining the scene and two or three sentences explaining why that scene was important for them.

Activity 5: Multicultural Messengers (Grades 3–12)

Research and completion of biographical sketches of "multicultural messengers" can give students the opportunity to discover individuals from different cultures, past and present, whose lives and words reflected humanitarian values. Some of the better-known messengers

Figure 5.8   Sample of an "Unsung" Multicultural Messenger

Robert R. Merhige, Jr. (1919–2005) was the federal district court judge who ordered the desegregation of many Virginia school districts. This occurred after school integration had lagged in the state for years after the U.S. Supreme Court's 1954 decision in *Brown v. Board of Education of Topeka,* in which segregated schools were ruled unconstitutional. Several cases had been combined in the *Brown* decision, one of which involved the Prince Edward County schools in Virginia.

Judge Merhige ordered that these schools be integrated, which led to dozens of African American, urban school systems merging with majority-white systems nearby in 1972. He also, in 1970, ordered the University of Virginia to admit women.

Because of his ruling approving crosstown busing in Richmond, the judge and his family received death threats and were placed under 24-hour protection by U.S. marshals.

Questions

1. Does Judge Merhige deserve to be called a multicultural messenger? Why? Is he an "unsung" hero?
2. On what did he base his decisions regarding integration?
3. Why did he receive death threats?

Source: "Judge Who Ordered Va. Schools Desegregated Dies." (March 2, 2005). *Education Week, 24*(25), p. 4.

are listed below, but students may do research on "unsung" heroes who live or have lived in their own community. For example, the woman who donated a building she owned for use as a drop-in center for teenagers or the retired gentleman who paid for buses and tickets so whole classes of students could travel to see Shakespeare and other plays in theaters located three hours away. (An example of a biographical sketch of a multicultural messenger is located in Figure 5.8. The length of this sketch will be a useful guide for students. The person described is likely not familiar to most people, but could be considered an unsung hero. Students can discuss the questions that follow the sketch.)

Their sketches could be shared with peers in other classes and even published in the local newspaper so that students can teach others about multicultural messengers who have made the world a more caring and equitable place.

A Very Brief List of Multicultural Messengers from Different Cultures, Past and Present

1. Muhammad
2. Maimonides
3. Albert Schweitzer
4. Nelson Mandela
5. Mahatma (Mohandas) Gandhi
6. Siddhartha (Gautama Buddha)
7. Martin Luther King
8. W. E. B. Du Bois
9. LaDonna Harris
10. Jane Addams

Sample Unit 2: A Comparative Study of Genocide

Grade Levels: 8–12
Content: Social Studies, Language Arts
Time: 3–5 weeks
Principles: 1, 2, 4

Genocide Studies is a fairly new concentration in colleges and universities and is often taught within the context of already established curricula on the Nazi Holocaust. Within the last ten years, there has been a proliferation of literature on the subject and teachers have a wide selection of material from which to choose (Balakian, 2004; Friedlander, 2008; Kimball, 2003; Malvern, 2004; Power, 2007; Sheehan, 2004; Stern, 2004; Valentino, 2004; Winter et al., 2004). Yale University is one of several institutions with a Genocide Studies program and the United States Holocaust Memorial Museum publishes a *Journal of Holocaust and Genocide Studies.*

An introduction to this topic for high school students in the form of a comparative study is appropriate for this chapter, since genocide is the most extreme form of prejudice (see Lesson 2 and the diagrams "Ladder of Prejudice" and "Pyramid of Hate"), and continues with all of its horrors to this very day in more than one part of the world.

In this unit of instruction students will be able to do research on one historic (or contemporary) example of genocide, defined as the systematic destruction of a group based on its race, religion, political views, culture, or other difference, and then compare that example to four others. While this research may not enable them to prevent genocide, information is included about how students can play a role in speaking out against such extreme acts of prejudice as well as how they can contribute to organizations that assist refugees and families who are suffering as a result of such prejudice.

Objectives

Students will be able to

1. Do research on one example of genocide, that is, find out the five Ws—and more—related to their topic (ELA 1, 8, 12).
2. Share their research with their research group and plan a presentation. (You can assign a paper to each student or simply evaluate their research based on their oral presentation and an annotated bibliography) (ELA 4, 5, 6, 7, 8, 11, 12).
3. Present to the larger class—and possibly others—their research on an example of genocide (ELA 4, 5, 6; SOCS-USH 3–8; SOCS-WH 6–9).
4. Complete a chart on which they place comparative data related to five examples of genocide (ELA 1, 7, 9, 12).
5. Identify one or more ways they can contribute to educating people about genocide or to speaking out against it (ELA 3, 6, 7, 11; SOCS-C 2, 3, 5).

Materials

- Online and library sources related to genocide studies
- Comparative chart (Figure 5.9)
- Films *Hotel Rwanda* and *Judgment at Nuremberg* or other film about one of the five genocides to be compared

Procedures

1. There are a number of ways to begin such a unit of instruction. This author has done the following and found it to be effective: Start with a film, either a documentary or a

motion picture, about one of the five examples of genocide to be compared (the Nazi Holocaust, the Armenian genocide, Rwanda, Bosnia, and Darfur). *Hotel Rwanda*, *Judgment at Nuremberg*, and *Schindler's List* are just three of the many possibilities. (*Note*: The five examples to be studied are *not* the only choices. You may wish to have students do research on others, such as in Ethiopia, Cambodia, and the attempt in this country to remove Native Americans.)

2. After viewing the film, discuss with students what they saw and how the film portrays genocide. (You can place the word and its definition on the board either before or after they view the film.) Ask them if they have seen other films or read books related to the topic of genocide. Have them share their experiences.

3. Divide the class into five groups and either assign one of the topics to each group or let them pick the topic out of a box in which you have placed the appropriate number of slips of paper with a topic written on each one.

4. Give them a copy of the chart (Figure 5.9) as a way to view the objectives of their research (i.e., five Ws and more). Explain that when the unit and the presentations have been completed, they should fill in the chart and submit it.

5. Provide time for groups to meet and plan their research.

6. After one to two weeks devoted to research, have students plan their presentations and prepare an annotated bibliography.

7. Hold panel presentations and remind students to take notes so they can complete their comparative charts.

8. Hold a discussion during which students get to debrief: talk about their work, the other presentations, what they learned.

9. (Optional) Follow up with a brainstorming session about the ways they could educate others or speak out against genocide and how they might contribute to organizations that are working with refugees, people who have fled their native countries in order to escape persecution, and others suffering from prejudice. (Compare their list of suggestions with the list in Figure 5.10.)

10. After approximately a week, collect their charts and annotated bibliographies (or research papers).

Assessment

- Participation in small research groups and large class discussions (Objectives 1, 2)
- Oral presentation of their research along with other panel members (Objectives 1, 3)
- Annotated bibliography (or, if you prefer, a research paper) (Objective 2)
- Comparative chart (Objective 4)

Figure 5.9   A Comparative Study of Genocide: The Highest Rung on The Ladder of Hate

What?	Who? (Oppressor/ Oppressed)	Where?	When?	Why?	How?	Aftermath? (Trials?)
Armenian Genocide	/					
Nazi Holocaust	/					
Rwandan Genocide	/					
Bosnian Genocide	/					
Darfur (Sudan)	/					

Note. Students should reproduce this chart and leave much more space for data.

Figure 5.10   Suggestions for Ways to Actively Respond to Acts of Genocide

1. Write a letter to request information, to arrange an interview, to tell people what you think, or to ask what you can do to assist in ongoing efforts (Hoose, 1993, p. 135). For example, write a letter to the editor of your local paper or organize a letter-writing campaign to your local representative or senator who may be dealing with the issue of what the United States should be doing.
2. Use a petition to build support for your position or activity—for example, asking government or legislators to speak out against genocide.
3. Speak out, such as by informing the student body about your research and educating peers about genocide.
4. Use the media by contacting the local paper or TV news media about your speech or about the panel presentations on genocide and asking them to cover it with a story and photos.
5. Do fund-raising by a bake sale, car wash, or other activity and send the money to such organizations as Doctors Without Borders or the International Rescue Committee (IRC) after finding out about their work online.
6. Boycott companies that do business with the perpetrators of genocide. (Some people protesting the human rights policy of China regarding its invasion of Tibet and its treatment of political prisoners have boycotted local businesses that trade with China.)
7. Protest and demonstrate by marching with signs in an area of town where you have permission to do so. Make posters that educate the public regarding the issue about which you are demonstrating. (The Constitution guarantees the right to demonstrate, but in some towns you may need to inform local police or local leaders.)

Summary Chart of Principles and Their Applications

Principle	Applications
1. Teaching at every level must reflect that Americans—no matter what their differences—are full and equal citizens, possessing the same rights and privileges.	1. There needs to be a coherent policy for dealing with bigoted talk among students. 2. Emphasize what is common to all humans. 3. Explore—and explode—stereotypes. 4. Teach about slavery as an institution with a long history involving many races, nationalities, and civilizations. 5. Clarify and research issues such as struggles for equal rights, to which students have likely already been exposed by the media.
2. One of the goals of a social studies program should be to convey to students many important points about socioeconomic differences.	1. Help students recognize that discrimination often deprives people of access to opportunities. 2. The nature of poverty and unemployment can be addressed using a variety of sources. 3. Show how our society has developed programs to address socioeconomic differences and needs.

3. Helping students to personalize prejudice is one way of helping them to connect with this subject. This can be done within the traditional humanities disciplines like history as well as in mathematics classes.	1. There are several examples of social justice math currently being employed in the work for equity. 2. Students may be more willing to honestly share their stories related to prejudice if the teacher reveals his or her own observations, stories, and attitudes. 3. Connecting certain holiday traditions to the topic of prejudice can help to personalize prejudice. 4. Discussing the racial past of the students' community or school can help to lessen prejudice.
4. Making use of the news media can enlarge students' awareness of local, national, and international examples of prejudice and its causes.	1. Use several kinds of media to gather data. 2. Explore with students ways they might respond to these examples of prejudice.
5. Choosing appropriate literature for teaching about other cultures—both within and beyond the United States—must be done with attention to criteria that can help prevent passing on inaccurate or stereotypical ideas. These criteria are also relevant to teaching about any group within the society who may be subject to stereotyping.	1. There are specific guidelines teachers can use for selecting bias-free texts and storybooks. 2. There is an emerging canon of transgender-inclusive young adult literature that allows topics once considered inappropriate for teen readers to become legitimate areas for exploration and debate.
6. Including material concerning any aspect of religion in the public school curriculum requires careful planning (if legal problems are to be avoided).	1. Objective study *about* religion as an important part of human life, culture, and history has a place in the public school. 2. Seek to discover where students' confusion about religious differences lies. 3. Teach comparative religion so students see the common elements of various faiths. 4. Help students understand that religion does not correspond to race or appearance. 5. Find out what guidelines exist in your school system for approaching topics or events related to religion. 6. Enlist the help of parents, religious leaders, and organizations in gathering information and materials appropriate for inclusion in the classroom.

 ## LINKS: Recording in Your Journal

1. *Before* looking back over this chapter, write down one idea or learning activity from this chapter that you recall. Why do you think this information made a lasting impression? (If

you do not come up with an idea, review the chapter and then identify research, a principle, or a lesson that you consider to be of value to you, and explain why.)

2. Bill Moyers, an outstanding journalist, said in an interview on the subject of racism: "This is in our bloodstream," meaning that human beings are naturally prejudiced and have to constantly try to overcome that part of their nature (Moyers, June 3, 2008). Do you agree with him? Or do you believe prejudice is learned from our environment or "Carefully Taught," as the song from the musical *South Pacific* suggests?

3. In this chapter you were introduced to Gordon Allport's simple formula explaining prejudice (F → A → D). What is your reaction to this formula? Would you teach it to your students? If so, in what context? If not, why not?

4. The poem about Emmett Till can reach students on the affective level (emotional level). Can you think of any other poems, stories, contemporary songs, works of art, dance, or film that convey messages about tolerance or that portray the painful effects of prejudice? How might you use the arts in helping your students recognize their own prejudices in order to overcome them?

5. Trace your own journey on the path of tolerance. What prejudices have you overcome? How did you overcome them? What work do you still have to do? (You may also want to interview relatives about their experiences with prejudice.)

6. What are some obstacles you see in carrying out the goals of this chapter? How might you overcome them?

References

Allport, G. W. (1958). *The Nature of Prejudice*. Garden City, NY: Doubleday.

Balakian, P. (2004). *The Burning Tigris, The Armenian Genocide and America's Response*. New York: Harper Perennial.

Brandwein, P. F., et al. (1972). "Man's Attitudes." In *The Social Sciences: Concepts and Values*. New York: Harcourt Brace Jovanovich.

Brooks, G., and G. Thompson. (September 2005). "Social Justice in the Classroom." *Educational Leadership*, 63(1), pp. 48–52.

Cameron, L., A. Rutland, R. J. Brown, and R. Douch. (September 2006). "Changing Children's Intergroup Attitudes towards Refugees: Testing Different Models of Extended Contact." *Child Development*, 77(5), pp. 1208–1219.

Cavanagh, S. (March 30, 2005). "Internet Postings Linked to Students Highlight Interest in Hate Groups." *Education Week*, 24(29), pp. 11–12.

Chideya, F. (August 29, 2005). "'Emmett Till': A Poem of Sorrow, and Hope." National Public Radio. Available at www.npr.org/templates/story/story/php?storyID=4818586

Cohen, R. (1968). *The Color of Man*. New York: Bantam Books.

Coles, R. (May 5, 1993). "When Earnest Volunteers Are Sorely Tested." *The Chronicle of Higher Education*, p. A52.

Denby, D. (May 2, 2005). "Angry People." *The New Yorker*. New York: Conde Nast Publications.

Derman-Sparks, L. (1989). *Anti-Bias Curriculum: Tools for Empowering Young Children*. Washington, DC: National Association for the Education of Young Children.

Friedlander, S. (2008). *The Years of Extermination: Nazi Germany and the Jews, 1939–1945*. New York: Harper Perennial.

Fromm, E. (1961). *May Men Prevail?* New York: Doubleday.

Gutstein, E., and B. Peterson (Eds.). (2005). *Rethinking Mathematics: Teaching Social Justice by the Numbers*. Milwaukee, WI: Rethinking Schools.

Halbfinger, D. M. (March 14, 2005). "A Filmmaker Finds His Métier Exploring the Gray Zone." *The New York Times*, Arts and Leisure Section, p. E7.

Haynes, C. C., and C. R. Kniker. (September 1990). "Religion in the Classroom: Meeting the Challenges and Avoiding the Pitfalls." *Social Education*, 54(5), pp. 305–310.

Hoose, P. (1993). *It's Our World, Too. Stories of Young People Who Are Making A Difference*. Boston: Little, Brown.

Jay, T. (1996). *What To Do When Your Students Talk Dirty*. San Jose, CA: Resource Publications.

Kimball, C. (2003). *When Religion Becomes Evil*. New York: Harper Perennial.

Loewen, J. W. (1995). *Lies My Teacher Told Me*. New York: The New Press.

Loewen, J. W. (Spring 2008). "Does My Town Have a Racist Past?" *Teaching Tolerance*, 33, pp. 23–27.

Malvern, L. (2004). *Conspiracy to Murder: The Rwanda Genocide*. New York: Verso Books.

Miel, A., and E. Kiester, Jr. (1967). *The Shortchanged Children of Suburbia: What Schools Don't Teach About Human Differences and What Can Be Done About It*. Pamphlet Series #8. New York: Institute of Human Relations Press.

Moyers, B. (June 3, 2008). Interview with Alan Chartock. Broadcast on WAMC, 90.3 FM.

Murrey, D., and J. Sapp. (Spring 2008). "Making Numbers Count." *Teaching Tolerance*, 33, pp. 51–55. Montgomery, AL: Southern Poverty Law Center.

Olson, S. (April 2001). "The Genetic Archeology of Race." *Atlantic Monthly*, 287(4), pp. 69–80.

Power, S. (2007). *A Problem from Hell: America and the Age of Genocide*. New York: Harper Perennial.

Rockefeller, E. (September/October 2007). "The Genre of Gender: The Emerging Canon of Transgender-Inclusive Literature." *The Horn Book Magazine*, 73, pp. 519–526.

Rodriguez, R. (2002). *Brown: The Last Discovery of America*. New York: Viking.

Sapp, J. (2006). *Rhinos and Raspberries: Tolerance Tales for the Early Grades*. Montgomery, AL: Teaching Tolerance.

Sheehan, S. (2004). *Genocide*. Chicago: Raintree (Juvenile).

Smith, N. W. (Fall 2005). "Reconstructing Race." *Rethinking Schools*, 20(1), pp. 31–34.

Stern, J. (2004). *Terror in the Name of God*. New York: Harper Perennial.

Valentino, B. A. (2004). *Final Solutions: Mass Killing and Genocide in the Twentieth Century*. Ithaca, NY: Cornell University Press.

Wilson, E. O. (May 30, 1993). "Is Humanity Suicidal?" *New York Times Magazine*, pp. 24–29.

Winter, J., P. Kennedy, and E. Sivan (Eds.). (2004). *America and the Armenian Genocide of 1915*. Cambridge, UK: Cambridge University Press.

Witzig, R. (October 2006). "The Medicalization of Race: Scientific Legitimization of a Flawed Social Construct." *Annals of Internal Medicine*, 125(8), pp. 675–679. Available at www.annals.org

Wynne, E. A., and K. Ryan. (Spring 1993). "Curriculum as a Moral Educator." *American Educator*, 17(1), pp. 20–48.

Recommended Resources

Aronson, E. (2000). *Nobody Left to Hate: Teaching Compassion after Columbine*. New York: Dial Books.

Derman-Sparks, L., and P. G. Ramsey. (2006). *What If All The Kids Are White? Anti-Bias Multicultural Education with Young Children and Families*. New York: Teachers College Press.

Eck, D. (2002). *A New Religious America: How a "Christian Country" Has Become the World's Most Religiously Diverse Nation*. New York: HarperOne.

Harry, B., and J. Klingner. (2006). *Why Are So Many Minority Students in Special Education? Understanding Race and Disability in Schools*. New York: Teachers College Press.

Noddings, N. (2006). *Critical Lessons: What Our Schools Should Teach*. New York: Cambridge University Press.

Pollock, M. (Ed.). (2007). *Everyday Antiracism, Getting Real about Race in School*. New York: The New Press.

Ponterotto, J. G., S. O. Utsey, and P. B. Pedersen. (2006). *Preventing Prejudice: A Guide for Counselors, Educators and Parents*. Thousand Oaks, CA: Sage Publications.

Sacks, J. (2002). *The Dignity of Difference: How to Avoid the Clash of Civilizations*. New York: Continuum.

Teel, K. M., and J. E. Obidah (Eds.). (2008). *Building Racial and Cultural Competence in the Classroom*. New York: Teachers College Press.

Tochluk, S. (2007). *Witnessing Whiteness: First Steps Toward an Antiracist Practice and Culture*. Lanham, MD: Rowman and Littlefield.

Videos

Hate Comes Home. (2003). Anti-Defamation League. A World of Difference Institute, 605 Third Avenue, New York, NY 10158
Find more information at www.adl.org

Mighty Times: The Children's March. (2005). Southern Poverty Law Center (and HBO). 400 Washington Ave., Montgomery, AL 36104
Also publisher of Teaching Tolerance Magazine. Find more information at www.splc.org and www.tolerance.org

The Murder of Emmett Till. (2003). PBS. American Experience Series.

Animated Films

All are available from Amazon.com.
Dumbo (DVD 2006)
Shrek (2001); *Shrek 2* (2004); *Shrek the Third* (2007)
Tubby the Tuba (1975)
The Ugly Duckling (DVD 2005)

Websites

www.algebra.org
    The Algebra Project, developed by Bob Moses, seeks to advance the struggle for citizenship and equality by enhancing mathematical literacy for students in inner city and rural areas.

www.ethnicdiversitycalendar.com
    Order a copy of the calendar "Ethnic Cultures of America" from Orison Publishers, P.O. Box 188, Grantham, PA 17027.

www.facinghistory.org/resources/lesson/emmett-till
    Facing History provides lessons that can be used with a study of the Emmett Till murder and the issues related to it.

http://ielhp.spokane.cc.wa.us/services/diversity/Diversity_Library.pdf
    The Institution for Extended Learning offers a lengthy and excellent list of materials to help teachers address

issues related to diversity and prejudice (based on race, religion, class, ethnicity, and gender).

www.radicalmath.org

This online tool, founded by Jonathan Osler, for teaching math and social justice that contains a searchable database of lesson plans, projects, articles, graphs, and websites.

www.nameorg.org

The National Association of Multicultural Education provides materials inclusive of all areas of diversity through its website, its newsletter, and its journal, *Multicultural Perspectives*.

www.pbs.org/wgbh/amex/till

The website of the Public Broadcasting System offers articles and photographs about Emmett Till.

Chapter Six

Strategies and Lessons for Addressing Diversity and the Needs of English Language Learners

Natasha Lorick, CATA 2007–2008 program year

*After English became my primary language, I no longer knew what words to use in addressing my parents. The old Spanish words (those tender accents of sound) I had earlier used—*mama *and* papa*—I couldn't use anymore.*

Richard Rodriguez, 1982

Haven't we always worked with the assumption that language learning—oral and written—is the key to parity, even as parity continues to elude so many?

Victor Villanueva, Jr., 1987

Regular classroom teachers who want to meet the language and content needs of their English language learners (ELLs) will find this chapter helpful. The research, principles, and teaching strategies provided will also have relevance to the learning needs of all other students as well. Preservice and in-service teachers will learn about the many approaches they can use to help students improve their English skills and their mastery of content in the core subjects.

This chapter calls attention to the increasing language diversity in the United States and proposes that it be viewed as an asset, one that, nevertheless, poses certain challenges for both the learners and the teacher. This chapter can assist teachers in successfully addressing those challenges.

How would you suggest the teacher in the following vignette deal with the student and the situation in general?

Imagine you are a student who cannot read, write, speak, or comprehend English. You are sitting in a classroom where only English is spoken. Yet you are expected to master the language *and* the academic course content—and on top of that to pass the standardized state tests mandated by the Elementary and Secondary Education Act (No Child Left Behind Act). While there is never a level playing field even for all of your native English-speaking counterparts, they are at least in a language comfort zone, while you struggle on two levels. It's not surprising that you feel nervous, confused, angry, frustrated, and afraid of sounding "like a dummy" (*Voices of Change,* 2004, p. 20).

Imagine also that your teacher is like nearly 90 percent of the teachers across the country who have never had training in techniques to help English language learners tackle their double load. Your teacher may be as frustrated as you are because of uncertainty regarding where to begin in order to meet your needs.

 **What the Research Says**

ONE Growth in Linguistic Diversity

Linguistic and ethnic diversity is growing in the United States, with new waves of immigrants arriving from such countries as Mexico, the Philippines, Korea, China, Taiwan, India, Vietnam, and Cuba (Azzam, 2004–2005, p. 7). Along with Hispanics, Asians, and Pacific Islanders, who form the largest segment of nonnative school students, the number of native speakers of Arabic, Armenian, Polish, Haitian Creole, and Russian has increased considerably. Nationally, the number of ELLs in public schools increased from approximately two million in 1993–94 to three million in 1999–2000, and continues to grow (National Center for Education Statistics, 2006). It is estimated that by the first quarter of the twenty-first century ELLs will make up nearly 50 percent of the total school enrollment (Carrasquillo and Rodriguez, 1996, p. 22; Pearlman, 2002).

Reflective question: What, if any, personal observations have you made about the growth of linguistic diversity?

TWO Majority of English Language Learners in Regular Classrooms

The majority of English language learners are enrolled in regular all-English classrooms (New Levine, 1993; Rossell, 2004–2005; Zehr, November, 2004). Fewer than 13 percent of regular all-English classroom teachers in the United States have been professionally prepared to teach the growing immigrant population (Carrasquillo and Rodriguez, 1996, p. 10; National Center for Education Statistics, 2006). Few schools have programs designed to address the language needs of ELLs, such as English as a Second Language (ESL) and bilingual education. While some educators like Christine Rossell believe that this fact is nothing to be concerned about (Rossell, 2004–2005), those others who favor bilingual programs disagree (Krashen, 2004–2005; Lindholm-Leary, 2004–2005). Rossell notes that "most immigrant children in the United States and throughout the world are in mainstream classrooms, and most of them seem to swim, not sink" (Rossell, 2004–2005, p. 36). While that may or may not be true, there is evidence that mainstream classroom teachers often classify very bright ELLs as learning disabled because of the teachers' lack of background in diagnosing the abilities of these students or in preparing to teach them.

On the other hand, outstanding teachers like Rafe Esquith, author of *There Are No Shortcuts* (2003) and recipient of the MacArthur Foundation's "Genius Award," teaches his ELLs in a mainstream inner-city Los Angeles classroom using only English, but he is not against his students being bilingual. "I don't want to rob a child of his past; I encourage the children to speak their native languages *at home*. I praise them for it. I honor their cultures and teach them that being bilingual makes them truly well educated" (Esquith, 2003, p. 59). This kind of encouragement contributes to the English language learner's self-esteem and reduces the stress level and anxiety that can impair the ELL's success in acquiring a new language (Cummins, 1986; Krashen and Terrell, 1983; McLaughlin, 1992).

Few would argue with Esquith about the advantages of being able to speak two languages. However, many have argued about formal bilingual programs in terms of their usefulness in helping ELLs learn English. *Bilingual education* refers to providing ELLs with instruction in their first language in order to facilitate their learning of both English and subject matter content. This program is based on the belief that instruction in the native language increases acquisition of the second language (Cummins, 1989; Garcia, 1993; McLaughlin, 1992).

In 1965 Congress passed the Title VII Bilingual Education Program or the Bilingual Education Act (BEA) as an amendment to the Elementary and Secondary Education Act of 1965, leading school districts to design and implement programs for ELLs. However, it was the Supreme Court decision *Lau v. Nichols* (1974) that raised awareness of the needs of ELLs. In *Lau* the Court ruled that school districts are obligated to provide for all children whose second language is English, but it didn't require a particular means for meeting their needs (Webb, Metha, and Jordan, 2003, p. 279).

All bilingual program models—and there are several—use the students' home language in addition to English instruction, but the proportion of instructional time in each language can vary from program to program. Those who have opposed bilingual education come from three primary groups: some immigrant parents, a certain percentage of teachers, and political conservatives opposed on philosophical grounds. Immigrant parents of ELLs have expressed frustration about the isolation of their children within ESL classrooms as well as the rigidity of some programs that restrict the English language learner from moving easily into all-English instruction when they are ready to do so. Teachers are also split on the issue, with many making the same arguments as the parents. Further opposition, however, comes from a very different source: conservatives who advocate English-only, a position believed by proponents to be intellectually defensible but thought by others to be simply a form of racism disguised as patriotism. English-only proponents have continually sought to have Congress declare English to be the official language of the United States. Such a law does not yet exist, although some states have passed such bills, including California, Florida, and Arizona (Crawford, 1989, p. 53).

Another source of controversy erupted in 1996 when the Oakland Unified School District Board adopted a policy recognizing Black English, or ebonics, as a second language and the primary language of some of its African American students (Webb et al., 2003, p. 280). The policy was later changed—after much debate—from actually teaching these students using ebonics to instead helping students become proficient in Standard American English, the means of communication used by academia, the marketplace, and political centers of power, and the English by which they will be measured and accepted in those places.

Reflective question: What is your position on bilingual education?

THREE ELLs and the No Child Left Behind Act

English language learners are at a disadvantage as a result of the No Child Left Behind Act (NCLB Act). The 2001 overhaul of the Elementary and Secondary Education Act requires testing in U.S. schools in order to assess the quality of those schools. Though the law was passed by Congress in order to improve education, it has resulted in penalizing schools with children from diverse backgrounds. Schools with children of lower socioeconomic status as well as schools with many ELLs "are at a disadvantage in almost any rigid standard of accountability" (Sternberg, 2004, p. 56). Of even greater concern, according to some analysts, including congressional officials, this already underfunded act has been cut by millions of dollars, and that cut has resulted in preventing "more than 32,000 children with limited proficiency in English from participating in federally supported English instruction programs" (Herbert, 2003). (See Chapter 2 for further discussion of, and changes in, the NCLB Act.)

Perhaps it is this lack of federal funding for such programs that has caused state departments of education such as the one in Massachusetts to add to their regulations for licensure the need for teachers to know "theories of first and second language acquisition and development" (Massachusetts Department of Education, 2004, pp. 19–20) and to be able to employ appropriate sheltered English or subject matter strategies for English learners (discussed elsewhere in this chapter). In addition, all teachers must be able to assess "the significance of student differences in home experiences . . . and proficiency in the English language for learning the curriculum at hand" and then to be able to use professional judgment to determine if instructional adjustments are necessary (2004, p. 41).

Reflective question: What kinds of accommodations do you think should be made for English language learners when taking tests?

FOUR Principles and Techniques for Addressing Needs of English Language Learners

Now for the good news. Experts in the area of addressing the educational and language needs of English language learners have identified principles and techniques that regular classroom teachers can use as they plan instruction relevant to English language development and performance in subject matter content and skills (Baruth and Manning, 1992; Carrasquillo and Rodriguez, 1995; Gray and Fleishman, 2004–2005; Herrell and Jordan, 2004; Milk and Supiens, 1992; New Levine, 1993; Ogulnick, 2000; Short and Echevarria, 2004–2005). (See the principles and their applications in the next section for some descriptions of these techniques.)

Reflective question: Are you familiar with any techniques for addressing the needs of ELLs? If so, which ones, if any, have you implemented?

FIVE Related Good News

On February 17, 2005, the United States endorsed an effort to promote programs that will assist Americans in speaking more than one language by passing a resolution establishing the "Year of Languages." Only 9.3 percent of Americans speak both their native language and another language fluently, according to the Census Bureau, compared with 52.2 percent of Europeans (Rivedal, 2005).

Reflective question: Should efforts be made to make learning a second language compulsory?

SIX More Good News: State Education Departments Are Developing Diversity Standards and Competencies Required for Teacher Certification

In general, diversity standards are very similar across state documents. Most explain the need for teachers to understand how students differ in their approaches to learning and the subsequent need to create institutional approaches adapted to diverse learners. The following excerpt from the Illinois standards is typical of the professional standards expressed by other states.

Standard 3—Diversity . . .

The competent teacher:
3A. Understands the areas of exceptionality in learning as defined in the Individuals with Disabilities Act (IDEA) and the State Board's rules for Special Education (23 Ill. Adm. Cod 226).
3B. Understands the process of second language acquisition and strategies to support the learning of students whose first language is not English.
3C. Understands how students' learning is influenced by individual experiences, talents, and prior learning, as well as language, culture, family, and community values.
3D. Understands and identifies differences in approaches to learning and performance, including different learning styles, multiple intelligences, and performance modes.
3E. Understands cultural and community diversity through a well-grounded framework and understands how to learn about and incorporate students' experiences, cultures, and community resources into instruction.
3F. Understands personal cultural perspectives and biases and their effects on one's teaching. (Illinois State Board of Education, 2002, p. 4)

Reflective question: Are these standards and competencies realistic? Why or why not?

 Principles and Applications
for Addressing Language Diversity
and the Needs of English Language Learners

Principle ONE

 The teacher's perceptions of English language learners affect the academic performance of these students.

The classroom teacher is the primary source of encouragement and support for ELLs and can contribute to the student's self-concept and academic development by identifying the specific needs of the ELL and *refusing to make any assumptions about the student's intelligence or ability to do academic work* (Waters, 2004). "Teachers must . . . view individual differences among students as more important to the strategic teaching than their similarities" (Carrasquillo and Rodriguez, 1996, p. 16). ELLs differ in their command of their native language and in the background knowledge they bring to their new classrooms. Further, responsible educators consider how their attitudes regarding language and other differences may affect their actions. Educators need to accept and respect the cultures from which ELLs come and help them ease their way into a new language and culture while still retaining their native culture.

Classroom Applications and Strategies

• Become familiar with the goals and standards established for English language learners by TESOL (Teachers of English to Speakers of Other Languages). Among these goals are the ability to both use English to achieve academically in all content areas and to use English in socially and culturally appropriate ways (TESOL, 2006). Many states have included in their licensure regulations the prospective teacher's (1) need to know theories of first and second language acquisition and development, (2) ability to assess the significance of student differences in home experiences, background knowledge, learning skills, and pace and proficiency in the English language for learning the curriculum, and (3) ability to use professional judgment to determine if instructional adjustments are necessary.

• Research the cultural norms of their diverse students by seeking sources in the library, the Internet, and from parents and community members with whom the students live. Even body language should be investigated so that embarrassing or insulting signals can be avoided.

• Assess their students' language proficiency by gathering information from other teachers, from test records (if available), from samples of content-related work, and from simply listening to and observing the students and recording in a journal data about the students' level of comprehension, speaking, writing, and reading proficiency (Fay and Whaley, 2004–2005, pp. 76–79). Two teachers at Bailey Elementary School in Virginia note that listening to students read and engaging in authentic conversation with them can often yield more clues about their strengths and needs than formal language assessments do (Fay and Whaley, 2004–2005, p. 76). And "sensitive mainstream teachers collaborate" and share information about the academic, cultural, and linguistic needs of their ELLs (Carrasquillo and Rodriguez, 1996, p. 17).

• Contribute to the students' self-esteem by emphasizing the values of knowing more than one language, the fact that English is only one among many languages in the world, and the knowledge that English, in fact, has borrowed many words from other languages.

• Exhibit patience and encouragement. Listen actively and try to resist the temptation to finish the learner's sentences. Errors are a natural part of language learning; teachers need to realize just how long it takes for students to become proficient enough in English to respond comfortably. Carrasquillo and Rodriguez note that teachers should be aware that ELLs go through a silent period before they begin to produce language orally. They usually show a "preproduction period" in which they can comprehend but say very little (Carrasquillo and Rodriguez, 1996, pp. 58–60). The teacher's belief in every student translates into their eventual success with their new language and the content (Ward, 2002).

Principle TWO

Teachers in English-only classrooms are the models of proficient English language usage (as are many of the English-proficient students in the class). Every native speaker is a temporary teacher and every conversation is a chance to learn something new (Zwiers, 2004–2005, p. 62).

Classroom Applications and Strategies

• Model correct usage and judiciously correct errors (Gray and Fleischman, 2004–2005, p. 84).

• Provide educational opportunities for ELLs to interact socially and academically with English-speaking peers. For example, small-group discussions, working on projects in committees, and pairing students (i.e., a buddy system) can help to eliminate social barriers and promote language acquisition (Carrasquillo and Rodriguez, 1996, pp. 17–18). A "buddy system" can minimize an ELL's fear of a new environment and has the added advantage of placing the ELL in the position of teacher by promoting the sharing of his or her language with a buddy.

• Specify vocabulary and technical terms associated with the subject matter and define those terms. Write them on the board. Consider having students make vocabulary charts or glossaries in their notebooks or make a bulletin board of academic terms. *Modified language* refers to the varied ways of making discipline-specific vocabulary comprehensible for ELLs (Dong, 2004–2005, p. 19).

• Pictures are the key to understanding new vocabulary as are real objects and actions, film, and hands-on demonstrations and activities (Carasquillo and Rodriguez, 1996, p. 164). Using visuals to make language more understandable is sometimes referred to as "visual scaffolding" (Herrell and Jordan, 2004, p. 19). Have students engage in role-plays, science experiments, pantomimes, construction activities, and drawings on which they can write simple labels. Visuals of all kinds are extremely helpful in making concepts clear. Use graphic organizers including graphs, timelines, Venn diagrams, tree diagrams, semantic mapping and charts; personal photographs; photos in newspapers, magazines, and catalogs; globes, maps, and other authentic materials; and audiovisual resources such as videos, CD-ROMs, and multimedia presentations. These visuals can reinforce information from lectures or from reading materials. And, finally, in terms of visual assists, be expansive in your gestures, facial expressions, and tone of voice (Josel, 1994, p. vii).

• Incorporate interactional routines during lessons that allow students to use the target language in context. For example, jazz chants, call-and-response games, and songs can support the acquisition of the target language (Carrasquillo and Rodriguez, 1996, p. 164; New Levine, 1993, pp. 1, 5; Short and Echevarria, 2004–2005, pp. 12, 13).

• Play games such as Simon Says to give the student practice in hearing commands (Waters, 2004), and other word games such as Scrabble and crossword puzzles as a fun way to learn words.

• Read aloud frequently to the students, speaking slowly so they can hear the sounds of the English language, or play stories on tape that have an accompanying printed version.

• Record the students reading aloud their own work on a regular basis. They will be able to hear their improvements.

• Write legibly on the board.

• Directly teach classroom survival skills such as study skills and simple rules for how to participate in class and organize materials (Payne, 1995).

• Accompany instruction with handouts and guidesheets for use by the students at home.

• When ELLs ask questions, repeat and paraphrase them before responding.

• Frequent use of language functions such as explaining, summarizing, rephrasing, classifying, and evaluating—for example, asking questions that require more than a yes or no answer—helps lead to greater understanding.

• Increase wait time after posing questions.

Many of the aforementioned techniques for modeling the English language are part of an approach referred to as the *sheltered instruction observation protocol* (SIOP), a research-based model that regular classroom teachers use to instruct ELLs in order to make academic content comprehensible while promoting the students' English language development (Short and Echevarria, 2004–2005). The SIOP model was tested over six years by the National Center for Research on Education, Diversity and Excellence before it was modified into a system for lesson planning and instruction (Hill and Flynn, 2006, p. 24). There are a number of different terms that refer to sheltered instructional techniques. For example, in California, the term used is "specially designed academic instruction in English" (SDAIE).

Research has confirmed that students in regular, that is, English-only, sheltered subject matter classes acquire an impressive amount of the second language and learn the subject matter as well (Carrasquillo and Rodriguez, 1996; Chamot and O'Malley, 1994; Hamayan, 1990; Rossell, 2004–2005; Short and Echevarria, 2004–2005). Still another writer on the subject of language acquisition by ELLs, Yvonne Pratt-Johnson, has coined the term *cognitive academic language proficiency* (CALP), which refers to the language required for formal academic learning and differs from language for social interaction or *basic interpersonal communication skills* (BICS) that ELLs attain much more quickly (Scherer, 2006, p. 2). The strategies that she suggests are also mentioned among the sheltering techniques listed under Principle 2.

Such simple instructional supports as those outlined in Principle 2 are also often referred to as *scaffolding strategies*. They not only facilitate language and content understanding for English language learners but these techniques are also "extensions of approaches that work well with all students" (Gray and Fleischman, 2004–2005). Every classroom can and should include sheltered instruction and scaffolding strategies since most students would benefit from them.

Briefly, here are the major sheltering techniques:

- Use of manipulatives
- Visuals
- Body movement, pantomime, and expansive facial expressions and gestures
- Clear enunciation and articulation
- Short, simple sentences
- Eye contact
- Vocabulary clearly defined
- Synonyms
- Building on prior knowledge
- Using introductory devices to let students know what they will be learning

Principle THREE

 The language learner's goals and a feeling of empowerment are essential in the process of second language acquisition.

Classroom Applications and Strategies

• In order to promote student empowerment and pride, provide instructional experiences that include the study of the students' cultures and the contributions made by members of these cultures. (In the next section of this chapter are lessons and strategies for culturally relevant teaching that include such experiences.) For example, multicultural literature, that is, literature across all subject areas from the students' ethnic backgrounds, is essential, "because these materials can meet the needs of *all* students and help them grow in understanding of themselves and others" (Carrasquillo and Rodriguez, 1996, p. 53).

• Use the ELLs themselves as resources since they can offer information about their countries and cultures and can expose native English speakers to other languages. Have ELLs share simple phrases and terms in their languages, such as appropriate greetings and phrases meaning "very good" and "thank you"; then use these terms on a regular basis (Gray and Fleischman, 2004–2005).

• Recommend appropriate television programs that ELLs can watch on their own so they can hear the English language spoken in conversation. (There are also many teaching videos available. See Additional Resources at the end of this chapter.)

• Meet the students' needs and prevent frustration while acquiring content and language skills. While a positive aspect of heterogeneous grouping is that it enables the English language learner to interact with English speakers, a drawback is the difficulty for teachers of addressing all of the diverse needs in the classroom simultaneously. Payne (1995) reports that one elementary school scheduled an hour for math at the same time in grades 1 through 3 as well as 4 through 6. Students were pretested and then moved to the appropriate group for that particular unit of instruction. Within two years the math scores in that building made a considerable gain (p. 149).

• Engage in conversations with high school–level *native* English speakers about their frustrations with trying to learn a foreign language—assuming many of them have taken or are taking such courses now. They will then be able to "walk in the English language learners' shoes" and recognize the problems they may be experiencing. These feelings of empathy can act to empower their ELL peers as they continue to work on their language skills.

• Establish support systems within the schools (Payne, 1995, pp. 145–152), such as

   a. Schoolwide homework support in the form of an extended day so that the teacher and older students can help ELLs for one to two hours after school.
   b. Schoolwide reading programs in which incentives are provided for improving reading skills and working cooperatively towards those ends.
   c. Keeping students with the same teacher for two to three years in situations where the teacher's knowledge of the students is likely to help them thrive.
   d. Instruction in coping strategies whereby groups of students meet with counselors or teachers during lunch to discuss common needs and issues.

• Be aware of potential *obstacles* to students' empowerment, warns Judith Waters (2004), former ESOL (English for speakers of other languages) coordinator for the Literacy Network of South Berkshire in Lee, Massachusetts. Potential obstacles about which teachers should be aware include

   • Transfer of patterns in students' native languages into English, such as placing adjectives after nouns, as in Spanish, instead of before nouns, as in English. Listen for such usage and be aware that these transfers may account for some of the errors that occur in speech or writing.
   • Instances of cultural bias either from the differences in cultural values, such as the gender issues in some cultures that might influence the male students' willingness to learn from a female teacher, or possible bias against a student's colloquial speech (e.g., Black English). Teachers need to be accepting of these alternatives but explain that the goal in this classroom is to respect everyone and also to learn Standard English, or academically acceptable English, so students can be successful in the mainstream society.
   • Isolation as an obstacle if a child is the only Hispanic or Asian in the classroom, or if there are so many that they form cliques.
   • The dilemma for ELLs about whether they should try to assimilate or remain separate. The idea of pluralism—whereby the students become part of the mainstream while retaining their native languages—should be shared and promoted.
   • The need for both teachers and students of all cultures to avoid stereotyping and making assumptions about each other's cultures.
   • The need to address mandated testing by the entire school working together to provide supports (such as those discussed previously) for their English language learners.

Principle FOUR

 In the case of students whose dialectical English differs from standard or academic English, teachers need to support the language that students bring to school while at the same time "provide them access to the politically popular dialect in this country, that is, Standard English" (Delpit, 1995, p. 53).

All languages contain words (*lexicon*) and conventions governing the use of those words (*grammar*). "The standardization of a society's lexicon and grammar, occurring over a period of time, mirrors the struggle for power within that society and finally reflects the language of its ruling class" (Mack, 1994, p. 1). This language is then codified in dictionaries. Alternate words, expressions, and grammar are no less important in terms of communication, but are considered nonstandard because they are the language of home and community as opposed to the marketplace. There are those who may classify and stereotype people because of their dialect or vernacular, based on the fact that the dialect speakers are members of an otherwise marginalized group. And, unfortunately, appropriate services may not always be provided because of lack of tolerance or insensitivity to those languages or dialects not considered to be legitimate forms of communication (Gollnick and Chinn, 2008).

The fact is that the language associated with the power structure, Standard English, is the language of economic success, and therefore "all students have the right to schooling that gives them access to that language" (Delpit, 1995, p. 68) in "contexts that are non-threatening, have real purpose, and are intrinsically enjoyable" (p. 54).

Classroom Applications and Strategies

• Students can be asked to "teach" the teacher and other students aspects of their language's variety. They can "translate" songs, poems, and stories into their own dialect (i.e., Ebonics or Black English) or into "book language" and compare the differences across the cultural groups represented in the classroom (Delpit, 1995, p. 67). The idea of the students teaching the teacher is made more significant by the fact that while the nonwhite student population is increasing, the teaching force is becoming more homogeneously white (p. 66). Delpit believes that in order for white preservice teachers to avoid negatively stereotyping the language patterns of their future students, their teacher education programs need to include interaction with diverse parents, community members, and faculty (p. 56).

• One teacher has high school students interview various personnel officers in actual workplaces about their attitudes towards divergent oral and written language styles. Students then discuss the impact of those styles on the messages being conveyed and their likely effect on different audiences. Students then prepare a talk or text using different styles intended for different audiences, such as their church group, academics, rap singers, politicians, small children, and others (Delpit, 1995, p. 68). In this way, students will learn to use the appropriate language, variety, register, and genre according to audience, purpose, and setting.

• According to African American teachers who have enjoyed success in teaching math to black-dialect-speaking students, the students were more likely to learn a new operation when they understood how it might be put to use in daily life or how that problem might be explained in terms of its relationship to the student's life, such as word problems that use names, places, and situations that the student is familiar with (Delpit, 1995, p. 65).

• Native Alaskan teacher Martha Demienstieff assists her students in dealing with the differences between the more wordy academic book language they struggle with and their briefer, more metaphoric style of Athabaskan. She has them write papers—working in pairs—using the more wordy style and then share their work to see if they have "sounded like a book." Next she has them reduce the messages to their essential meanings and produce those phrases on paper T-shirts which are then hung around the room (Delpit, 1995, p. 62).

• Create bidialectical dictionaries of the students' own language form and Standard English.

• Dramatizations in which students have to memorize parts for a play allow them to try out Standard English while not under the threat of correction. Putting together news reports for the school eliminates the possibility of implying that the child's language is inadequate "and suggests, instead, that different language forms are appropriate in different contexts" (Delpit, 1995, p. 53).

• Show examples of various writing systems, including pictographic (Mixtec), ideographic (Egyptian, Chinese), and phonetic (Liberian syllabary and Latin, both derived from Sanskrit) symbols (Mack, 1994, p. 2) to emphasize the diversity of language in terms of written format to contrast with the fact that there are even more varieties of spoken languages, including standard forms, slang, or colloquial versions of a language. There are over 2,200 Native American languages alone (Baruth and Manning, 1992; Wax, 1971).

Principle FIVE

 Where there is parental involvement, English language learners are more successful (Bernstein, 2005; Carrasquillo and Rodriguez, 1996; Green, 2005; Zehr, 2005).

Establishing connections with the English language learner's family can help prevent the kind of alienation that often develops when a student is caught between two cultures, wanting on the one hand to become part of the mainstream, and on the other, not wanting to reject or break with their native culture. When the family joins the school in securing the best education for the student, learning a second language can be a win–win experience, an enriching process without the loss of emotional connections with their family.

Classroom Applications and Strategies

• Regular classroom educators may think that the parents of English language learners are not interested in their children's education because of their reluctance to communicate with the school. The likelihood, however, is that this reluctance stems from a feeling of insecurity in their own abilities to speak English. Carrasquillo and Rodriguez advise teachers to invite these parents to the school and make them feel welcome. Then explain—with the assistance perhaps of the children themselves or an adult who speaks both languages—what they can do to help improve their child's educational performance (Carrasquillo and Rodriguez, 1996, p. 55). Eventually some of these parents might be asked to become aides in the classroom.

• The school librarian along with the teachers can establish family literacy programs that enable parents to learn *with* their children. "It gives them more dignity," said an organizer of such a program in Queens, New York. "And reading to your child is the single most important thing a parent can do for their child's success in school" (Bernstein, 2005).

• Before planning collaborative activities with family members, first learn about the family's experiences prior to and since their arrival, their beliefs and practices, parenting policies, and the roles ascribed to family members and friends.

• K. W. Barrett Elementary School in Arlington, Virginia, with a student population that is nearly 70 percent Asian, responds to parental outreach by

    a. Inviting parents to attend PTA meetings while their children are accessing computers.

    b. Giving students bilingual "Friday Folders" to give to their parents, who return comments in their native language. Whenever possible, schools should translate all written communications to families into their native language. Smaller school districts may not have the resources to do this. However, many translation resources are available on the Internet at no cost, including http://babelfish.altavista.com and www.itools.com. In addition, the school should identify bilingual contacts within the school system and the community as well as foreign language instructors in local colleges and universities.

Other resources include local intercultural institutes, social service agencies, and state bar associations (Gray and Fleischman, 2004–2005, p. 85).

c. Having Friday Family Breakfast meetings for parents for conversations over coffee.

d. Establishing "Project Interaction," which ties activities together with high-tech, student-animated bilingual broadcasts that air on hallway monitors during parent pick-up and drop-off times.

e. Holding monthly Library Nights during which the library media specialist shares the school's collection of multicultural books (Green, 2005).

• Invite immigrant families to participate in meaningful activities, such as classroom demonstrations of their culture, or—as in the case of K. W. Barrett Elementary School mentioned previously, which maintains a full-time family program coordinator—have teachers visit the homes of English language learners to cook and eat while demonstrating hands-on math. Such an activity was, in fact, described in an online NEA cover story (Green, 2005), as follows: "Maria Mendoza mashes the *endredo de yuka*, Edwin measures the *masa*, and teacher Amy Sack, with the help of a translator, takes careful notes. . . . Edwin, a third grader . . . may sit in teacher Amy Sack's class . . . but it's Amy who's learning valuable lessons about Central American culture—in Edwin's home kitchen."

• Follow the example of one teacher, who held annual international potluck picnics at which both current ELLs and their families and her former ELLs, some of whom were then attending college, came together (Ward, 2002, p. 15).

• Ruby Payne (1995) observed several types of successful support systems that address communication between teachers and parents. One approach used by a principal in Illinois involved parent training and contact through video, based on the idea that most, if not all, immigrant parents have a VCR. In this school each teacher made a 15-minute videotape giving a personal introduction and an overview of instructions for the year while identifying the expectations of the class and encouraging parents to visit or call. This was successful because (1) parents who were not literate could understand, and those who did not speak English could get assistance from family or friends; (2) it provided a kinesthetic view and feel for the teachers; (3) the parent was not dependent on transportation to have contact with the school; and (4) the videos did not cost much. Short videos can also be made for parents about specific topics, such as participating in extracurricular activities, discipline, and homework (Bradley, 2005, p. 3; Payne, 1995, pp. 150–157).

Strategies and Lessons for
Addressing Diversity and the Needs
of English Language Learners

While the multicultural and interdisciplinary activities that follow have been designed and selected with the English language learner in mind, they are also appropriate for *all* learners. Each lesson or series of lessons addresses both language acquisition skills and multicultural content within core subject areas. The lessons are activity-oriented and enable students to engage in listening, reading, writing, and speaking in ways that are sensitive to students' varied language backgrounds while also enabling them to learn about their own and others' cultures.

Most of the activities can be done by pairing or grouping English language learners with native English-speaking students, since such collaboration can increase the learners' confidence in the process of acquiring English language skills. Cooperative learning provides a nonthreatening method during which "friendships develop among students of different backgrounds" (Carrasquillo and Rodriguez, 1996, p. 118). All of the strategies incorporate the seven practices listed below that have been identified as beneficial to English language learners no matter what subject area they are studying.

- Provide opportunities for sharing information about the subject orally and in writing, as well as using physical or pictorial forms such as graphic organizers and hands-on approaches.
- Make connections between the content and the students' own experiences.
- Enable the students to tap into information about their native countries and to share it with peers.
- Address the diverse language issues of the students and make accommodations that assist students in communicating their knowledge.
- Use cooperative learning and pairing.
- Promote critical thinking and study skills development.
- Diversify instruction to meet the needs of students' varied learning styles (Carrasquillo and Rodriguez, 1996).

"Rather than viewing linguistic diversity as a deficit, we need to see it as an asset on which further learning can be built" (Nieto, 2000, p. 368). In his review of the book *Do You Speak American?* (MacNeil and Cran, 2005), Ted Anthony, who appears to agree with the preceding assertion, refers to the authors' assertion that, while mass media creates a large pool of people who understand each other, it can also foster "tolerance and appreciation of the linguistic diversity of this country." And according to Anthony, that's an attractive alternative: "Unity and diversity, intelligibility and regional flavor functioning together—an outcome befitting to a land of people who combined their linguistic traditions into one bubbling, evolving, constantly shifting language" (Anthony, 2005, p. E2). For English language learners and everyone else within the schools throughout the country, healthy attitudes like Ted Anthony's can lead to celebrating language diversity instead of viewing it as an obstacle.

Under the No Child Left Behind Act (2001), each state is to develop standards defining English language proficiency for English language learners. Teachers of English to Speakers of Other Languages (TESOL) established English Language Proficiency Standards (revised in 2006), organizing them around five proficiency descriptions. They include both social and academic uses of the language that students must acquire for success in and beyond the classroom. One or more of these standards, listed below, is included in the Objectives of each of the following lesson plans. It is critical to combine language objectives with content objectives, since content knowledge cannot grow if there is only focus on learning the English language (Hill and Flynn, 2006, pp. 22–23). All five of the following standards involve students in demonstrating the English language skills of listening and reading, as well as writing and speaking (TESOL, 2006).

Standard 1: English language learners *communicate* for *social, intercultural,* and *instructional* purposes within the school setting.

Standard 2: English language learners *communicate* information, ideas, and concepts necessary for academic success in the area of *language arts.*

Standard 3: English language learners *communicate* information, ideas, and concepts necessary for academic success in the area of *mathematics.*

Standard 4: English language learners *communicate* information, ideas, and concepts necessary for academic success in the area of *science.*

Standard 5: English language learners *communicate* information, ideas, and concepts necessary for academic success in the area of *social studies.*

These standards are meant to supplement, not replace, the standards developed in the major content areas. In the document TESOL expresses the belief that all education personnel should assume responsibility for the education of linguistically and culturally diverse learners (LCDL). To that purpose the 2006 revisions also specify "Five Levels of Language Proficiency" as follows:

> The five levels of language proficiency reflect characteristics of language performance at each developmental stage. The language proficiency levels are intended to highlight and provide a model of the process of language acquisition that can be adapted by individual districts and states.

> *Level 1–Starting.* At L1, students initially have limited or no understanding of English. They rarely use English for communication. At the earliest stage, these learners construct meaning from text primarily through illustrations, graphs, maps, and tables.
> *Level 2–Emerging.* At L2, students can understand phrases and short sentences. They can communicate limited information in simple everyday and routine situations by using memorized phrases, groups of words, and formulae. Errors in writing are present that often hinder communication.
> *Level 3–Developing.* At L3, students understand more complex speech but still may require some repetition. Proficiency in reading may vary considerably. Students are most successful constructing meaning from texts for which they have background knowledge on which to build.
> *Level 4–Expanding.* At L4, students' language skills are adequate for most day-to-day communication needs. They communicate in English in new or unfamiliar settings but have occasional difficulty with complex structures and abstract academic concepts. They can read independently but may have occasional comprehension problems, especially when processing grade-level information.
> *Level 5–Bridging.* At L5, students can express themselves fluently and spontaneously on a wide range of personal, general, academic, or social topics in a variety of contexts. They are poised to function in an environment with native speaking peers with minimal language support or guidance.

Lesson 1: Languages of the World*

Grade Levels: K–12
Content: Language Arts, Social Studies, Mathematics
Principles: 1–5

This activity allows students to share their native languages with their peers and also to learn about other languages. Since only a few languages are likely to be represented, it's important to point out that there are *many, many* more languages in the world and that language provides a window through which we can learn about other cultures.

Objectives

Students will be able to

1. Answer questions about languages of the world by studying a graph (ELA 9; MAT-N/O 3; MAT-COM 2; MAT-CONN 3; MAT-PS 3; MAT-REP 3; TESOL 1, 2, 3, 5).
2. Share their knowledge about languages of the world with their peers through discussion (TESOL 1, 2, 5; SOCS-USH [K–4] 4).
3. Teach and learn the meanings of certain words in other languages (ELA 9, 10).
4. Develop appreciation and respect for one another's language differences (TESOL 1).

Materials

- Handout of graph with top languages spoken in the world and questions
- (Optional) Index cards

*Adapted from Josel, C. (1994). *Ready-to-Use ESL Activities for Every Month of the School Year* (pp. 222, 231). West Nyack, NY: The Center for Applied Research in Education.

Procedures

1. Make a list of the languages spoken in your classroom by English language learners and others whose families may speak another language.
2. Have the students write on cards—or say—common phrases or words in their native languages: *hello* or an equivalent greeting, *goodbye, I love you, thank you*, and teach them to one another. (All languages have greetings but do not always use a word equivalent to *hello* or *goodbye*. For example, in Navajo you greet at all times of the day with the Navajo equivalent of "It is good," and the appropriate reply is "Yes, it is good." Ask ELLs about possible differences that may exist between their native language and American English.)
3. Share the list of languages in Figure 6.1 with the students and have them respond to the questions below it with yes or no answers.

Assessment

- Students' written and oral responses to the graph (Objective 1)
- Discussion about languages of the world (Objectives 2, 4)
- Participation in teaching and learning phrases from different languages (Objective 3)

Extension

- This activity can be expanded to include a mathematical component to help English language learners and others practice their calculation skills. In pairs you can pose the following problems for students and have them show how they arrived at their answers. Note that the underlined words imply the mathematical operation.

Figure 6.1   List of World Languages

Languages	Approximate Number of Speakers
Mandarin (Chinese)	1,075,000,000
English	514,000,000
Hindustani (encompasses multiple dialects, including Hindi and Urdu)	496,000,000
Spanish	425,000,000
Russian	275,000,000
Arabic	256,000,000
Bengali	215,000,000
Portuguese	194,000,000
Malay-Indonesian	176,000,000
French	129,000,000

Answer yes or no referring to the chart:

1. Do more people speak English than any other language?
2. Is Mandarin (Chinese) spoken by more than 800 million people?
3. Do more people speak Spanish than speak Russian?
4. Do approximately 200 million people speak Portuguese?
5. Do more than 100 million people speak Bengali?

Source: Infoplease. (n.d.) "Most Widely Spoken Languages in the World." Retrieved October 12, 2006, from www.infoplease.com.

1. Approximately how <u>many more</u> people speak Arabic than French?
2. If you <u>combined</u> Russian speakers with Hindu speakers, approximately what total would result?
3. If the total of English speakers <u>doubled</u> by the year 2020, approximately how many English speakers would there be?

- The following activities represent meaningful ways to incorporate *writing* with the same three questions:

1. Restate the problem in your own words. What are you trying to find out?
2. How do you think you might solve the problem?
3. Explain how you solved the problem. Include all the steps so that someone else can use your method.
4. How do you know your answer is right? Is there more than one possible answer to this problem? Why? Why not? (Carrasquillo and Rodriguez, 1996, pp. 154–155).

Lesson 2: Comparing Countries*

Grade Levels: K–12
Content: Social Studies
Principles: 1–5

This simple research-oriented activity accomplishes two goals. English language learners (and others) are motivated to do research around a multicultural topic that personally relates to them. At the same time, all learners begin to recognize similarities and differences between their countries and others and start to gain a global perspective.

Objectives

Students will be able to

1. Compare and contrast their native (or their ancestral) country with the United States (SOCS-USH [K–4] 2, 4; TESOL 1, 5).
2. Identify the locations on a map or globe of the countries represented in their classroom (SOCS-GEO 1; ELA 7, 8).
3. Expand their global perspective (SOCS-USH [K–4] 4; SOCS-GEO 1).

Materials

- Globe or wall map of the world or individual copies of a world map
- Library sources, especially *World Almanac*, encyclopedia, Internet
- Chart (Figure 6.2)

Procedures

1. Point to world map or globe. Ask students to identify the location of the country they or their ancestors come from. (If they can't find it, help them locate the country.)
2. Discuss the countries they mentioned by asking questions about which is closest to, furthest away from, north of, south of, east of, west of the United States, or other variations.

---

*Adapted from Josel, C. (1994). *Ready-to-Use ESL Activities for Every Month of the School Year* (pp. 248). West Nyack, NY: The Center for Applied Research in Education.

Figure 6.2   Chart on Comparing Countries

My Native Country (or My Ancestors' Native Country)	The United States
1. City and country I (my ancestors) came from:	City and state where I live now:
2. Population of that country:	Population:
3. Capital of the country:	Capital of the United States *and* the state I live in:
4. Major languages spoken:	Major languages spoken:
5. Unit of money:	Unit of money:
6. National anthem:	National anthem:
7. One other basis of comparison of your choice:	

3. Have the students do research in order to complete the chart in Figure 6.2. Consider having them work in pairs.
4. After they complete the research and the chart, discuss their findings.
5. Then, next to a wall map on the bulletin board, place a vertically arranged list of the students' names. Pin lengths of yarn from each child's name to their or their ancestor's country of origin. (Though a single child may have links to several countries, you might want to limit their identifications to one or two major countries.)
6. Students can find the answers in the library or on the Internet. They may want to make several other comparisons and add to the chart. When the class comes together you may want to record some of the responses on a Venn diagram (see Figure 6.3) or have them orally compare and contrast the countries they researched.

Assessment

- Completion of chart (Objective 1)
- Sharing their findings during class discussion (Objectives 2, 3)

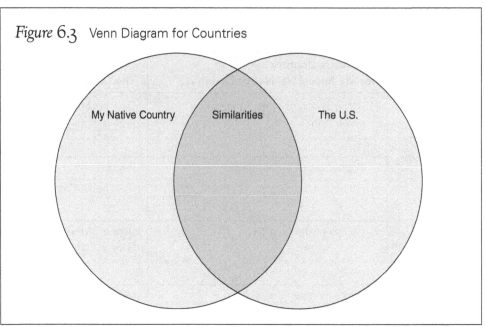

Figure 6.3   Venn Diagram for Countries

My Native Country   Similarities   The U.S.

Lesson 3: Using a Song as a Springboard for Multicultural, Interdisciplinary Activities*

Grade Levels: K–6
Content: Language Arts, Social Studies, Science
Principles: 1–5

By using a song such as "Old MacDonald Had a Farm" teachers can introduce several interdisciplinary activities and at the same time convey culturally relevant ideas—for example, that animals, too, speak different languages and belong to different cultures that are characterized by different habitats, diets, and family patterns, among other components. (Multicultural picture books can also be used as springboards for interdisciplinary activities. See the school librarian for examples of such books as well as books that are bilingual.) The varied strategies included within this lesson can help the English language learner acquire both content knowledge and language skills and they are appropriate for other students as well.

Objectives

Students will be able to

1. Participate in a variety of interdisciplinary activities (see Procedures) that relate to a song with multicultural content (TESOL 1, 2, 4, 5; ELA 1; SOCS-USH [K–4] 3; NS 6; NA-M 1; NA-T 2).
2. Express the knowledge they have gained in a variety of ways (TESOL 1, 2, 4, 5).

Materials

- (Optional) Copies of the song or chart with words of the song; multicultural picture books; copies of animal pictures
- (Optional) Drawing tools and tools for making booklets
- Graphic organizer (see Figure 6.4)

---

*The strategy described in Lesson 3 can be done in one lesson if there is sufficient time. It can also be developed as a unit of instruction.

Procedures

1. Ask students what sounds different animals make. (*Note:* In some cultures the sounds animals make are described differently than those traditionally denoted in Western cultures. Ask English language learners in the class if they can share the sounds certain animals make according to their language.) Explain that animals, too, have languages and communicate within their species, but, unlike humans, don't have the ability to learn other species' languages. However, there are exceptions that would be fun to discuss. For example, have any students trained a parrot to speak their language? Have they taught their dog to understand certain commands? Have they ever read about or seen chimpanzees use sign language?
2. After the preceding discussion, read the song aloud. (Have it written on a chart or transparency or distribute individual copies.)
3. Sing the song together. (The repetition within this song makes it useful for a student who is learning English.)
4. Role play: Students can act out the animals they are singing about.
5. Students can draw the animals and label the pictures and include on the pictures the sounds the animals make either according to English or their native language.
6. Engage the students in conversation about their pictures.
7. Make booklets of their labeled drawings to share with parents and other students.
8. Make a graphic organizer (Figure 6.4) on which students can place relevant information.

Assessment

- Students' completion of two or more of the activities listed in the Procedures (Objectives 1, 2)
- Students' participation in discussion (Objectives 1, 2)

Extension

- Take students to a farm or a museum of natural history or a zoo.
- Have students draw pictures of their lives and cultures as compared with their favorite animal. For example, they could make pairs of pictures labeled: My Favorite Food/The Animal's Favorite Food, My Home/The Animal's Home, and so on. They can include labels written in both their native language and in English as well as orally describe their pictures for their peers.
- (Grades 7–12) Have a world music celebration in which students or the teacher, including the music teacher, bring in CDs of music from other cultures, particularly from cultures represented in the class. Have students teach peers the chorus (and translation)

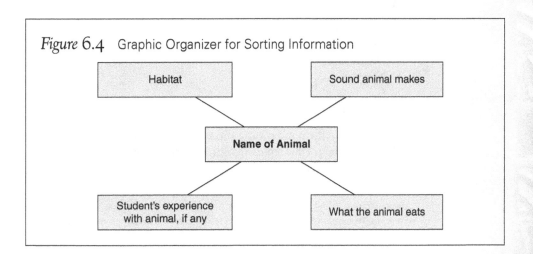

Figure 6.4   Graphic Organizer for Sorting Information

of one of the songs. Perhaps print it out phonetically so everyone can learn to sing the refrain together. If there are dances that go along with the music—as in salsa danced to Latin American songs—these can also be taught to peers.

Adaptation of This Strategy

Because certain sociopolitical songs, like "We Shall Overcome," are familiar to many minorities within the country, such songs can also be used as a springboard to multicultural, interdisciplinary activities.

Lesson 4: Nouns (Related to Culture) and Where They Are Found*

Grade Levels: K–12
Content: Language Arts
Principles: 1–5

Language is one of the components of a culture and is usually codified in dictionaries. Words considered nonstandard because their use is limited to home or community are no less important than those comprising standard usage. Meaningful use of a language can be enhanced by learning the grammar (rules governing the use of words) of the language and by referring to dictionaries that contain information about meaning and usage.

Objectives

Students will be able to

1. Identify five nouns that refer to the components of a culture (language, religion, art, values, food) and add to those nouns others that have meaning for them (TESOL 1, 2, 5; SOCS-GEO 4).
2. Use a dictionary to locate nouns (ELA 8).
3. Produce a dictionary in which they record the five nouns that are cultural components, as well as nouns related to their own and others' cultures, nonstandard nouns, and non-English nouns (TESOL 2, 5; ELA 6).
4. Use the five nouns (and other nouns) in speech and in writing (TESOL 1, 2; ELA 6).
5. Demonstrate initiative in expanding their dictionaries with nouns—and other parts of speech—learned during the course of the class (ELA 6, 8; TESOL 2).

Materials

- Index cards with nouns
- Drawing tools
- Dictionaries
- Notebooks

Procedures

1. Introduce the noun *culture* and see if students can identify components of a culture.
2. List five nouns that represent components of a culture, such as language, religion, values, art, and food, and also explain that these are not the only nouns that comprise culture.

---

*Adapted from E. Mack. (1994). *Lesson Plans for Cultural Inclusiveness and Relevance* (pp. 1–2). Milwaukee: Wisconsin Technical College System. This lesson can be carried out over several days, much like a unit of instruction.

3. Explain that nouns are the class of words representing names of people, places, and things (concrete nouns), and feelings or states of being (abstract nouns).

4. Then demonstrate examples—with students' input—of the five nouns listed on the board. (Students will probably mention examples directly connected to their respective cultures, which you can then list under the five nouns.)

5. Offer other examples of nouns that relate to specific subject matter content or to nouns that the students may have used or expressed interest in learning. (Sylvia Ashton-Warner, in her book *Teacher*, 1975, created a unique system of teaching English to native Maori children in New Zealand. The children created their own stories that the teacher recorded and illustrated in the form of big books, which then became the reading materials for the children. She referred to the words that had meaning for these children, that is, the ones they used in their stories, as "Key Vocabulary.")

6. Divide students into groups of four or five and give each student a card with a different one of the five words (cultural components) on it. (In some cases one student may have two cards.) Give them drawing supplies and have them play "Pictionary." Players look at the word on their card, then sketch an example of or symbol of that word as it looks or is represented in their own culture, and then others in the group guess the noun (cultural component). The player will then be able to teach the others about the meaning of the cultural symbol reflecting the noun. Encourage students to sketch other nouns after they complete their initial card.

7. Help students to alphabetize the five nouns and then begin a discussion of the uses and parts of a dictionary, calling attention to

   - Alphabetic organization and guide words
   - Pronunciation guide
   - Word origin information and part of speech
   - Definition with usage example

8. Assist students as they enter the five words (five cultural components) into their dictionary (notebooks). Tell them that after they include the lexical information, they can include culture-specific examples—their culture or others—along with the more formal entries. Remind them also that, since these are *their* personal dictionaries, they can at any time add nouns of their choice—nouns that may be in English, slang, colloquial speech, or in languages other than English.

9. Have students use the words they learned with friends and family and within class conversation.

Assessment

- Student's ability to follow directions (Objectives 1–5)
- Student's dictionary of nouns (Objectives 1, 3, 5)
- Student's use of the nouns (Objective 4)

Extensions

- Synonyms
  1. Explain the concept of a synonym and generate lists of words that are equivalent to the five words they have entered into their dictionaries. Again, these may be English, slang, colloquial speech, or in other languages.
  2. Ask students to choose *one* of the words and write a poem using it and its synonyms.
- Have students act out or dramatize certain nouns.
- Continue using the dictionary to teach other parts of speech.
- Set aside a section of the dictionary for terms associated with a specific topic or subject under study.

Lesson 5: Learning about Language Diversity and Culture Through Film*

Grade Levels: 7–12
Content: Language Arts, Social Studies
Principles: 1–5

Students can learn about different cultures and the languages of the English language learners in their class by viewing foreign films with English subtitles. A few of these films are suggested below, but you can discover many more by going to a film catalog or video store. Children or young adults play meaningful roles in each of the films mentioned. Teachers should, of course, preview a film before showing it so they can decide if it is appropriate for their class and so they can create learning activities to go along with the film.

Objectives

Students will be able to

1. Listen to the sound and rhythm of the language spoken in the film (NA-VA 6; ELA 9; NA-T 7).
2. Read the subtitles on the screen (ELA 1, 9; NA-T 7).
3. Summarize the story told in the film in their own words (TESOL 1, 2, 5; NA-VA 6; SOCS-USH [K–4] 4).
4. Discuss how true to life the portrayal of the culture shown in the film seems (TESOL 1, 2, 5; NA-VA 6; NA-T 7; SOCS-USH [K–4] 4).
5. Identify the culture portrayed in the film as well as significant characteristics and historical events related to the culture (TESOL 1, 5; NA-T 7; SOCS-USH [K–4] 4).
6. Explain the connections between the characters they observed and themselves and the connections between the events and lifestyle portrayed and their own lives (TESOL 1, 2, 5; NA-VA 6; SOCS-USH [K–4] 4).
7. Demonstrate empathy for the characters in the films (TESOL 1; ELA 1, 9).

Materials

- Film or video of choice
- Notebooks

Procedures

1. Ask if anyone has ever seen a film made in another country in another language. (English language learners may have seen American movies with subtitles in their native language.) Discuss their experiences and views related to these films. Discuss what kinds of information one can learn about different cultures from such films.
2. Show the students one of the following films or another one that appears to be suitable. (Consider stopping the film every half hour to determine what the students are grasping and to answer their questions. You may want to stop more frequently and read the subtitles together until you are sure the ELLs are able to follow the script. Perhaps showing just a small portion of the film will serve your purposes.)
   - *Children of Heaven*, Majid Majidi, 1997, Iran. Nominated for Best Foreign Language Film at the 1998 Academy Awards, *Children of Heaven* is the simple story of two children in Tehran and their efforts to cover up the loss of a pair of shoes from their impoverished parents.
   - *El Norte*, Gregory Nava, 1983, Guatemala/North America. A saga of a brother and sister who leave their violence-torn village in Guatemala to find a better life in the

---

*This strategy will require more than one class session and is appropriate as a unit of instruction.

North, El Norte. Getting to America is half the story; making a life there is the other half.

- *The Two of Us,* Claude Berri, 1968, France. A charming film about the growing relationship between a Jewish boy sent away for safety from World War II Paris by his parents and his anti-Semitic grandfatherly guardian who lives in the country.
- *Windwalker,* Keith Merrill, 1970, Native American. Deceased Indian patriarch returns to life to save his family from the vengeance of his son, a twin who was stolen at birth and raised by an enemy tribe. Filmed in the Cheyenne and Crow languages. There are some very violent scenes.

3. Ask students to write in their notebooks answers to these (and other) questions:
   - Whom did you like in the film and why?
   - What did you learn in the film about the culture portrayed?
   - What role did prejudice play in the film directly or indirectly (if any)?
   - What questions do you have about the film? (This can be done in class or for homework.)

4. After they write answers, you can have students share their answers in small groups with a recorder who then will share with the rest of the class the views of his or her group, or you can have a discussion of the questions with the whole class.

5. Evaluate together the value of learning about a culture from watching a film made within that culture's environment. How might the culture have been portrayed differently if the picture had been made by members of another cultural group?

Assessment

(See also Objectives for expected outcomes.)
- Summaries of the films in their own words in their notebooks (Objective 3)
- Answers to the questions in item 3 under Procedures (Objectives 4–6)
- Participation in discussions of the questions and of the value of watching the films (Objectives 1–7)

Lesson 6: Multicultural Foods, Windows to Culture: Making Matzo*

Grade Levels: K–12
Content: Interdisciplinary
Principles: 1–5

The exploration of foods associated with different cultures can lead students to an awareness of the historic events and people that help tell the story of those cultures, including their own. While there are many other foods that teachers could choose to teach about and prepare, the following description can serve as a model for teachers to follow. Working together on following multicultural recipes helps students learn about teamwork, about following directions, and, of course, about other cultures. (And they get to eat at the conclusion of the lesson.)

(*Note:* There are critics who say that teaching about diversity through the 2 *F*s, food and festivals, is superficial. On the contrary, food is grounded in culture, and scholars have written dissertations about the connections between food and culture. While there are, of course,

---

*Adapted from Josel, C. (1994). *Ready-to-Use ESL Activities for Every Month of the School Year,* Lesson: "Multicultural Foods . . ." pp. 220, 228. © 2002 Prentice Hall, Inc. Reproduced by permission of Pearson Education, Inc. If time prevents you from carrying out this lesson during a single class session, it can easily be divided up into two or more lessons.

many more approaches to diversity, using foods and festivals can motivate students to go further in their understanding of cultures.)

Objectives

Students will be able to

1. Identify foods from their own and other cultures that are associated with special observances and celebrations (TESOL 1, 2, 5; SOCS-USH [K–4] 3; SOCS-GEO 4).
2. Prepare one of those foods, in this case, matzo, or flat bread (SOCS-USH [K–4] 3; MAT-MEA 2; MAT-CONN 3).
3. Express what they learned as a result of this activity (TESOL 1, 2, 5; SOCS-USH [K–4] 3).
4. Share recipes with their classmates for the foods *they* have enjoyed associated with their cultural background (TESOL 1, 2, 5; SOCS-USH [K–4] 3; ELA 5; MAT-MEA 2).

Procedures

1. Discuss the special foods they eat that are associated with their cultural celebrations and whether or not they have helped prepare them.
2. Explain that matzo is like a cracker and is eaten by many Jews during Passover, the celebration of the delivery of Jews from slavery in Egypt thousands of years ago. Matzo doesn't require yeast or "rising" since the Jews, led by Moses, had no time to wait for regular bread to rise as they hastily escaped from Egypt and traveled through the desert to safety.
3. (Optional) Ask them to bring in recipes for their special foods to put in a booklet of recipes to be reproduced for each family.
4. Prepare the matzo with the class.

Materials

- Flour
- Cold water
- Large bowl
- Measuring cup
- Fork
- Rolling pin
- Baking tray

Steps in Making Matzo

1. Place two cups of flour in a bowl. Make a well in the center.
2. Pour a half cup of cold water into the well.
3. Mix the flour and water with your fingers. Add more water if needed. Keep mixing until the dough is soft and smooth.
4. Divide the dough into four pieces. On a floured table, *knead* each piece 10 times. If the dough is too sticky, add more flour. To knead dough:

   - Place dough on lightly floured table. Fold it toward you.
   - With your palm, push it away. Give the dough a quarter turn.
   - Continue until dough is smooth and not sticky.

5. Roll each piece out with a floured rolling pin so it is one-eighth inch thick or less. Prick with a fork.
6. Place the rolled dough on a baking tray. Bake at 500 degrees for four to eight minutes on each side, depending on thickness. The matzo is done when it is dry and has golden-brown patches and edges.
7. Enjoy the matzo with peanut butter or jam and butter (Josel, 1994, p. 228).

Assessment

- Students' participation in the activity (Objective 2)
- Discussions held both before and after (debriefing) the matzo-making activity or paper in which students express what they learned and how they felt about the activity (Objectives 1, 3)
- The contribution of a recipe from their cultural heritage (Objective 4)

Sample Unit 1: Putting Cameras in the Hands of English Language Learners and Their Peers

Grade Levels: 3–12
Content: Social Studies, Language Arts, Art
Principles: 1–5

Cameras are learning tools when they are used to tell stories related to subject matter and the students' lives. The additional advantage of cameras is that most students feel comfortable with them, and they enable the student to construct knowledge and then share it with peers. In addition in their role as photographers, the students are also expressing themselves as artists.

Objectives

Students will be able to

1. Capture on film stories about their families and their cultural experiences or images that depict the diversity of their town or school (TESOL 1, 2, 5; NA-VA 1, 3, 4).
2. Share these pictures by providing oral or written descriptions of the contents of these photographs (TESOL 1, 2, 5; NA-VA 4; ELA 4, 5, 12).
3. Prepare a bulletin board or book of their families' stories (TESOL 1, 2, 5; NA-VA 1; ELA 4, 5, 12).

Materials

- Cameras (Purchase "throw away" cameras or buy them after holding a fundraiser, such as a multicultural bake sale, or students can use their own cameras.) Access to digital cameras may be possible. The value of digital photography is not only the ease in printing the picture but also the possibility of other screen applications including PowerPoint presentations. However, if film is used, then funds for developing film, and the film itself, may be available from PTAs or other organizations that want to support local schools. (Perhaps a local camera shop owner would provide a discount—or even donate services—if approached about the class project. Or you can inquire if a local college has a darkroom.)
- Materials on which to write labels for the photographs
- Construction paper for booklet-making
- Pens or magic markers for labeling
- Computer (if PowerPoint presentation is created)

Procedures

1. This activity might begin with your showing the students photographs from texts in which a variety of cultures are portrayed or by sharing photos from *your* family's cultural activities. Then encourage them to look in magazines for pictures portraying

different cultures and their practices, as well as in their family's photo albums. Note that they will have the opportunity to continue telling those family stories by becoming photographers, actual artists creating original pictures for public display.

2. Converse with students about the teaching role that photographs can play and how they can illustrate families and cultural practices. Discuss this project in which they will take on the role of artist and, with cameras, capture their family's cultural activities or those taking place in the community. The content of the photos might also include the diverse nature of their town and its neighborhoods, buildings, and institutions.

3. Perhaps invite a local photographer to share his or her photos and speak to the class about how to prepare for taking pictures.

4. Help students plan their projects by listing with them—on the board or using the overhead—a series of steps they'll need to take—for example, deciding which activities, places, and people they want to capture, where will they find them, what kinds of simple labels they can provide for their pictures, where will the images be displayed, and with whom do they want to share the pictures besides their peers.

Assessment

- The photos and labels prepared by the students (Objective 1)
- The display on the bulletin board or in booklet form (Objectives 2, 3)
- Oral presentations (Objective 2)

Sample Unit 2: Heroes, the Five Ws, and the News

Grade Levels: K–12
Content: Interdisciplinary
Principles: 1–5

Heroes are people who do brave deeds and sometimes put their lives at risk trying to help others. Heroes can be found in all cultures and throughout history. They may be famous or "unsung" or found within one's own family.

The five Ws approach refers to a useful, organized, and simple method of gathering and presenting vital information about people and events. The five Ws refer to asking questions: using *who, what, when, where,* and *why* in doing research or interviews. (*How?* is also often added to the list.)

For this activity students become news reporters and share their findings about heroes in the form of a newspaper in which all of their articles appear. To carry the simulation further, they could give the newspaper an appropriate name and distribute copies of their newspaper throughout the school and even the community.

Objectives

Students will be able to

1. Identify heroes from their own and others' cultures from the past and present (TESOL 1, 2, 5; ELA 7; SOCS-USH [K–4] 4).

2. Do research in the library or do interviews using the five Ws to investigate the biographies of, and the contributions made by, certain heroes (ELA 1, 7; SOCS-USH [K–4] 4).

3. Share the information they gathered in the form of a newspaper (a simpler way of sharing their findings can also be used, such as simply doing reports or, in pairs, having structured conversations with one student taking the role of interviewer (news reporter) and the other being the interviewee (the hero) (TESOL 1, 2, 5; ELA 1, 5, 7; SOCS-USH [K–4] 3, 4).

4. Describe (orally or in writing) the characteristics of the heroes that they most admire and explain why (TESOL 1, 2, 5; ELA 5, 7; SOCS-USH [K–4] 3, 4).
5. Describe activities they might pursue to emulate some of these heroes (TESOL 1; ELA 7; SOCS-USH [K–4] 3).

Materials

- Materials needed for interviewing, including cassette tape recorders
- References, such as in the library or on the Internet
- Several newspapers
- (Optional) A flip chart for writing down potential questions

Procedures

1. Discuss the meaning of heroes and heroines.
2. Brainstorm to see if they know any heroes past or present from their own cultures, American culture, other cultures, or their families.
3. Explain the five Ws approach to gathering key facts about people and events. Show how, for example, they could describe themselves in this way in terms of their role as student. Have a few students respond to the five Ws (i.e., who are they, where are they in school now, when did they enter school, what do they do in school, why do they go to school).
4. Read the first two paragraphs of two or three news stories from the local paper and have the students listen for—and jot down—the five Ws they hear in each story. Discuss the fact that most newspaper reporters answer those questions about their topic in the first two paragraphs. Invite students to become newspaper reporters seeking to reveal information about multicultural heroes.
5. Have them pick someone from within the categories of heroes listed in the next section and prepare their articles for the class newspaper. (Remember that if you choose not to put together a newspaper, you can instead have students do such visuals as a poster or a mobile in which they include the five Ws with illustrations, using photos of the person or sketches of what that hero accomplished. In cases where the person did many significant deeds, the student can choose one or two to discuss and illustrate.)
6. Model the five Ws for the students by identifying a hero such as Martin Luther King, Jr., and see if they can answer the five Ws about him with your assistance. Suggest that the following questions are useful:

   - Who is the hero? (name, birth, death, origins)
   - What did this person do that was heroic?
   - Where did the hero do it?
   - When did this person make her or his contributions?
   - Why is he or she a hero?
   - How did he or she accomplish heroic deeds?

   In the case of a family hero, the student can interview family members using the five Ws. In addition, students can ask parents, "Who are your heroes—real or in literature—and why are they your heroes?" Students can share the conversations they had with their parents.
7. Emphasize the importance of writing down where they got their information from. It's never too early to teach students about documenting their sources. If you are requiring a bibliography, then show students examples of such entries where they appear in their texts.
8. On completion of their articles, assist students in putting together the newspaper and printing and distributing copies (or simply have students share their research and interviews with one another).

Categories of Multicultural Heroes (Past and Present)

1. A family member whom the student considers to be a hero—for example, a relative who came to this country under difficult circumstances.
2. Heroes from America who share a common heritage or identity with the student, such as Mexican Americans Cesár Chavez or José Angel Gutierrez; African Americans such as Thurgood Marshall, Harriet Tubman, and W. E. B. Du Bois; or gay activists like Harvey Milk, who fought to end discrimination against people with diverse sexual orientations.
3. Heroes from outside of America such as Nelson Mandela, Anwar Sadat, or Aung San Suu Kyi, or people who were heroes in the student's native country that Americans have never heard about.
4. Heroes who made humanitarian contributions to the world through their deeds or words, such as Mother Teresa, Raoul Wallenberg, Jane Addams, Mother Jones, and so many others.

Assessment

- The results of the student's research or interview portrayed in either a newspaper article, report, poster or mobile, oral presentation, or role-play (Objectives 1, 2, 3)
- A written list of sources where they found their information (Objective 3)
- Discussion of community service or other activities they might participate in that relate to the behaviors of people they learned about (Objectives 4, 5)

Summary Chart of Principles and Their Applications

Principle	Applications
1. The teacher's perceptions of English language learners affect the academic performance of these students.	1. Become familiar with the goals and standards established for English language learners by TESOL. 2. Research the cultural norms of diverse students. 3. Assess students' language proficiency. 4. Contribute to students' self-esteem by emphasizing the value of knowing more than one language. 5. Patience and encouragement are useful techniques.
2. Teachers in English-only classrooms are models of proficient English language usage (as are many of the English-proficient students in the class). Every native speaker is a temporary teacher and every conversation is a chance to learn something new.	1. Model correct usage and judiciously correct errors. 2. Provide educational opportunities for ELLs to interact socially and academically with English-speaking peers. 3. Specify vocabulary and technical terms associated with the subject matter and define those terms. 4. Use pictures as the key to understanding new vocabulary along with real objects, film, hands-on demonstrations, and interactional routines. 5. Record the students' reading aloud their own work on a regular basis so they can hear their improvements.

3. The language learner's goals and a feeling of empowerment are essential in the process of second language acquisition.	1. Include the study of the ELLs' cultures and the contributions made by members of these cultures. 2. Use the ELLs themselves as resources about their own countries and cultures. 3. Recommend appropriate television programs that ELLS can watch on their own so they can hear English spoken in conversation. 4. Establish schoolwide support systems (i.e., homework support in the form of an extended day so teacher or older students can help ELLs after school). 5. Teach coping strategies whereby groups of students meet with counselors or teachers during lunch to discuss common needs and issues.
4. In the case of students whose dialectical English differs from standard or academic English, teachers need to support the language that students bring to the school while at the same time "provide them access to the politically popular dialect in this country, that is, Standard English" (Delpit, 1995, p. 53).	1. Students can "teach" the teacher and other students aspects of their language's variety. 2. Students can prepare a talk or text using different language styles for different audiences. 3. Explain the subject matter in terms of its relationship to the student's life, using where appropriate the names, places, and problems that the student is familiar with. 4. Create bidialectical dictionaries of the student's own language form and Standard English. 5. Engage students in dramatizations in which they have to memorize parts that allow them to try out Standard English.
5. When there is parental involvement, English language learners are more successful.	1. Invite parents to school and make them feel welcome. (Then explain—perhaps with assistance of the children themselves—what they can do to help improve their child's educational performance.) 2. Establish family literacy programs that enable parents to learn with their children. 3. Provide other translation resources (e.g., bilingual adults within community, foreign language instructor at local colleges, social service agencies). 4. Hold an international potluck picnic for ELLs and their families. 5. Make a video for parents explaining your expectations for the class and encouraging parents to visit or call.

 LINKS: Recording in Your Journal

Reflect on the research and principles presented in this chapter and the lessons and strategies that address diversity and the needs of English language learners.

1. What, if any, is your *personal* connection to language diversity? (For example, this author recalls her grandmother conversing in Yiddish, a combination of German and Hebrew, and feeling frustrated at not being able to comprehend the meaning of the words. She also recalls asking her African American fifth graders to teach her the meanings of some of their

expressions. Finally she can remember traveling to countries where she communicated with non-English speakers using signs, body movements, facial expressions, and song.)

2. Which lessons and strategies do you think will help you (or have helped you) improve your teaching of culturally and linguistically diverse students? Why?

3. As you peruse again the five principles and their applications contained in the first part of this chapter, identify

   a. The one most meaningful to you and why you chose it.
   b. The one you know least about and want to research further.

4. Arrange the principles in their order of importance or usefulness—in your opinion—in terms of addressing the needs of English language learners to grasp language skills and content knowledge.

5. As you peruse again the lessons and strategies in the second half of this chapter, which appear to be most useful in terms of your subject specialty or the grade level you will be teaching?

6. What is your personal perspective on the following issue that was described in a column in 2006:

   "The airing on Hispanic radio stations of 'Nuestro Himno,' a Spanish-language adaptation of the American national anthem, has been greeted with an unprecedented and, indeed, astonishing wave of denunciations all over the United States" (Dorfman, 2006, p. A6). Both conservatives and liberals alike responded by declaring that "The Star-Spangled Banner" should be sung exclusively in English. For Dorfman, a professor of literature at Duke University, the adaptation is an indication that Spanish is a language that has come to stay and that "our better angels should welcome the wonders of Spanish." And he concludes his argument with the words, "Sí, se puede" (Yes, it can be done) (Dorfman, 2006).

   Discuss your point of view on this debate with your peers. Consider the *implications* of both perspectives.

References

Anthony, T. (March 6, 2005). "Take a Road Trip through American English." *The Berkshire Eagle*, p. E2.

Ashton-Warner, S. (1975). *Teacher*. New York: Bantam.

Azzam, A. M. (December 2004–January 2005). "A Look at Language Learning." *Educational Leadership*, 62(4), p. 7.

Baruth, L. G., and M. L. Manning. (1992). *Multicultural Education of Children and Adolescents*. Boston: Allyn & Bacon.

Bernstein, N. (January 12, 2005). "Immigrants Discover English and the Delight of Learning Together." *New York Times*. Available at www.nytimes.com

Bradley, A. (March 2, 2005). "Short Takes, Video Explains Schools for Latino Parents." *Education Week*, 24(5), p. 3.

Carrasquillo, A. L., and V. Rodriguez. (1996). *Language Minority Students in the Mainstream Classroom*. Clevedon, UK: Multilingual Matters.

Chamot, A. U., and J. M. O'Malley. (1994). *A Cognitive Academic Language Learning Approach: An ESL Content-Based Curriculum*. Wheaton, MA: National Clearing House for Bilingual Education.

Crawford, J. (1989). *Bilingual Education: History, Politics, Theory and Practice*. Trenton, NJ: Crane Publishing.

Cummins, J. (1986). "Empowering minority students: A framework for interaction." *Harvard Review*, 56, pp. 18–36.

Cummins, J. (1989). *Bilingualism and Special Education: Issues in Assessment and Pedagogy*. San Diego, CA: College-Hill Press.

Delpit, L. (1995). *Other People's Children: Cultural Conflict in the Classroom*. New York: W.W. Norton.

Dong, Y. R. (December 2004–January 2005). "Getting at the Content." *Educational Leadership*, 62(4), pp. 14–19.

Dorfman, A. (May 12, 2006). "A Language That Is Here to Stay." *The Berkshire Eagle*, p. A6.

Esquith, R. (2003). *There Are No Shortcuts*. New York: Pantheon.

Fay, K., and S. Whaley. (December 2004–January 2005). "The Gift of Attention." *Educational Leadership*, 62(4), pp. 76–79.

Garcia, E. E. (1993). "Language, Culture, and Education." In L. Darling-Hammond (Ed.), *Review of Research in Education* (pp. 51–98). Washington, DC: American Educational Research Association.

Gollnick, D. M., and P. C. Chinn. (2008). *Multicultural Education in a Pluralistic Society*. Boston: Allyn & Bacon.

Gray, T., and S. Fleischman. (December 2004–January 2005). "Successful Strategies for English Language Learners." *Educational Leadership*, 62(4), pp. 84–85.

Green, M. Y. (January 10, 2005). "Beyond Taco Tuesdays." *NEA Today online*. Available at www.nea.org/neatoday

Hamayan, E. V. (1990). "Preparing mainstream classroom teachers to teach potentially English proficient students." In *Proceedings of the First Research Symposium on Limited English Proficient Students' Issues*. Washington, DC: Office of Bilingual Education and Minority Language Affairs.

Herbert, B. (August 28, 2003). "The Kids Left Behind." *New York Times*. Available online at www.nytimes.com

Herrell, A., and M. Jordan. (2004). *Fifty Strategies for Teaching English Language Learners*. Columbus, OH: Pearson.

Hill, J. D., and K. M. Flynn. (2006). *Classroom Interaction That Works with English Language Learners*. Alexandria, VA: Association for Supervision and Curriculum Development.

Illinois State Board of Education. (2002). *Illinois Professional Teaching Standards* (2nd ed.), p. 4. Available at www.isbe.state.il.us

Krashen, S. (December 2004–January 2005). "Skyrocketing Scores: An Urban Legend." *Educational Leadership*, 62(4), pp. 37–39.

Krashen, S., and T. Terrell. (1983). *The Natural Approach: Language Acquisition in the Classroom*. Oxford, UK: Pergamon Press.

Lindholm-Leary, K. J. (December 2004–January 2005). "The Rich Promise of Two-Way Immersion." *Educational Leadership*, 62(4), pp. 56–59.

MacNeil, R., and W. Cran. (2005). *Do You Speak American?* New York: Doubleday.

Massachusetts Department of Education. (2004). Professional Standards for Teachers. In *Regulations for Educator Licensure and Preparation Program Approval*. Boston: Massachusetts Department of Education.

McLaughlin, B. (1992). *Myths and Misconceptions About Second Language Learning: What Every Teacher Needs to Unlearn*. Santa Cruz, CA: National Center for Research on Cultural Diversity and Second Language Learning.

Milk, R., C. Mercado, and A. C. Supiens. (1992). *Rethinking the Education of Teachers of Language-Minority Children: Developing Reflective Teachers for Changing Schools*. Washington, DC: National Clearinghouse for Bilingual Education.

National Center for Education Statistics. (2006). *The Condition of Education*. Washington, DC: Author.

New Levine, L. (1993). "Sharing the Wealth: The Collaboration of ESL and Mainstream Teachers." *Idiom*, 23(3), pp. 1, 5.

Nieto, S. (2000). *Affirming Diversity: The Sociopolitical Context of Multicultural Education*. New York: Longman.

Ogulnick, K. (2000). *Language Crossings: Negotiating the Self in a Multicultural World*. New York: Teacher's College Press.

Payne, R. (1995). *Poverty: A Framework for Understanding and Working with Students and Adults from Poverty*. Baytown, TX: RFT Publishing.

Pearlman, M. (2002). "Measuring and Supporting English Language Learning in Schools: Challenges for Testmakers." Presentation at CRESST Conference. Los Angeles.

Rivedal, K. (March 6, 2005). "Breaking the Language Barrier, New Effort Underway to Help Create a More Multilingual America." *Boston Globe* online. Available at www.bostonglobe.com

Rodriguez, R. (1982). *Hunger of Memory*. New York: David R. Godine.

Rosell, C. (December 2004–January 2005). "Teaching English through English." *Educational Leadership*, 62(4), pp. 32–36.

Scherer, M. (June 2006). "Increasing Reading Comprehension of English Language Learners." *Education Update*, 48(6), p. 2.

Short, D., and J. Echevarria. (December 2004–January 2005). "Teacher Skills to Support English Language Learners." *Educational Leadership*, 62(4), pp. 8–13.

Sternberg, R. J. (October 22, 2004). "A Dozen Reasons Why the No Child Left Behind Act Is Failing Our Schools." *Education Week*, p. 55.

Teachers of English to Speakers of Other Languages (TESOL). (2006). *Pre-K–12 English Language Proficiency Standards*. Alexandria, VA: Author. Available at www.tesol.org

United States Department of Education. (1993). *Descriptive Study of Services to Limited English Proficient Students*. Washington, DC: Planning and Evaluation Service.

United States Public Law 100-297. (April 28, 1988). *Bilingual Education Act. Title VII Bilingual Education Programs*. Washington, DC: United States Government Printing Office.

Villanueva, V., Jr. (December 1987). "Whose Voice Is It Anyway?" *English Journal*, 76(8), pp. 17–21.

Voices of Change: Students' Collected Writings. (2004). Lee, MA: Literacy Network of South Berkshire.

Ward, D. H. (June 19, 2002). "Alzheimer's Cannot Silence a Teacher's Legacy." *New York Teacher*, pp. 14–15.

Waters, J. (2004). *Literacy Network Tutor Manual*. Lee, MA: Literacy Network of South Berkshire.

Wax, M. L. (1971). *Indian Americans: Unity and Diversity*. Englewood, NJ: Prentice Hall.

Webb, L. D., A. Metha, and K. F. Jordan (2003). *Foundations of American Education* (4th ed.). Upper Saddle River, NJ: Merrill/Prentice Hall.

Zehr, M. A. (November 17, 2004). "Tests of Youngest English-Learners Sparks Controversy." *Education Week*, 24(17), pp. 1, 16.

Zehr, M. A. (January 5, 2005). "Report Faults Immigrant Instruction in 3 States." *Education Week*, p. 12.

Zwiers, J. (December 2004–January 2005). "The Third Language of Academic English." *Educational Leadership*, 62(4), pp. 60–63.

Recommended Resources

Bazin, M., M. Tamez, and the Exploratorium Teacher Institute. (2002). *Math and Science Across Cultures*. New York: New Press.

Delpit, L., and J. K. Dowdy. (2002). *The Skin That We Speak: Thoughts on Language and Culture in the Classroom*. New York: New Press.

Faltis, C. J. (2006). *Teaching English Language Learners in Elementary School Communities: A Joinfostering Approach* (4th ed.). Columbus, OH: Merrill/Prentice Hall.

Garcia, E. E. (2005). *Teaching and Learning in Two Languages: Bilingualism and Schooling in the United States*. New York: Teachers College Press.

Perry, T., and L. Delpit (Eds.). (1998). *The Real Ebonics Debate: Power, Language and the Education of African-American Children*. Milwaukee, WI: Rethinking Schools.

Stavans, I. (Ed.). (2005). *Wáchale ("Watch Out"), Poetry and Prose about Growing Up Latino in America*. New York: Cricket Books.

Strickland, D. S., and D. E. Alvermann (Eds.). (2004). *Bridging the Literacy Achievement Gap, Grades 4–12*. New York: Teachers College Press.

Videos

The following 3 videos are provided by Insight Media: www.insight-media.com, 2162 Broadway, New York, NY 10024   (800) 233-9910

"Educating Culturally and Linguistically Diverse Students" (2003). Association of Supervision and Curriculum Development.

"The Ebonics Controversy" (1998).

"Conversations for Three: Communicating Through Interpreters" (2000).

Films

Children of Heaven. (1997). Majid Majidi, Iran.

El Norte. (1983). Gregory Nava, Guatemala/North America.

The Two of Us. (1968). Claude Berri, France.

Windwalker. (1970). Keith Merrill, Native American.

Websites

www.ncela.gwu.edu

The National Clearinghouse for English Language Acquisition (NCELA) provides *In the Classroom* toolkits designed to bring research and practice together for teachers of English language learners (www.ncela.gwu.edu). The toolkits offer specific strategies for addressing content needs on both the elementary and secondary levels and for facilitating instruction by involving parents.

http://iteslj.org

TESL Journal, a Teachers of English as a Second Language Web magazine, includes articles and teaching ideas.

www.tesol.org

The Teachers of English to Speakers of Other Languages website provides access to online publications, standards, and professional development resources for teachers.

Chapter Seven

Strategies and Lessons for Increasing Global Perspectives

Eric Schumann, CATA 2007–2008 program year

I wanted, with all my heart, a peaceful world. And I knew it would never be achieved on a lasting basis without greater understanding between peoples.

Eleanor Roosevelt, 1946

The new education . . . must teach man the most difficult lesson of all—to look at someone anywhere in the world and be able to see the image of himself.

Norman Cousins (1915–1990)

*T*he purpose of this chapter is to provide research and principles related to the meaning, importance, and application of global education across the curriculum. Also included are several lessons, strategies, and interdisciplinary units of instruction that will help you to internationalize K–12 curricula and teacher education courses.

Each lesson satisfies one or more of four goals of global education: to expand opportunities for students to learn about the world beyond the borders of the United States, to recognize the interdependence between nations, to learn about American society's relationship to, and place in, the larger world, and to see things from the perspective of other peoples of the world (Tye, 1991, p. 14). Satisfying these goals is challenging, but making the effort to do so is crucial in a world still plagued by conflicts of all kinds. The intent of these lessons is to help lay an initial foundation for students in the area of global perspectives so that they may begin to tackle these larger issues.

While state mandates may vary, all have embraced global studies, often emphasizing the countries to which their state is connected socially, economically, or historically. And the No Child Left Behind Act (see Chapter 2) requires that global education be integrated, not as an add-on, but as a regular part of the K–12 curricula.

Do any of the group numbers or percentages listed below surprise you? Why or why not?

If we could shrink the earth's population to a village of precisely 100 people, with all existing human ratios remaining the same, there would be

57 Asians
21 Europeans
14 from the Western Hemisphere, both north and south
8 Africans

52 would be female
48 would be male

70 would be nonwhite
30 would be white

70 would be non-Christian
30 would be Christian

89 would be heterosexual
11 would be homosexual

6 people would possess 59% of the entire world's wealth and all 6 would be from the United States

80 would live in substandard housing
70 would be unable to read
50 would suffer from malnutrition
1 would be near death
1 would be near birth
1 (yes, only 1) would have a college education
1 would own a computer.

If you can read this message . . . you are more blessed than over two billion people in the world that cannot read at all (Smith, 2002).

What the Research Says

ONE The World as a Global Village Made Closer by Technology

David Smith's children's book represents the world as a global village (2002). Smith compiled the previous statistics using a broad range of primary sources and studies (Smith, 2002, p. 32). He suggests that we imagine "the whole population of the world—nearly 7 billion in all—as a village of just 100 people, each person representing about 62 million people from the real world" (Smith, 2002, p. 7). On each page he indirectly encourages readers to view the world as a village where they get to know their neighbors and where and how they live so that together they can live in peace.

In his book, we learn about the numbers of people within various different categories, including nationalities and languages. His village of 100 in terms of religions, for example, shows the following divisions:

> 32 are Christian
> 19 are Muslims
> 13 are Hindus
> 12 practice shamanism, animism, and other folk religions
> 6 are Buddhists
> 2 belong to other global religions, such as the Baha'i faith, Confucianism, Shintoism, Sikhism, or Jainism
> 1 is Jewish
> 15 are nonreligious (Smith, 2002, p. 15).

Advanced communications and technology have transformed the world into a global village. The Internet has provided a multitude of ways for both students and teachers to travel electronically to nearly every country on earth and to address several global problems in meaningful ways.

In a project involving Google for Educators and a variety of online interactive tools, resources, and lesson plans for teachers, the company invited students and teachers to brainstorm ideas to combat global warming. Ideas came from upwards of 80 schools—more than half of them outside the United States, according to a Google spokeswoman (Borja, 2006, p. 9). At Ghana's Opoku Ware School, for example, 11- to 13-year-old students suggested that farmers allow land to lie fallow to enable soil nutrients to regenerate, and high school students in Romania suggested that scientists create hybrid plants that can survive in extreme conditions.

Electronic technology of all kinds reminds us on a daily basis that we live in a world of the immediate. For example, hand-held TV cameras with direct uplinks to satellites enable us to receive live coverage of any event anywhere in the world; we can see and talk with people like telephone operators in India who ironically handle our business transactions here in the United States; and for better or worse we can view a war as it is being waged. With this kind of immediacy and firsthand look at other cultures, it becomes difficult to ignore the oppression and problems some of these cultures and nations face, as well as how much we have in common with those who are suffering (Jennings, 1994, p. 11).

The most immediate connection Americans have to other countries, however, has little to do with the speed of modern media. The fact is that all Americans are connected through their heritage to other parts of the world, including Native Americans who migrated from

Asia. And immigration continues to be one of the major links between the United States and countries all over the world.

Reflective question: How has the Internet brought *you* in closer touch with the world?

TWO Becoming Citizens of the World

There are approximately 7 billion people in the world and approximately 95 percent of them don't live in the United States (Manzo, March 2005, p. 5). Because students in the United States are living in a world where their country comprises only a minority of the world's peoples, Catherine W. Scherer, an educator and president of a Washington-based publisher of books with international themes, believes that "our students have to have an awareness and acknowledgment of the world beyond . . . [their own] country" (Manzo, 2005, p. 5).

In an attempt to make global studies more than a single case of highlighting the food, flags, and festivals of other countries, the International Studies Schools Association offered suggestions at its 2005 conference in Littleton, Colorado, on how to integrate—not add on—such studies in science, math, business education, physical education, history, language arts, and service learning. Michael H. Levine, executive director of the National Campaign for International Education in the Schools, an arm of the New York City–based Asia Society, noted also, "The curriculum in the 'Leave No Child Behind' world requires that global education not be a separate subject" but rather become integrated within state-mandated content, especially because there is such a huge emphasis now on high-stakes standardized testing in core subjects and limited classroom time for new subjects (Manzo, 2005, p. 5).

The state of North Carolina has been a leader in trying to educate their portion of the 5 percent about the rest of the world. Four secondary schools have been created there that focus on international studies with the goal of preparing students for the global marketplace (Manzo, 2005, p. 12) and preparing them to be "citizens, workers, and leaders in the global age of the 21st century" (Manzo 2005, p. 12). In addition, North Carolina boasts a number of global studies elementary and middle schools, as well as the Center for International Understanding, which sponsors training on international issues and study trips abroad for thousands of teachers. The state received an award from the Asia Society in 2003 for its commitment to international education.

Reflective question: Did your high school incorporate global education strategies? If so, compare them to the approaches just described.

THREE Introducing Global Education to Young Children

Research indicates that not only are elementary school-age children developmentally ready for a global perspective, but that this may be a more appropriate age at which to introduce it (Evans, 1987). There are age-appropriate curricula and methods for introducing global education to young children (Lacks, 1992).

The monthlong project, "Sharing a World of Difference in Early Education," a combined effort of two early childhood teachers in the Ferguson-Florissant School District in Missouri, is an example of an early childhood/parent international and cultural program expressly for 4- to 5-year-olds. With the assistance of the district's International Cultural Center (ICC) the teachers established the following objectives:

- To teach specific skills identified in the early childhood curriculum including seriation (ordering by size), such as when the teacher holds up a mango and pineapple and asks if the mango is bigger or smaller than the pineapple or when students put different-sized wooden dolls from Bangladesh into different baskets for little, big, and biggest.

- To verbalize how things are alike and different.
- To expose children and their parents to objects from other cultures in such a way that they begin to value and appreciate them.
- To develop in American children an awareness of their own everyday objects as compared to what children use in other places (Lacks, 1992, pp. 6–8, 30). Different kinds of kits were developed for the project. One of them contained musical instruments from around the world. There were home visits during which children and their parents could play and listen to the instruments and their sounds and discuss what materials they were made of and where they came from.

Judy Brown, one of the teachers who developed the project, said she "wanted children to experience delight in differences rather than fear, withdrawal, or making fun of someone who is not like them" (Lacks, 1992, p. 6).

Charles Evans's (1987) summary of the research on the developmental readiness for a global perspective of children 10 to 13 years old reveals that they are receptive to learning about people from other countries. After age 14, however, attitudes formed about people from other countries are somewhat negative. He found that students involved in social studies programs with a strong global education focus saw more similarities than differences between themselves and others.

Reflective question: What are some arguments in favor of global education for young children? Are there any arguments against this idea?

FOUR Controversies around Global Education

Global education, like multicultural education, has spawned controversy. The controversies that have arisen around global education are usually related to one of the following: (1) whether or not certain controversial global issues and sources, for instance, access to Al Jazeera, the Arab news agency, are antithetical to the nation's self-interest and thus inappropriate for inclusion in the curricula, (2) cultural relativism, and (3) globalism.

Below are responses to these sources of controversy:

Controversial Global Issues

Several years after the September 11 terrorist attacks, and in the midst of intensifying debate over the nation's approach to battling terrorism, many teachers around the country were "trying to determine how, and when, to teach about events . . . still fresh in the nation's collective memory, even as they [worried] about the likelihood of controversy and conflict" (Manzo 2006, p. 22). A case in point involved a social studies teacher in California who claimed in a lawsuit in August of 2006 that he began receiving negative reviews from the principal at San Fernando High School, where he taught history, because of his antiwar views. He testified that he offered objective discussion about the Iraq war but was taken to task for presenting antiwar films and lessons to balance out what he saw as one-sided messages from military recruiters on campus, according to the *Los Angeles Times* (Manzo, 2006, p. 22).

There are ways of negotiating the controversy and emotion surrounding these issues. The Foreign Policy Research Institute has solicited lesson plans from teachers around the country and compiled some of the best ones to distribute to schools. The Watson Institute for International Studies at Brown University in Providence, Rhode Island, also distributes materials on terrorism and on Islam. The Institute posts resources and teaching tips on its website, and the Teaching With the News link aims to help teachers link today's headlines with their curriculum content and includes lessons on terrorism, immigration, the violence in Sudan, nuclear weapons, and global environmental policy (Manzo, 2006, p. 24). Christopher Gavin, a teacher at New Jersey's Haddonfield High School, who runs professional workshops for teachers on the topic of 9/11, is concerned about the fact that many of the teachers he has encountered shy away from digging deeper into global issues, and, as a result, have done little to incorporate them into their curricula. "Knowing the truth about the world is ultimately in our national self-interest," said Mary Swenson, who in 1990 was the coordinator of the Education Outreach Project at the Central American Resource Center in St. Paul, Minnesota (ASCD, 1990, p. 7). She shares the view of many teachers that the more citizens of every country know about each other, the more likely we are to have global justice and global peace. Our mutual well-being is connected to political, economic, and cultural happenings throughout the world (Cotes, 2005, p. 6).

Cultural Relativism

Cultural relativism is in essence an approach to the question of the nature and role of values in culture (Herskovits, 1972, p. 14). It is quite natural for a cultural group to believe that the values and habits with which they grew up are the only viable and real ones. However, with education in cultural awareness and competency, students learn that there are many ways of understanding reality and that reality is relative to one's cultural upbringing.

Ethnocentrism—the view by members of a particular culture that their beliefs and habits are superior to all others—is one of the beliefs that students need to understand in order to move from an ethnocentric mindset (negative attitudes toward other cultures) to a culturally sensitive view that promotes healthy attitudes about others.

While behavior varies from culture to culture, we can, nevertheless, establish basic moral principles to which nearly everyone will subscribe. That is what the United Nations did when it created the Universal Declaration of Human Rights (see Figure 7.1), a document endorsed by countries with extraordinarily diverse cultures. When, however, a local custom contrary to those principles persists, the first step in bringing about change is to work with or enlist the aid and advice of local groups making a similar effort. It is they who are likely to have both the insight and moral standing to lead reform in their own land.

Globalism and Globalization

Joe Nye, the former Dean of Harvard University's Kennedy School of Government outlined the fundamental difference between globalism and globalization. *Globalism* attempts to understand all of the interconnections of the modern world and to highlight patterns that underlie and explain them. In contrast, *globalization* refers to the increase or decline in the degree of globalism and focuses on the forces and speed of these changes (Nye, 2002). In short, globalism can be considered the underlying basic network, while globalization refers to the dynamic shrinking of distance on a global scale.

Thomas Friedman, a proponent of globalization, defines it in *The Lexus and the Olive Tree* (1999) as the integration of capital, technology, and information across national borders, a faceless system searching for profit and innovation. Writes Marge Scherer, "The Lexus in his title is the robot-built, luxury car over which half the world lusts, and the olive tree is the gnarled bit of nature over which the other half is fighting" (2002, p. 5). The result of this tension can leave some people with unfathomable potential while leaving others uprooted and brutalized.

All dimensions of globalism/globalization—economic, military, environmental, and social—continue to arouse controversy, especially among students and others whose concern for justice has led them to protest against multinational firms and first world countries whom they accuse of caring only about profit at the cost of social and economic justice. While there are many diverse voices involved in the debate about globalization, most participants claim to be in favor of alleviating human suffering through spreading knowledge about the world and balancing the diverse needs and desires of its inhabitants.

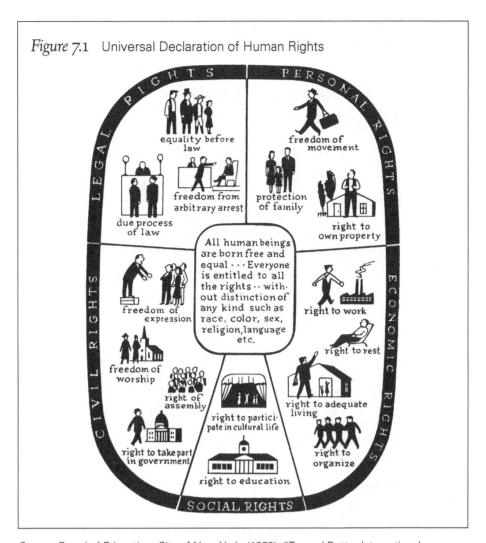

Figure 7.1   Universal Declaration of Human Rights

Source: Board of Education, City of New York. (1959). "Toward Better International Understanding A Manual for Teachers." Curriculum Bulletin No. 4. New York: Author. Reprinted by permission of the Board of Education of the City of New York.

In some cases, professional teacher organizations have become participants in some of the controversies related to globalism. For example, in December 2006, the National Science Teachers Association rejected the offer by the producers of former Vice President Al Gore's film about global warming, *An Inconvenient Truth*, to distribute 50,000 free copies of the film to its members. The association said their decision was based on a policy against endorsing outside organizations' products and messages, but one of the film's producers noted another possible motive, the fact that the NSTA receives contributions from oil companies that have disputed certain assertions about climate change (Cavanagh, 2006, p. 17). The controversy grew to the point that organizations on all sides of the political spectrum contributed their views. Mr. Gore himself criticized the NSTA in an appearance on "The Tonight Show with Jay Leno." The head of NSTA noted that the organization's position on distributing materials from outside organizations would remain firm.

Perhaps the most visible of globalization's injustices—because of famous companies like Nike and Walmart that are associated with them—are the factories, more like sweatshops, located in countries like China, where some women work as long as 70 hours a week for very low pay and under questionable conditions (Miller, 2001, p. 9). On the other hand, noted economists like Paul Krugman believe that low-wage export factory jobs will, in the end, better the lives of workers and their families in the developing world.

Reflective question: Weigh in on the controversial issues related to global education and globalization, as well as on cultural relativism.

FIVE Replicating Models for Teaching about the World

There are several schools across the country that have established models of learning and teaching about the world that can be replicated. The schools featured in *Schools for a Global Age: Promising Practices in International Education* (Asia Society, 2005) provide models of learning and teaching about the world that hold the promise of developing an internationally literate generation. For example, at Newton North and South High Schools in Massachusetts, the student exchange program with Beijing, China, promotes the study of Asia throughout the curriculum (Cotes, 2005). The John Stanford International School in Seattle, Washington, offers its students a half-day language immersion program in Spanish (K–5) and Japanese (K–4). And Morikami Park Elementary School in Delray Beach, Florida, an International Baccalaureate magnet program, follows a student-led inquiry-learning model. Its purpose is to prepare students "to be citizens, workers, and leaders in the global age of the 21st century" (Manzo, 2005, p. 12).

Long before the concept of global perspectives gained national attention, the teachers, administrators, and parents in Muscatine, Iowa, developed a global studies model that acknowledged the need for students to learn how to operate in an interconnected and interdependent world (DeKock and Paul, 1989). As far back as 1974, the Stanley Foundation, a private foundation dedicated to working toward peace, began working with interested teachers, and eventually the goal of developing global perspectives became part of the Muscatine district's mission statement and philosophy, equal in weight to learning the three Rs (DeKock and Paul, 1989).

Reflective question: Do you think these models for teaching about the world can be easily replicated in any school? Why or why not?

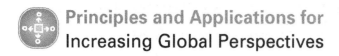

Principles and Applications for Increasing Global Perspectives

Principle ONE

There is a place for global perspectives in every discipline.

If teachers in any subject area want to integrate global education all they would have to do is have students do research on the many significant individuals whose contributions have enhanced that field of study. Biographies of, among others, Einstein (sciences), Shakespeare (literature), Mozart (music), Picasso (art), historical figures from many cultures (history), and Euclid (mathematics) would reveal to students that the content of every discipline is the result of a multitude of global influences. And the origin and history of every discipline has roots in many cultures, from Greco-Roman to Mayan to Chinese, to name a few.

Whenever possible, teachers of all disciplines can choose to use texts and materials that reflect an international perspective by including historical and current events from multiple points of view (Bergman and Young, 1989). For example, issues such as global warming or human rights, and such concepts as the interdependency of nations can be integrated within social studies and science courses as well as within other subject areas.

Classroom Applications and Strategies

- Have students participate in a model United Nations program within your school or between groups of schools. (Social Studies)

- Establish pen pal relationships with a class at a school overseas. Include in the letters—or communications via e-mail—drawings and other artwork that portrays cultural stories. As a result of these exchanges, students come to see the similarities as well as the differences between their lives and those of children in other countries. Students also discover how art can convey cultural values and social conditions. (Language Arts and Social Studies)

- Encourage school or class support of a worldwide humanitarian project such as those sponsored by UNICEF, Heifer International, and Oxfam America and discuss their roles in fostering internationalism and social justice. (This author teaches near a school system that researched and fund-raised on behalf of a primary school built in Afghanistan, after a local couple had initiated the project. The couple wanted to do something that would help increase understanding and forge relationships between their local area and the third world after their son was killed aboard one of the flights on 9/11.) (Social Studies)

- Do simulations of global problems. For example, hold a hunger banquet in which students are separated into "nations" and the students representing the wealthy nations are fed well, and those from poor nations who suffer from famine and malnutrition are fed little or nothing at all. Use this "banquet" to have students share their research on the unequal distribution of food among the world's children. This nutrition lesson can affect students on literally a gut level. They also can learn that poor diets typify not only remote areas of the Amazon but also many American cities where poor families do not have enough food on the table. The fact is that the more students learn about other countries, the more they learn about their own. (Social Studies, Home Economics)

- Identify and research a global problem, such as war, pollution, terrorism, nuclear proliferation, or prejudice, and discuss its current and future impact and then brainstorm solutions (Bergman and Young, 1989). (Social Studies)

- Do research on the origins and content of the "Universal Declaration of Human Rights" (1948). (See Figure 7.1.) (Social Studies)

- Watch films from other countries or films *about* other countries, as well as cross-cultural films (films that depict two or more cultures coming together). If the film is about cross-cultural connections, analyze the behavior of each group toward the other. What can you learn about how to achieve successful cross-cultural communication? Mark Salzman's 1991 film *Iron and Silk* is a good example of the value of crossing cultures (Summerfield, 1993). (Social Studies, Film Studies)

- Have students do research, write, and present plays dramatizing biographies of men and women who have worked for or written about human rights and internationalism around the world (i.e., Eleanor Roosevelt, Nelson Mandela, Albert Schweitzer, Bill Gates, Nicholas Kristof, the Dalai Lama, and entertainers like Bono and Angelina Jolie). Have students write to Amnesty International for information about human rights issues around the world (see Recommended Resources at the end of this chapter). (Language Arts, Social Studies)

- Have students collect political cartoons from the world's press as well as the American media (students don't necessarily have to be able to read the words to get the picture). Collect cartoons related to a particular event or action taken by the U.S. government. In groups students can analyze the cartoons using these questions:

   a. What are similarities and differences in how the United States is viewed or in how the event is depicted?

b. Which cartoons tend to be critical of or supportive of the action? Why? This activity leads students to do research on the people, governments, and cultures of other nations (Drum, Hughes, and Otero, 1994, p. 75). (Social Studies)

• The Center for Human Interdependence at Chapman College in Orange, California, helped to organize an "International Sports Day," in which the physical education teachers from four middle schools and one K–8 school made plans for teaching their seventh graders eight games from around the world that stressed cooperation instead of competition (Tye, 1990, p. 105). And in some gym classes, students get a physical workout by doing African and other ethnic dances. (Physical Education)

• Take students to a museum in which the art of many cultures is housed and where a docent can explain the relationships between the art and artifacts and the cultures that produced them. Despite the argument by some that museums present only a narrow range of artistic expression, it is worthwhile for students to learn about the needs, history, and beliefs of groups through their art (Blandy and Congdon, 1987). Students can also learn about world cultures by making examples of traditional art and crafts from different countries. By doing so, they can learn about the different media—beads, feathers, fibers—that comprise the works of art and the relationship the materials have to the geography of those countries (Ryan, 1989). (Art, Social Studies)

• Have students go to a music store—or simply do research on the Internet—to find out about performers of world music and where they come from. Then on a classroom map, indicate the various locations where the music originated. (Music, Social Studies)

• Students can learn folk songs and read folk tales from different countries and do research on the connection between the content of the songs or stories and the cultures from which they come. If possible have musicians and storytellers from different countries perform in the classroom. Students who have little or no knowledge of countries in Africa, for example, except what they may hear or see on the news in terms of disease, wars, or poverty, will come to see the creativity and beauty of African musical culture, and in so doing, alter the stereotypes that may exist. (Music, Social Studies, Language Arts)

• Research the origins of familiar fairy tales. (Literature)

• The metric system, used in many countries, can be a focus of study as well as comparing the values of foreign currency to those of U. S. money. (Mathematics)

• Study of environmental and population issues that affect the whole world—pollution, soil depletion, global warming, overpopulation in certain areas, and causes of disease—bring to life the contemporary problems that require problem solving and critical thinking. (Science, Social Studies, Mathematics)

Principle TWO

Establishing geographic knowledge is a good way for students to begin their global education.

When the National Geographic Society periodically polls students about their geographical knowledge, Americans from 18 to 24 years old score below their counterparts in other countries (Roper, 2002).

Several years ago McDonald's got involved in an effort to feed customers some geography and history along with Chicken McNuggets. Their "Fiesta" packet came with a real coin from Argentina, Costa Rica, Ecuador, Guatemala, Peru, or Venezuela, plus a map of all Latin America, plus explanations of the coins (centavos, centimos, sucres, and colones) and the flags of the six countries. Along with the coins were questions like "Who owns the Gala-

pagos?" and "Where are the Quechua Indians?" A coin holder who cared enough to find out the answers to these questions might also develop a desire to study third world debt or the difference between totalitarian or authoritarian regimes and democratic governments.

Classroom Applications and Strategies

• While maps may not be as tasty as McNuggets, they can become quite exciting vehicles for stimulating students' interest in other countries, and, what's more, they are interdisciplinary. For example, if students are studying India they might use maps to carry out the following activities: Indicate on a map the large cities in India and the seaports with lines pointing to icons of the different products imported and exported from each one (Social Studies); describe in writing an imaginary trip to India mentioning the chief points of interest and people they met along the way (Language Arts); explain the role of science in combating malaria, cholera, and tuberculosis in India or indicate climate differences in the country (Science); plot the air distance from one of the large cities of India to some of the capitals of the world, including Washington, D.C., or call different airlines to find out cost of a round-trip ticket to India and calculate the differences in costs among the airlines for airfare (Mathematics); play a selection of folk songs from various parts of India that are noted on the map and explain how the songs typify life in those areas (Music); show slides of the Taj Mahal and Hindu temples and other architectural wonders and note their locations on the map (Art).

• Have students bring in everyday products from home, such as clothing or small appliances that were made in other countries; then find those countries on a map and, if there is time, do research on the reasons why those items are manufactured in those areas, who is doing the work, and what the working conditions are. This may lead students into playing a role of expressing their concerns publicly about child labor and, in some cases, harsh working conditions. Several companies, from Nike to Walmart, have been made accountable because of public opinion regarding the sources of their products. At the very least, students will learn about the interdependence between the United States and other countries.

• Use a world map on the wall on a daily basis and locate places in the news, countries where friends or relatives live or are traveling, areas where the books they are reading take place, and so on (Smith, 2002). It's also helpful to have available at least one atlas with a good index so that students can find places in the world more easily.

• Play geography games like What's Next, in which one person names two contiguous countries and the others have to figure out what the next contiguous place is. Or Name the Capital/Country, in which one person names a capital or a country and the other players have to name the missing capital or country. Or Details, in which one person names a country and each player has to give one detail about it. Another game involves Making Up Puns, using the name of countries on the map. For instance, Pakistan might become "Pack his tan suitcase."

Or Madagascar might become "I'm really <u>mad: a gas car</u> is expensive," or "When I'm in a hurry, I <u>Russ-ia</u> lot." Students could be divided into groups, each with a map, and compete (or not) in creating as many puns as they can. (This author tried the game with several groups of teacher education students. All together the groups came up with 45 puns; many admitted they had never heard of some of the countries they found on the map.)

• Find out about R. Buckminster Fuller's World Game, sometimes called the World Peace Game. Originally it was played on a basketball-court size "Big Map." Students could learn in a very visual way about population distribution, food supply inequities, consumption of the planet's energy, military expenditures, and other global issues. In 2001, a company, O.S. Earth, purchased the assets of Fuller's World Game Institute and offers Global Simulation workshops (see Recommended Resources).

• Encourage passion for exploring the world through maps, travel, literature, and languages by demonstrating your own passion for these routes to learning about other cultures.

Principle THREE

 Developing interpersonal, international relationships is one of the most effective ways for teachers to bring the world into their classrooms (Keller, 2003) and decrease ethnocentrism.

Establishing international relationships as a way of increasing students' global awareness is easier now than ever before. With the search engines on the Internet, international educators and educational institutions are at the fingertips of any teacher seeking to make such connections. (This author created International Student Teaching Opportunities, ISTO, at her college and has placed student teachers at K–12 schools in seven countries. By googling "American schools" or "International schools" and the name of the country you are interested in, you will be able to locate—and then contact—dozens of schools.)

Classroom Applications and Strategies

• Perhaps the simplest way of developing international relationships is by inviting foreign-exchange students in the community to visit your classroom and share information about their countries. Find out if there are professors from other countries teaching nearby and invite local immigrants to speak about their native countries. Dozens of connections to other countries can be found in most communities.

• Using the "Professional Development Resources for International Studies" in the "Recommended Resources" section at the end of this chapter, teachers can begin to pursue travel–study fellowships, teaching abroad for a summer or a semester, hosting students or teachers from other countries, teleconferencing, e-mail, and communications by letter with classrooms and educators in other countries.

• Tap into iEARN, the International Education and Resource Network, a worldwide program that allows teachers and students to work collaboratively on classroom projects and share basic cultural information through the Internet and other technologies (Cavanagh, 2006, p. 10). The nonprofit global network serves 20,000 schools and youth organizations in 115 countries, including 600 schools in the United States. Teachers and students design all of the projects and, with the administrative help of iEARN officials, communicate with peers in other countries. An example of such a collaboration is a project that involved exchanging data about water habitats between an elementary school in Seattle and students in the Republic of Vanuatu, an island nation in the South Pacific.

• Consider putting an ad in the local paper to find someone who has visited or who comes from a country your class is studying. (Many years ago, this author's fifth-grade class was studying explorers. She put an ad in the local paper for a "modern day explorer," resulting in a visit to the class by the son of a man who was a member of the National Explorer's Society. He brought with him the two sled dogs that accompanied him and his father on expeditions to Antarctica. Years later, when her high school students were studying apartheid in South Africa, her ad seeking someone who had been there resulted in a response from a retired Foreign Service diplomat who had lived in South Africa and assisted in efforts to end apartheid.)

Principle FOUR

 Understanding the concept of interdependence, or the mutual dependency that exists between countries, as well as between people and their environment, is central to students' appreciation of global diversity.

While every community has many kinds of links to the world, most people are unaware of just how much they are affected by other countries.

Classroom Applications and Strategies

• Have students trace the origins of products that, while "made in America," are really a composite of materials that were made in other countries. For example, some refrigerators may include steel from Japan, handles from Taiwan, icemaker trays from Hong Kong and South Korea, and motors made by European companies located in Brazil. And cars, for example, even when manufactured in Japan, include components from 34 countries (Goldman, 1989, p. 18).

• Have students go to one or more of the following locations on a kind of scavenger hunt for links to other countries: an appliance store, a grocery store, a toy store, and their own closet. Ask them to find at least ten items in each place that were made in other countries and to then list those items. Next to each item they can record the brand name of the item and, in a third column, the country of origin. When they share their lists, have a map of the world posted so markers or labels can be placed in those locations with the name of the items made there. You may also want to have students list the raw materials that make up the products, which would then lead to a discussion of the geography, economy, and climate of each country listed.

Strategies and Lessons for
Increasing Global Perspectives

What are the outcomes that teachers can *realistically* expect from integrating some of these interdisciplinary lessons and strategies into their regular curriculum? Perhaps it is not realistic to expect all of your students to become humanitarians who actively seek out international relationships and undertake projects that can help to make the world a healthier and fairer place in which to live (although the next Albert Schweitzer may be sitting in your classroom). But it *is* very possible that as a result of the following strategies, students will begin to question their own ethnocentric attitudes—based largely on ignorance—and come to recognize that American culture is not better than every other, that there is much of value to be learned from other cultures, that we are connected to the world in so many important and vital ways, and that they are, in fact, not simply citizens of the United States but of the world.

You will know you have succeeded in increasing the global perspectives of your students when, instead of reacting to different cultural characteristics with fear or attitudes of superiority, they seek instead to understand the differences, identify commonalities, and demonstrate an ongoing curiosity and desire to explore further.

Lesson 1: The World in a Chocolate Bar

Grade Levels: 4–12
Content: Social Studies, Science
Principles: 1, 2, 4

Where did the chocolate bar come from (besides a candy store)? This favorite treat of children and adults alike provides a wonderful way for students to learn about the world and the idea that the world is an interdependent place. This lesson, adapted from one developed by the American Forum for Global Education, conveys the fact that it takes a lot of nations and a lot of people to create something that has been a sweet source of enjoyment for many years (Goldman, 1989).

Objectives

Students will be able to

1. Explain the concept of interdependence as it relates to the production of a chocolate bar (SOCS-EC 6; SOCS-GEO 5).
2. Work together in groups to determine which countries produce the products that contribute to a chocolate bar; provide reasoning for their choices (SOCS-EC 6; SOCS-GEO 4; NS 6).
3. Identify the map locations of the countries that provide the ingredients for making the chocolate bar and its wrappers (SOCS-GEO 1).

Materials

- Copies of a map of the world (for each student)
- Wall-size map
- List of the products that make up a typical chocolate bar
- Chocolate bars

Procedures

1. Begin the lesson by holding up a chocolate bar in its wrapper and asking the class, "Where did this chocolate bar come from?"
2. As students contribute their ideas you might ask them how they arrived at their answers. Then ask if anyone has ever been to a chocolate factory (e.g., in Hershey, Pennsylvania), if they ever saw or read *Charlie and the Chocolate Factory*, or if they knew that different kinds of chocolate bars are made in countries noted for their chocolate (e.g., Switzerland, Belgium, Germany, Austria, Italy, Sweden, and many others).
3. Then ask which ingredients they think go into making chocolate bars. Again ask why they mentioned certain ingredients.
4. Divide the students into groups; give each group a copy of the world map and a list of the products (see Figure 7.2) that go into creating a typical candy bar. Ask them to look on the map for the various countries from which each of the eight items might have come from. Through consensus each group should reach agreement on which country—or at least which continent—produced the ingredient and why they chose those locations. (A recorder chosen by each group will document their conclusions.) (You will have the answer key; see Figure 7.2.)
5. After the groups have met and made their decisions (around 15 minutes), have the group recorders share their answers and why the group chose certain countries or continents. Where there is disagreement, have the class decide which choices appear

Figure 7.2   Handout Listing Materials for Creating a Candy Bar

Ingredients	Country (or Continent) of Origin
1. Cocoa	
2. Peanuts	
3. Corn syrup	
4. Coconuts	
5. Sugar	
6. Paper wrapper	
7. Tin foil	
8. Truck that brought candy to the store	

Possible Answers:

1. Ghana   2. Sudan   3. Iowa   4. Philippines   5. Ecuador   6. Canada
7. Thailand   8. Japan

Source: Based on Goldman, A. L. (April 9, 1989). "World Affairs Can Be Child's Play." *Education Life, The New York Times Supplement* (4A), pp. 18–31.

to be most logical. Indicate final answers on a large wall-size world map by placing a Post-it on each of the countries that students have agreed on as the sources of the eight products listed on their sheets.

6. Share with students your answers (also using Post-its). Let them know that there are *many* countries that produce the same products, and that they should—for homework—find out if, in fact, the countries *they* chose might also be producers of those ingredients. Tell them to report back to class tomorrow with their data and the sources of their findings.

7. Review with students the idea that there are many countries involved in the making of popular products and that without interdependence among countries, we might not have the pleasure of enjoying many items that we take for granted.

8. Distribute chocolate bars to the students so they can share in the final product.

Assessment

- Participation in the discussion about interdependence and in their small groups (Objectives 1, 2, 3)
- One-page written summary of the lesson they participated in, its purpose, and what they learned about where a chocolate bar comes from (Objectives 1, 2, 3)
- Homework assignment in which they try to determine if their group's choices were correct as sources of the ingredients (Objective 2)

Extension

After students complete their homework of determining whether the countries they selected produced the products in the ingredients list, have them share their findings with the class. Then as a class compose a letter—or an e-mail—in which they inquire of a local candymaker (if there is one) or from the Hershey Company or other international candy company about their current sources for certain ingredients listed on their most popular candy bars.

Lesson 2: Reaching Consensus*

Grade Levels: 9–12
Content: Social Studies
Principle: 1

Subconscious *ethnocentrism*—the belief in the superiority of one's own ethnic group or culture—pervades many societies, and in order to decrease its negative effects, it is helpful to introduce students to the idea that their cultural conditioning may narrow their ability to think objectively about cultural differences. The value of this lesson lies not so much in whether or not the statements the students will be responding to are valid, but in the discussions they spark. In particular, it provides the teacher with the opportunity to underscore certain key points, that is, how pervasive ethnocentrism is and how difficult it is to form nonjudgmental or nonethnocentric statements.

Objectives

Students will be able to

1. Participate in groups in which they discuss, and take a position on, a list of statements (ELA 11).
2. Discuss the reasons for their positions on the statements (ELA 3).
3. Debrief with the class about the concept of cultural conditioning and its influence on subconscious ethnocentrism (SOCS-GEO 2, 4).
4. Express in writing what they learned in this lesson (ELA 3).

Materials

- A copy of the list of statements (see Figure 7.3) for each student

Procedures

1. Divide the class into groups of three to five and give them the following instructions:
    - *Individually*, place an A or D beside each statement on the handout (Figure 7.3) to indicate whether you *personally* agree (A) or disagree (D) with it.
    - Then in groups go over each statement in order; check to see if anyone in your group disagrees with it. If even one person disagrees, the group should change the wording so that the statement becomes acceptable, as recorded, to *all* members of the group. The same applies when *everyone* in the group disagrees with the statement; it must be changed so as to make it acceptable.
    - You may not simply "agree to disagree."
    - Choose one member to record the revised, acceptable document.
2. Ask each group to report orally on a couple of the statements, and ask for alternative revisions from other groups (Kohls and Knight, 1994, p. 25).
3. Review the concept of ethnocentrism: the belief in the inherent superiority of one's own ethnic group or culture.

---

*Adapted from a lesson by Kohls, L. R., and J. M. Knight (1994). *Developing Intercultural Awareness.* Yarmouth, ME: Intercultural Press.

Figure 7.3 Handout of List of Statements

Directions: Agree or Disagree by placing an *A* or *D* after each statement.

1. The fact that the first man on the moon was an American is proof of U.S. technological superiority.
2. Many third world countries are "underdeveloped" through lack of initiative on the part of their inhabitants.
3. Everyone should learn English as it is the one unifying language.
4. The Iraqis do not place as much value on human life as Americans do.
5. Other people in the world should learn to do things the way Americans do so that we will all be able to get along and understand each other better.

4. Ask group members to identify ethnocentric attitudes evident in the statements.
5. Explore how each group reached consensus on the rewording of the statements and which attitudes were challenged in the process.

Assessment

- Participation in the group responses to the list of statements (Objectives 1, 2, 3)
- A one-to-two page reaction paper explaining what they learned from this "Reaching Consensus" lesson (Objective 4)

Lesson 3: The International Pencil, an Illustration of Global Interdependence*

Grade Levels: 5–12
Content: Social Studies (Geography), Science
Principles: 1, 2, 4

As the world economy has expanded, interactions among people and groups both within regions and between regions have increased in number and complexity. They involve people with different national origins, who speak varied languages and live under contrasting social, political, and economic systems. As nations try to improve their standard of living, they further develop their natural resources and seek ways to use them more effectively. But because most resources are not uniformly distributed among the countries of the world, nations trade with one another for the resources they need, and this exchange leads to the creation of products that may be used locally or shipped to consumers around the world. As this cycle continues, the result is often an increase in the standard of living for all countries involved as well as a tremendous increase in global interdependence, the meaning of which will become clear in the following lesson about how the pencil, a very familiar object, is the result of complex interactions involving people and resources from all over the world.

*Adapted with permission from a lesson by L. C. Wolken. (November/December 1984). "The International Pencil: Elementary Level Unit on Global Interdependence." *Journal of Geography* 83(6), pp. 290–293. Reprinted by permission of the publisher (Taylor and Francis Group, www.informaworld.com) and Lawrence Wolken, Department of Finance, Mays Business School, Texas A&M University. To view a PowerPoint presentation created by Lawrence Wolken to accompany his lesson, go to http://sage.tamu.edu/topics/topic_resources/I/intl_pencil/pencil.htm.

Objectives

Students will be able to

1. Explain the meaning of global interdependence as it applies to the production of a pencil (SOCS-GEO 4; SOCS-EC 6; NS 6).
2. Identify the geographical sources of the materials that go into making a pencil (SOCS-GEO 1; SOCS-EC 6).
3. Describe how metals and minerals are used in making a pencil and where they are from (NS 2, 6).

Materials

- Map (or globe) of the world and the United States
- Three or four pencils
- A sharp knife or razor blade
- Chart of materials that comprise a pencil and the places they come from (see Table 7.1)

Procedures

You may want to do just one of the following activities or several, depending on the time you have available for carrying out the objectives and on the age level of the class. You may want to combine several activities or use them separately.

Before you have students do any of these activities, share with them the list of materials needed to make a pencil as well as the pencils you have split in half lengthwise so the lead is ex-

Table 7.1   The "International Pencil" (the Mongol Pencil produced in Wilkes-Barre, Pennsylvania)

The Part of the Pencil	Materials Used to Make That Part	State or Country That Produces the Raw Material
Exterior of the pencil	Wood (cedar trees), cut into 7" slats	Oregon, northern California
Lead (which is actually a scientifically produced mixture)	Mixture: • Graphite • Clay • Gums	Sri Lanka Mississippi Mexico
Lacquer that coats the pencil	Castor oil from castor beans	Brazil, east Africa (also California, Oregon)
Black lettering on the pencil	• Carbon black • Resins	Texas (where there is a plant that makes carbon black)
Ferrule (the metal that holds the eraser)	Brass, a combination of • Zinc • Copper	United States, Canada, Australia, or Ireland Bolivia, Chile, or Zambia
Rings on the ferrule	Black nickel	Canada, China
Eraser	• Pumice • The product of a chemical reaction between sulfur chloride and oil from seeds	Italy Indonesia

posed for the students to see. (It should also be noted here that thousands of people are involved in the production of the pencil from the lumberjacks who cut down the trees to the truck drivers who transport the materials to the workers and scientists involved in producing the lead.)

Activities

Activity 1: Map Skills
Give each student a map of the world and of the United States. Have them locate all of the places listed on the chart. Students may work individually or in groups.

Activity 2: Collage
Have students use brochures from travel agencies and magazines to collect pictures of the places mentioned. The class can then make a collage that can be placed on the bulletin board next to a world map. Use thumbtacks and yarn to connect the collage pictures to the appropriate locations on the map.

Activity 3: Quality of Life
Have the students compare the wealth (the GNP or gross national product per capita or the GDP, gross domestic product) and the quality of life in the nations involved in making the pencil.

Activity 4: Transportation
Students can determine the transportation routes for zinc from Australia, copper from Chile and Zambia, and pumice from Italy (or the possible routes used to transport other materials from their origins) to the factory in Pennsylvania.

Activity 5: Longitude and Latitude
Have students determine the longitude and latitude of the capitals of each nation involved in producing the pencil.

Activity 6: Regions
Place the countries mentioned on the chart within these categories:

  a. by continent
  b. Northern or Southern Hemisphere
  c. north of Tropic of Cancer, between the Tropic of Cancer and Capricorn, south of the Tropic of Capricorn
  d. east of the Prime Meridian to the 180E meridian, west of the Prime Meridian to the 180E meridian

Assessment

  • Completion of one or more of the activities that involve using map skills (Objectives 2, 3)
  • Participation in a discussion of how the production of the pencil is an example of global interdependence (Objective 1)

Extension

The lesson can be extended beyond one session by assigning activities that were not completed during the initial lesson.

Lesson 4:   Endangered Species*

Grade Levels: 4–6
Content: Science, Social Studies, Language Arts
Principles: 1, 2, 4

This lesson reflects the philosophy and values of Dr. Albert Schweitzer (1875–1965), the Nobel Prize–winning medical doctor and humanitarian. His philosophy—reverence for life—influenced everything Schweitzer did for humankind, including establishing in 1924 a hospital in Lambaréné, a small village in the jungles of what is today the nation of Gabon in West Africa. His legacy there continues.

While it is not necessary for students to do research on Schweitzer's life in order to complete the lesson successfully, you may want them to know more about this global Renaissance man. The Internet and the school library are destinations you can recommend to students who want to learn more about Schweitzer's life and deeds.

Objectives

Students will be able to

1. Develop a positive attitude toward solving social, economic, and environmental problems (NS 6, ELA 11).
2. Recognize how human activity threatens the existence of many species not just in the United States but worldwide (NS 3, 6; SOCS-GEO 5).
3. Discover steps being taken to protect endangered species (SOCS-EC 15; ELA 8).
4. Recognize that individual actions can create change (NS 6, ELA 11).
5. Identify ways in which Schweitzer's example is relevant to today's world and to their own lives (NS 6; ELA 5, 7, 8, 11).
6. Practice skills in researching, making connections, and problem solving (ELA 5, 7, 8, 11).

Materials

- Research Report Form
- Internet, library, and other sources of information about endangered species

Procedures

1. Tell the class a few details about Dr. Albert Schweitzer given in the introduction to this lesson. Then read the excerpt in Figure 7.4 aloud to the students.
2. After reading the paragraphs in Figure 7.4 aloud to students, divide the class into pairs or groups of three. Each team should select one endangered species from the list (Figure 7.5) to research. Give them the "Research Report Form" (Figure 7.6 on p. 196) to use in preparing their reports to the class. Allow students to name their first and second choices, but make sure each team has a different species. If information on one species is difficult to locate, let the team choose another one.
3. After the teams have given their reports, talk about what is lost when species disappear. Why isn't it enough to keep these animals in zoos? Do other living things have as much right to live as humans do? How does the loss of open space and of animal species reduce the quality of life for humans? How can Dr. Schweitzer's idea of reverence for life be applied to this problem?

---

*Adapted from a lesson on endangered species in King, D. C., F. Daniels-Thompson, and A. Hanchett Boland. (1992). *An Albert Schweitzer Activity Book, Curriculum Guide for Grades 1–6* (pp. 34–35). Great Barrington, MA: Albert Schweitzer Center.

Figure 7.4   Albert Schweitzer and Environmentalism

Albert Schweitzer loved and helped animals. He took care of both tame and wild animals who were sick or hurt or who had no mothers. At night they liked to listen to his music. He saved the cat Sizi's life when she was a kitten. She grew up on his desk and lived to be 23 years old. Parsifal was a pelican whose mother had been shot when he was a baby. Dr. Schweitzer raised him, and taught him how to fish for himself. Parsifal never flew away with the other birds. Every night he stood guard on Dr. Schweitzer's roof. When he was a boy, Dr. Schweitzer made this promise: "I will try never to hurt any living thing." All his life, he kept that promise.

Hundreds of species of wildlife have become endangered because of the activities of humans. Some species are close to extinction because of overhunting, or from the effects of pesticides. And one of the greatest human-generated threats is loss of habitat. As humans pave over, build, farm, cut, and mine ever-increasing areas of the planet's surface, animals find their living space (and food supplies) shrinking at disastrous rates.

Fortunately, a growing number of people are taking part in efforts to protect what remains of our wildlife. Nonprofit organizations, universities, and some government agencies, along with thousands of concerned citizens are working to reverse the tragic trends of the past century. Species that were on the verge of extinction—like the brown pelican, the bald eagle, and the American peregrine falcon—have been the beneficiaries of concerted preservation efforts. The banning of DDT enabled the pelicans to make a startling comeback. Captive breeding has been used to reintroduce bald eagles and falcons into the wild and the outlook for both species is hopeful.

This work only scratches the surface of what is needed—but it is a start. This activity will enable you to find out more about some of the animals and birds in greatest danger. By sharing your findings, you will gain an understanding of the situation and you will discover what you can do to help.

Source: King, D., F. Daniels-Thompson, and A. Hanchett Boland. (1992). *An Albert Schweitzer Activity Book: Curriculum Guide for Grades 1–6.* Great Barrington, MA: Albert Schweitzer Center.

Assessment

- Completion of a report on an endangered species (Objectives 1–6)
- Participation in a class discussion of the questions posed in step 3 of the procedures (Objectives 1–6)
- Written response paper in which students express what they learned about endangered species and what, if any, change in attitudes they experienced (Objectives 1–6)

Figure 7.5   List of Endangered Species

Atlantic salmon	Monarch butterflies	Snow leopards
Corals	Pandas	Tigers
Elephants	Pikes	Whales/dolphins
Great apes	Polar bears	West African ostrich
Marine turtles	Rhinos	

Source: From list posted by World Wildlife Fund (www.worldwildlife.org/endangered/2006)

Note: The World Endangered Species site (1998) of Thinkquest lists over 50 endangered species: 10 amphibians, 10 birds, 6 fish, 5 insects, 16 mammals, and 6 reptiles. Students might consult this site and others.

Figure 7.6   Endangered Species Research Report Form

• Name of species:

• Locations (find them on a map):

• Reasons for becoming endangered:

• How this species lives (i.e., food sources, raising young, etc.):

• Why we think this species should be protected:

• Steps being taken to save this species from extinction:

• Things we can do to help:

Extension

• Ask students if they would like to choose one of the endangered species, or environmental concerns, as a class fund-raising project and send money to an organization that protects animals or habitats (such as The Nature Conservancy, World Wildlife Fund, or Digit Fund).
• Have students read newspapers and magazines and visit Internet sites that describe current legislation relating to animals, habitat, and environment. Then have them write to legislators in support of current bills concerning these issues.
• Finally, have students respond to the following:

   Thousands of people would volunteer to go to Lambaréné to assist Schweitzer and his staff at the hospital. Often, however, Dr. Schweitzer discouraged them from coming to Lambaréné. "Everyone has his own Lambaréné," he said.

   1. What does his quote mean?
   2. Do you have "your own" Lambaréné?

Lesson 5: Global Munchies: Snack Foods and Where They Come From

Grade Levels: 3–12
Content: Science, Social Studies, Language Arts
Principles: 1, 2, 4

At the dawn of civilization, humans established two behaviors, among others: the practice of rituals and the cultivation of food. Add a television set thousands of years later, and you get the ritual of snacking (although a television isn't required). People in other cultures also practice the ritual of snacking, although the snacks may not be the same. In the lesson that follows, students will learn about global munchies, and, in so doing, come to recognize similarities and differences among various cultures.

Objectives

Students will be able to

1. Write about their snack foods and where they think they came from originally (ELA 12; SOCS-GEO 2, NS 6).
2. Discuss certain global snack foods and where they're from, as well as where the countries that enjoy those foods are located on a map (SOCS-GEO 1, 2, 6; ELA 9).
3. Try to determine the connection between the climate and geography of each country and its favorite snacks (SOCS-GEO 2; NS 6).
4. Describe some of the similarities and differences among various cultures and how snacks from one culture "travel" to others (SOCS-GEO 2; ELA 9).

Materials

- World map
- Chart of global munchies
- Notebooks

Procedures

1. Start with a prewriting activity before students discuss, read, or pursue information in various ways. Ask students to write for five minutes about what comes to their minds when the concept of "snack foods and where they come from" is presented to them as a topic.
2. After they complete their prewriting activity, have pairs of students read their work to one another. Then have each student tell the rest of the class one or two of the most interesting ideas they heard from their partner.
3. Make a list on the board of the foods that were mentioned in the students' writing.
4. Then share the chart on "Global Munchies" (see Table 7.2). Were any of the global munchies mentioned in their own writing?
5. Locate on a map the different countries listed on the chart. Discuss why the foods listed might be popular in those countries, and why the snack foods *they* wrote about are popular in the United States or in their region. Are snack foods *from other countries* sold in stores near them? Have them look for stores—or sections of a grocery store—where foods from other countries might be sold. Perhaps the students in the class who come from other countries or whose families enjoy foods from other cultures wrote about such global munchies and thus know where they are sold.

If students react with laughter or squeamishness to the kinds of snacks listed on the chart, ask them how someone from another culture might react to some of their snacks. Can they put themselves in the other's place? (*Note:* You might want to purchase some examples of these foods and share them with the students, as suggested in the Extension.)

Assessment

- The prewriting assignment completed before the lesson begins (Objective 1)
- Participation in the discussion of global munchies, their connections to geographical locations, and how they "travel" to other cultures (Objectives 2, 3, 4)
- A short paper on the similarities and differences among the cultures on the chart in terms of snacks (Objectives 2, 3, 4)

Table 7.2   Global Munchies

Country	Common Snacks
Canada (Quebec)	Poutine—a combination of French fries, brown gravy, and curd cheese
Mexico	Carnitas—fried pork cutlets
	Chicharrón—fried pork skin
	Pozole—a pork broth with a floating hunk of corn on the cob
	Menudo—a stew of cow stomach and chile
	Pizza
	Hamburgers
	Potato chips
Germany	Erdnussflips—a light brown peanut-flavored corn snack
	Potato chips
South Africa	Pap and mutton—pap is the country's staple corn mash; meat from sheep
	Pap and amathumbu—corn mash and tripe, or stomach tissue of the ox
Britain	Crisps—potato chips
	Mini chocolate bars
France	Camembert cheese
	Paté
	Cold pork sausages
	Roast chicken eaten with baguette (bread)
The Philippines	Adidas—grilled chicken feet
	Walkmans—pig's ears
	Unhatched duck eggs boiled and eaten from the shell with a sprinkling of rock salt
Japan	Peanuts
	Salty fried peas
	Rice crackers (called osembei)
	Dried sweet potatoes warmed in a toaster
China	Roasted watermelon seeds, prepared salty or sweet
Israel	Pitzuhim—anything that can be cracked open and shelled, including sunflower or watermelon seeds or pistachios
Saudi Arabia	Fava beans with olive oil, eggs, and basturma (a spicy Armenian cured-beef specialty)

Source: Adapted from "A Global Guide to TV Munchies." (January 26, 1997). *New York Times,* Section E, p. 3.

Extension

- Consider purchasing the ingredients of several global munchies in a local store or restaurant and either preparing the foods and sharing them or simply purchasing the foods already made and holding a Global Munchie Snack Fest.
- Have students do research on some of the munchies popular in other countries.

Lesson 6: Word Origins

Grade Levels: 3–12
Content: Language Arts
Principles: 1, 2, 4

The English language is made up of thousands of words with origins in dozens of other languages. Do your students realize to what extent English words come from one or *more* languages? If they have studied foreign languages, they probably already know this fact to some extent, but they may be surprised to find out just how many different sources have contributed to English.

Objectives

Students will be able to

1. Explain the origins of the English language and specifically the origins of at least ten words (ELA 3, 6, 8, 9).
2. Use a dictionary to find out the history of the English language and the origins of several words; use the "Abbreviations" section of the dictionary to help decipher dictionary entries (e.g., ME: Middle English) (ELA 8, 9).
3. Develop an interest in doing additional research on the origins of the English language (ELA 6, 9).

Materials

- Dictionary for each student (or they may use Internet sources for the same purpose)
- Map of the world

Procedures

1. Ask students if they would like to become *etymologists*. After some curious looks, define the term for them and place the definition on the board: someone who traces the development of words from their earliest recorded occurrence.
2. Ask students if they know where the English language comes from. After some responses, ask them what they think the origins of the word *students* might be. Then have them find the word, and together try to identify the meaning of the abbreviations that indicate the word's origins. Direct them to the front of the dictionary where the list of abbreviations appears; they will be able to use the list to translate the abbreviations that follow each dictionary entry.
3. Give each student a different letter. Have them find ten words that start with their letter. They should find ten words each with different origins and then, on a chart, record the words, their origins, and their meanings (pronunciations also, if you like). Mention that some words will have multiple origins.
4. Then divide the students into groups of three or four in which they can share their findings. Each group should then decide through consensus which two words from their group they want to share with the rest of the class.
5. List the words in chart form on the board. Discuss the origins of the words. Find the countries of origin on the map that you have hung on the bulletin board. Discuss how these words may have "traveled" to English-speaking countries and the United States in particular.
6. Consider having the students create a "Global Dictionary" made up of *all* the words the class recorded in their respective charts.

Assessment

- Completion of a chart with ten English words and their origins prepared with the assistance of a dictionary (Objectives 1, 2)
- Participation in a discussion of the origins of English words (Objectives 1, 3)

Extension

- As mentioned, you may want to have students work together on preparing a "Global Dictionary," one that is partially illustrated.

- Consider having students share their knowledge about the origins of the English language with another class.

Lesson 7: Writing Simple Poems

Grade Levels: 2–12
Content: Language Arts, Social Studies
Principles: 1, 3

This lesson appears simple enough, but it can have the profound effect of arousing your students' interest in the world and other cultures. At the same time, they will come to see that they have the ability to write a poem that may become a springboard for exploring their global interests in a more formal way.

Objectives

Students will be able to

1. Write a simple poem using the "I wonder why" format (ELA 4, 5, 12).
2. Share their poem with the class by reading it aloud (ELA 4, 5).
3. Invite one or several people to the class who might be able to answer their questions about the world and other cultures (ELA 9; SOCS-GEO 4).

Materials

- Pencil and paper

Procedures

1. Explain to the students that there is much they may already know about the world and its cultures, such as that people speak many languages or that different reasons led many people from different countries to come to the United States.
2. Then ask them to write down five questions they have about the world and other cultures. They should write each question beginning with "I wonder why . . ." Their sixth line should be the same as their first.
3. Ask the students to read their poems aloud. (Optional: Have students comment on each other's poems or say something positive about each one or ask a question of the poet.)
4. Discuss with students how they might try to find out answers to their questions. Do they know of someone they might invite to the class who might have some responses?
5. Have students—for homework—try to find the answer to *one* of their inquiries.

Assessment

- Completion of the "I wonder why" poem (Objectives 1, 2)
- Share their poems with peers (Objective 2)
- (Assuming a guest or guests visit the class) Interact with guest speaker(s) who come to class to address the student's poetic inquiries (Objective 3)

Lesson 8: What Is "Developed"?*

Grade Levels: 5–12
Content: Social Studies
Principles: 1, 2, 4

The term *development* has become increasingly popular in referring to the process of change in Africa, Asia, Latin America, and the Middle East. What does it mean to be "developed" or "underdeveloped"?

Countries like the United States, Canada, France, and Japan are often referred to as being among the developed nations while most countries in Asia, Africa, Latin America, and the Middle East are often referred to as underdeveloped, developing, or less-developed countries in an economic sense. The so-called *developed countries* are more industrial and wealthier in that their gross national product (GNP) per capita is larger (Drum et al., 1994, p. 63). (*GNP* refers to the estimate of the total value of goods and services produced by residents of a country, regardless of where that production takes place.)

But is this all there is to it? Maybe overall economic improvement must precede other developments. But it is also possible that economic growth, by itself, is not enough, and maybe it is even the wrong goal. For example, for some people, *development* refers to projects to help the poor. For others, it may mean adaptations which involve minimal disruption of traditional values, as in *sustainable development,* which refers to economic growth that doesn't damage the ecological and social systems it serves. And there are still other views. This lesson on development can begin in a number of ways, with the information just given or with the ideas listed first under the Procedures.

Objectives

Students will be able to

1. Explain the concept of development from a variety of different perspectives (ELA 1, 9; SOCS-C 4; SOCS-EC 12, 14, 18).
2. Identify on a map the areas of the world that are referred to as "developed" and "underdeveloped" and how they came to be labeled that way (ELA 9; SOCS-GEO 1, 4, 5; SOCS-WH 9).
3. Share the many different ways a nation or culture can be "developed" (ELA 9; SOCS-EC 12, 14, 18; SOCS-GEO 2, 4, 5).

Materials

- Map of the world
- Handout titled "Eight Views of Development" (Figure 7.7)

Procedures

1. Show students pictures of places or scenes from different countries. A good way to provoke some controversy is to show pictures that challenge the students' stereotypes. For example, scenes from so-called developed countries might include a bullfight arena in Houston or a sharecropper in Alabama or a homeless person in inner-city Los Angeles. Conversely, you might include pictures of gleaming skyscrapers in Brazil or a factory in India (Drum et al., 1994, p. 65).
2. Share the information in the introduction to this lesson with the class.

*Adapted from a lesson in Drum, J., S. Hughes, and G. Otero. (1994). *Global Winners*. Yarmouth, ME: Intercultural Press.

3. Identify on a wall map of the world where the regions mentioned are located.
4. Give students the handout "Eight Views of Development" (see Figure 7.7) and read them aloud together. They contain some definitions and statements by various experts in the area of international development.
5. Then hold a discussion in which you pose questions similar to the following: What are the differences between the points of view? With which do you agree or disagree? In what ways is the United States developed or undeveloped? Do you think that there is an assumption in the language used that to be more like the United States is to be better and that it is better to be developed? What students may need to understand is that there are many ways that a nation or a culture can be "developed."

Figure 7.7   Eight Views of Development

Development is improvement of the quality of life of people; it is not synonymous with economic growth, though such growth is necessary to achieve it. The people whose quality of life needs to be improved are mainly the poor.

—Martin McLaughlin, Interfaith Action for Economic Justice

The basic goal of development is the attainment of high mass consumption.

—W. W. Rostow, Professor of Economics

Development is a process. No one person, community or nation is fully developed. We are all at different stages of development. Development should always be based on the values of human dignity and justice.

—Nicole Mendoza, Catholic Relief Services

What does development mean? I believe it to be the building of a more equitable society; one in which people have access to the resources to work and prosper.

—Laurence Simon, American Jewish World Service

The question is whether Americans can create policies and institutions that suit an interdependent world—whether they will recognize that the development of countries overseas is a crucial component of their own welfare.

—John Hamilton, World Bank

Development is people working together for the well-being of the global community.

—Mary Hill Rojas, Virginia Polytechnic Institute

The environment is a critical variable in the development process. In fact, protection of the life support system, or the ecosystem in which development is taking place, has become one of the most critical factors in the process.

—Helen Vukasin, Development Institute, UCLA

I hold that economic progress is antagonistic to real progress. . . . I have heard many of our countrymen say that we will gain American wealth but avoid its methods. I venture to suggest that such an attempt if it were made is foredoomed to failure. We cannot be wise, temperate, and furious in a moment.

—Mahatma Gandhi

Source: "What Does Development Mean?" (1988). In *The Development Kit.* New York: Catholic Relief Services.

Assessment

- A short paper in which students present their views on development using as evidence and as a reference the handout "Eight Views of Development" and the information shared in class (Objectives 1, 2, 3)

Sample Unit 1: Local Links to the World*

Grade Levels: K–12
Content: Interdisciplinary
Time: 2–4 weeks
Principles: 1, 2, 3, 4

The bonds that connect us to others in the human family are easily found in every community and can be used to design instruction that heightens students' local and global awareness (Chartock, 1991, p. 50). The idea that global education can and, in fact, should begin with local links to other countries appeared in journalist Jack Hamilton's book, *Main Street America and the Third World* (1988). He was concerned that many people were not reading his or other reporters' stories about faraway places because they seemed irrelevant to their lives. He began experimenting with the "links" concept and noticed that when he uncovered all kinds of local links to developing nations, from banks to colleges to restaurants, people were interested; these faraway places were, indeed, present in many vital ways in their own backyards.

This unit of instruction will enable students to discover the many connections between their own communities and the world and, at the same time, engage in various methods of research.

Objectives

Students will be able to

1. Do research in their own communities to uncover local links with other countries (ELA 8, 9, 12; SOCS-GEO 2, 4; SOCS-USH [K–4] 1, 2, 3).
2. Interview people connected with the local links to the world that they uncover (ELA 5, 8, 9, 12; SOCS-USH [K–4] 2).
3. Identify the locations on a map of the countries with whom there are local links (SOCS-GEO 2, 4).
4. Express their findings in a well-organized, documented paper or packet and in a panel presentation (ELA 5, 12).
5. Work cooperatively with their committee (ELA 5, 11, 12).

Materials

- Questionnaire—"Local Links to Developing Countries and the World" (see Figure 7.8 on p. 205)
- Wall map of the world
- Handouts of a world map
- Cameras or sketchbooks
- Notebooks

*Adapted from article by the author, Chartock, R. K. (April 1991). "Identifying Local Links to the World." *Educational Leadership*, 48(7), pp. 50–52.

Procedures

1. Introduce the concept of "Local Links" by referring to the opening paragraph of this unit of instruction.
2. Brainstorm with students about the links they already know about. Then have them respond to the list of questions in the handout (Figure 7.8) that will help them think of still more links.
3. Decide on research committees you want to organize, perhaps three or four, with each one pursuing a different category of links (or more than one category), for example, one committee on business links, another on educational links.
4. Decide which tasks each committee member will pursue. Will the whole committee go into the field and locate still other links within their category? Who will interview the "links" that have been identified? Who will photograph or sketch the "links"? Who will invite one or more of their "links" to the class as guest speaker? Who will do additional research in local newspapers and on the Internet? Who will perform the other tasks that are included?
5. Have students meet in their committees to decide how they'll evenly share tasks; then give them one week (possibly two) to complete their research.
6. Provide time for students to meet with their committee and share their findings. At these meetings students can assist one another and decide how they want to organize and present their findings to the class.
7. Students should do some research on the countries they have identified as local links and locate them on individual maps. Some of that research can be done when they listen to guest speakers, "links" that they themselves have invited to class.
8. *Every student* should then prepare a packet that includes their findings in the form of a paper, their map, and any photos or sketches they completed.
9. Each committee then presents their research in class in the form of a panel (Chartock, 1991, p. 51).

Assessment

- Cooperative behavior within their committee (You might want to have each student write a simple self-evaluation in which they explain (1) their contributions to the project, (2) what they might have done differently, and (3) what was their most important learning experience) (Objective 5)
- The individual tasks completed by each student that contributed to the whole project (Objectives 1, 2, 3, 5)
- Their final project: packet of research and participation in oral presentation (Objective 4)

Extension

- Student panels could do a public presentation of their projects for parents and community and invite *all* of the "links" they uncovered.
- The class could write an article or editorial for the local paper explaining the importance of recognizing how much their community can learn about the world by looking right in their own backyard.
- Consider having students do a mural for the classroom wall—or school corridor—that illustrates their "Local Links to the World."

Figure 7.8 Questionnaire: Local Links to Developing Countries and the World

Directions: Links to other countries exist in your own community. Next to each question, try to identify by name real links in each category.

Nature of the Link	Name(s) of the Links
A. Community/Family Links	
1. Immigrants living in your town or city?	
2. Family members who come from another country?	
3. People who are familiar with immigrant groups that settled in your area?	
4. Veterans of military service?	
B. Educational/Recreational Links	
1. Faculty in schools or colleges in your area who come from another country?	
2. Students who come from another country?	
3. Students or faculty who have traveled to other countries?	
4. Teams that have players from other countries?	
5. Teams that have traveled to other countries to play?	
6. Peace Corps returnees?	
C. Environmental Links	
1. Experts who can discuss global or local environmental problems such as pollution or acid rain?	
D. Business/Trade/Industrial Links	
1. Small businesses that import goods (gift shops, flower shops, for example)?	
2. Large businesses that import or export goods (factories, for example)?	
3. Banks?	
4. Ethnic restaurants?	
5. Rotary Club exchanges?	
E. Religions/Social Links	
1. World religions in your community?	
2. Church/synagogue/mosque organizations with links to other countries?	
3. Festivals that celebrate origins?	
4. Organizations attempting to solve local problems related to hunger, homelessness, and refugee placement?	
F. Medical Links	
1. Hospitals with doctors or nurses from other countries?	
2. Experts on global diseases (AIDS, for example)?	
3. Experts on good or bad drugs coming in and going out of this country?	
4. Experts familiar with population issues?	
G. Cultural Links	
1. Visiting artists or performers in your community?	
2. Museums with exhibits from other countries?	
3. Plays or films from other countries?	
4. Musical groups from other countries?	
5. Sister City visitors?	

Source: Chartock, R. K. (1991, April). "Identifying Local Links to the World." *Educational Leadership, 48*(7), p. 52. © 1991 by ASCD. Used with permission. Learn more about ASCD at www.ascd.org.

Sample Unit 2: Creating a Classroom Museum of Global Art

Grade Levels: K–12
Content: Interdisciplinary
Time: Approximately 3 weeks
Principles: 1, 2, 3, 4

Art transcends all languages, geographic barriers, and age levels. While painting, sculpture, pottery, photography, collage, posters, videos, and other art forms may reflect the cultures from which the artists come, these works can speak to all peoples on levels both historical and aesthetic.

This unit involves students in learning about other cultures by viewing global art as well as making global art. The culmination of these activities is the establishment by the class of a museum in which they hang their own art and copies of the works of noted artists from other cultures, Western and non-Western.

The many learning activities in this unit of instruction can be simplified as needed, but there is no question that students of every age can participate in many, if not all, of them, to some extent.

Objectives

Students will be able to

1. Do research on global art, both Western and non-Western, and collect examples of art from many cultures (ELA 2, 7, 8, 9; NA-VA 3, 4, 6).
2. Work with a committee on establishing a classroom museum of global art (ELA 2, 7, 8, 9, 11; NA-VA 3, 4, 5, 6).
3. Become an expert on one work of art and present information about it both orally and in writing (ELA 8; NA-VA 1, 3, 4, 6).
4. Produce one or more works of art related to global perspectives (NA-VA 1, 3, 4, 6).

Materials

- Paper
- Markers or crayons
- Clay
- Paper for lining the bulletin boards
- 3 × 5 cards
- Map of the world
- Pictures of works of art from different cultures

Procedures

The art activities that comprise this unit of instruction are presented in the following list (of ten steps you can take toward creating a classroom museum of global art). Feel free to choose the steps or activities that are most appropriate for your grade or subject area, and feel free to carry them out *in any order*.

1. Ask students about their personal experiences making art and viewing art in museums. Ask them if they believe that all art reflects the culture from which the artists come. Ask them to be specific in terms of art they've made and viewed and where, besides museums, they have viewed art. Discuss the idea that art, like music and folk tales and obviously nonfiction, are all ways they can learn about other cultures and time periods.

2. Invite the art teacher to the class to share examples of art from other countries (in a PowerPoint presentation or by bringing photos or pictures of art from different cultures).

3. Invite a curator from a local art museum who can explain what is involved in putting together an art exhibit.

4. Have students begin collecting works of global art either from their own homes, art books (photocopies), museum catalogs, photos they have taken in a museum, postcards purchased from museums, art contained in library books, or from the art department. Be sure to tell them to document every item they collect, that is, the title of the artwork, the artist, when and where it was created, materials used, and a brief biography of the artist if possible.

5. Organize the students into committees and have them share their inventory of items. Each committee should select items for their class museum based on a number of criteria: items representing Western as well as non-Western artists, items representing different art forms, and items from different time periods. (The total number of items in the "museum" will vary. Aim for depth, not breadth; perhaps no more than 20 to 25 global items is appropriate, *not* including the students' personal creations. The art works produced by each student should *all* be exhibited.)

6. Have each committee share their selections with the class and encourage critiques based on the criteria mentioned.

7. Once the final decision is made on which works of art will be exhibited, have each student become an expert on *one* of those items in order to give a factual description of the item from a historical, artistic and aesthetic perspective—based on the research they have done. Each student will be responsible for preparing a label for the work of art that includes information listed in step 4. You may decide to have students prepare a catalog for the exhibit in which there is a photo of each item and a brief description. Finally, have students locate on a map the country of origin of the work of art they selected for the exhibit. Yarn can extend from the map locations to a list posted on the bulletin board of all of the artworks.

8. Based on the information students learned from the curator about mounting an exhibit, have them hang the works they selected. Provide tables for three-dimensional items. (They may want to cover the bulletin boards with some colored paper. Curators may be helpful in explaining how decisions are made about the colors of the walls in museums.)

9. Once the exhibit has been mounted, have each student become a docent, or guide, by preparing remarks on a 3 × 5 card about the item they researched. They can use the notes when standing up next to the work of art and reporting on it to the rest of the class. In their remarks, they should, of course, explain the relationship of the item to its cultural origins.

10. Invite other classes to the "museum" and have the "docents" walk them through the exhibit.

Hands-on Art Activities

- Bring students to an art museum that contains non-Western art and art from beyond the United States. (In New York City, for example, there are separate museums that contain art from African cultures, Asian cultures, Latin American cultures, European cultures, Afro-Cuban exhibits, and many others. In the Metropolitan Museum of Art—and in many fine arts museums—there will be examples of art from *many* cultures in one building. In one exhibit related to African art, for example, the objects shown tell a story of how rice-growing techniques were transported from Africa through the slave trade to America (Cotter, 2005, p. 14).

- "The Shape of . . ." is an activity that can help students get in touch with their world view and their feelings, biases, and beliefs. "The Shape of . . ." can refer to the shape of the world, the shape of Latin America, the shape of *anything*, for that matter, as demonstrated in the following list.

1. Ask students to close their eyes and think about some part of the world, say Africa, or the planet itself, about its conditions, a particular problem in the world, the oceans, or any other aspect of the globe.
2. As soon as an image pops into their heads, they should open their eyes and draw the image.
3. After they have drawn their pictures, randomly assign them to groups of five to eight people.
4. In their groups, students should explain their pictures to each other.
5. When they finish, each group should then draw a group poster incorporating the ideas of each member. (Each group will need a large piece of blank paper and colored markers or crayons.)
6. Finally, each group should place its poster on a wall and have a spokesperson explain it to the class. This activity can become the basis of a discussion, an essay, or other project (Drum et al., 1994, p. 35). What will become apparent are the accurate, as well as inaccurate, conceptions held by students—and the influence of their imaginations.

- "Nature Designs of Mexico" is an activity that demonstrates how art can transform items such as chairs, bowls, and spoons into festively colored works of art by using shapes from nature (e.g., animal and plant motifs) or materials from nature (e.g., seeds, twigs, and other natural resources). Craftspeople from many cultures often use environmental resources to produce unique designs and crafts. Have students do research on the plants and animals of Mexico (and other cultures such as Egyptian, Greek, or their own region). Have them collect pictures of those animals and plants and use the items as the basis for their *own* craft designs. You may want to work with the art teacher on planning this activity. Clay may be the best medium for this activity, that is, students can make bowls on which to paint or shape their versions of the global motifs they have gathered (Ryan, 1989, p. 161).

Assessment

- Their research and presentations on global art (Objectives 1, 2, 3)
- Contributions to their committee related to creating the classroom museum (Objectives 1, 2)
- Creation of their own works of art (Objective 4)

Extension

Visit an artist's studio and interview the artist about what, if any, connection his or her work has to their cultural origins.

Summary Chart of Principles and Their Applications

Principle	Applications (partial list)
1. There is a place for global perspectives in every discipline.	1. Organize a model United Nations program (Social Studies) and discuss the Universal Declaration of Human Rights.

2. Watch films about or from other countries. (Social Studies, Film Studies)
3. Hold a "hunger banquet" after doing research on the nutritional problems of certain countries and how they affect children. (Home Economics, Social Studies)
4. Organize an "International Sports Day." (Physical Education, Social Studies)
5. Have students research, write, and present plays about individuals who have worked for human rights around the world. (Language Arts, Social Studies)
6. Explore issues related to environment and population. (Science, Social Studies, Mathematics)

---

2. Establishing geographic knowledge is a good way for students to begin their global education.

1. Indicate on a map the products imported from and exported from certain countries that trade with the United States.
2. Show slides of major architectural wonders in the world and then locate them on a map.
3. Indicate on the map such things as countries in current news items, places you or your relatives have traveled, where books they are reading take place, and other relevant locations.
4. Play geographic games like What's Next, Name That Capital/Country, Details, Making Up Puns, and explore Buckminster Fuller's World Game.
5. Share your own (teacher) experiences with travel and global literature.

---

3. Developing interpersonal, international relationships is one of the most effective ways for teachers to bring the world into their classroom and decrease ethnocentrism.

1. Invite foreign-exchange students or teachers to the class to speak.
2. Tap into iEARN, a worldwide program that allows teachers and students to work collaboratively on classroom projects through the Internet.
3. Consider putting an ad in the paper to find someone who has visited or who comes from a country the class is studying.
4. Apply for travel study fellowships (for teachers) to other countries and bring back information from your firsthand experiences.

---

4. Understanding the concept of interdependence, or the mutual dependency that exists between countries, as well as between people and their environment, is central to students' appreciation of global diversity.

1. Have students trace the origins of products that, while "made in USA," are really a composite of materials from other countries.
2. Have students go to the following locations and take an inventory of the various places that common objects come from:
   - a grocery store
   - a toy store
   - their own closet
3. Connect yarn from the list of items gathered in step 2 to the areas on a map where the items were made.

 ## LINKS: Recording in Your Journal

This chapter has hopefully taken you on the kind of journey that will enable you to motivate your students to learn more about cultures beyond their borders, and, in so doing, learn more about themselves. Review the research, principles, and lessons, and then reflect on the following questions. Record your responses in your journal, and consider including sketches to illustrate your thinking.

1. World music, like global art, can arouse interest in other cultures. Likewise, current events can stimulate interest, as in the case of the deadly tsunami that struck parts of the world (in December 2004) that your students may never have heard of, such as Sumatra, the Maldives, or Sri Lanka. How might you organize a global perspectives lesson using current events or music as a springboard?

2. As you reflect back on this chapter, try to identify what is the *most important* idea you would want your students to learn. (You might want to compare your answer with those of your peers.)

3. Without looking back at the chapter, see if you can recall one activity for increasing global perspectives that could easily be integrated into almost *every* subject area. Then review the chapter for examples of other such activities.

4. Has this chapter changed your attitudes in any way about the world? Other cultures? Anything? If so, how are you different? What, if anything, can you point to as having influenced that change?

5. Ongoing wars in the world bring the United States into direct or indirect contact with many other regions. To what extent should students engage in discussion or debate regarding the causes and direction of current wars, and at what age is it appropriate for students to confront world conflicts and the efforts to resolve them? What is the basis for your thinking?

6. What has been your personal experience with art from other cultures? With producing art? If you have, in fact, created art, analyze one or two examples. Do you see any connection between your art and your own culture and cultural views?

7. Have you traveled beyond the borders of the United States? If so, how has that influenced the way you teach (or how do you think it will)?

References

Asia Society. (2005). *Schools for a Global Age: Promising Practices in International Education.* New York: Asia Society and Goldman Sachs Foundation.

Association for Supervision and Curriculum Development. (January 1990). "Issue." *Update, 32*(1), p. 7.

Bergman, D., and S. Young. (September 1989). "Internationalizing Your School." *Educational Leadership.* Alexandria, VA: Association for Supervision and Curriculum Development.

Blandy, D., and K. G. Congdon (Eds.). (1987). *Art in a Democracy.* New York: Teachers College, Columbia University.

Borja, R. R. (2006). "'Google for Educators' Unveils Interactive Tools for Schools." *Education Week, 26*(13), p. 9.

Cavanagh, S. (February 8, 2006). "Network Sponsors Worldwide Sharing of Curricula." *Education Week, 25*(22), p. 10.

Cavanagh, S. (December 6, 2006). "Critics Accuse NSTA of Having Conflict Over Film." *Education Week, 1,* p. 17.

Cotes, G. R. (April 2005). "Schools for the Global Age." *Education Update,* p. 6. Alexandria, VA: Association for Supervision and Curriculum Development.

Cotter, H. (March 30, 2005). "Outside In: Non-Western Art Moves into the Main Gallery." *New York Times,* pp. E1, 14.

DeKock, A., and C. Paul. (September 1989). "One District's Commitment to Global Education." *Educational Leadership.* Alexandria, VA: Association for Supervision and Curriculum Development.

Evans, C. (1987). "Teaching a Global Perspective in Elementary Schools." *Elementary School Journal, 87,* pp. 545–555.

Friedman, T. (1999). *The Lexus and the Olive Tree: Understanding Globalization.* New York: Farrar, Strauss, Giroux.

Goldman, A. L. (April 9, 1989). "World Affairs Can Be Child's Play." *Education Life, The New York Times Supplement* (4A), pp. 18–31.

Hamilton, J. M. (1988). *Main Street America and the Third World.* Washington, DC: Seven Locks Press.

Herskovits, M. J. (1972). *Cultural Relativism: Perspectives in Cultural Pluralism.* New York: Vintage Books.

Jennings, T. E. (Spring 1994). "Global Communications, Identity and Human Rights Advocacy." *Proteus: A Journal of Ideas, 11*(1), pp. 11–14.

Keller, B. (December 3, 2003). "Teachers Travel the Globe for Professional Development." *Education Week, 23*(14), p. 8.

Kohls, L. R., and Knight, J. M. (1994). *Developing Intercultural Awareness.* Yarmouth, ME: Intercultural Press.

Lacks, C. (January–February 1992). "Sharing a World of Difference: International Education in the Early Years." *Social Studies and the Young Learner, 4*(3), pp. 6–8.

Manzo, K. K. (March 2, 2005). "Group Promotes Global Studies in Curriculum." *Education Week, 24*(25), p. 5.

Manzo, K. K. (July 27, 2005). "North Carolina to Open Four International-Studies Schools." *Education Week*, 24(43), p. 12.

Manzo, K. K. (September 6, 2006). "Teachers Tiptoe into Delicate Topics of 9/11 and Iraq." *Education Week*, 26(2), pp. 1, 22–24.

Miller, J. (Summer 2001). "Teaching about Sweatshops and the Global Economy." *Radical Teacher*, No. 61, pp. 8–14. Baltimore, MD: Center for Critical Education.

Nye, J. (2002). "Globalism versus Globalization." *Globalist*. Available online at www.globalist.com

Roosevelt, E. (2006). Remarks at United Nations, 1946, in Brochure for the *Eleanor Roosevelt Center at Val-Kill*. Hyde Park, NY.

Roper Global Geographic Literacy Survey. (2002). Washington, DC: National Geographic Society.

Ryan, M. W. (1989). *Cultural Journeys: 84 Art and Social Science Activities from Around the World*. Holmes Beach, FL: Learning Publications.

Scherer, M. (October 2002). "The World Is With Us." *Educational Leadership* 60(2), p. 5.

Smith, D. J. (2002). *If the World Were a Village: A Book About the World's People*. Tonawanda, NY: Kids Can Press. Available online at www.kidscanpress.com

Summerfield, E. (1993). *Crossing Cultures Through Film*. Yarmouth, ME: Intercultural Press.

Tye, K. A. (Ed.). (1991). *Global Education: From Thought to Action*. The 1991 ASCD Yearbook. Alexandria, VA: Association for Supervision and Curriculum Development.

Recommended Resources

Anderson, M., and K. Kraco (Eds.). (1997). *Good Things Happen When Students Take Action*. Minneapolis, MN: Partners in Human Rights Education. Order from Human Rights USA Resource Center, 310 Fourth Avenue South, Suite 1000, Minneapolis, MN 55415–1012. E-mail: hrusa@tc.umn.edu

Byrnes, R. S. (Spring 1997). "Global Education's Promise: Reinvigorating Classroom Life in a Changing, Interconnected World." *Theory Into Practice*, 36(2), pp. 95–101.

Collinson, V. (Ed.). (November 2006). *Learning, Teaching, Leading: A Global Perspective* (Vol. 45). Mahwah, NJ: Lawrence Erlbaum.

Flowers, N. (Ed.). (1998). *Human Rights Here and Now*. Minneapolis, MN: Amnesty International USA, Human Rights USA Resource Center, and the Stanley Foundation.

Gaudelli, W. (1996). *World Class: Teaching and Learning in Global Times*. Thousand Oaks, CA: Corwin Press.

Merryfield, M., E. Jarchow, and S. Pickert (Eds.). (1997). *Preparing Teachers to Teach Global Perspectives: A Handbook for Teacher Educators*. Thousand Oaks, CA: Sage Publications.

Rotberg, I. C. (Ed.). (2004). *Balancing Change and Tradition in Global Education Reform*. Lanham, MD: Rowman and Littlefield.

Scherer, M. M. (Ed.). (October 2002). *The World in the Classroom* issue of *Educational Leadership* 60(2). Alexandria, VA: Association for Supervision and Curriculum Development.

DVD

Global Studies. (2006). Princeton, New Jersey: Films for the Humanities and Sciences.

Workshop

Global Simulation Workshops available from O.S. Earth, P.O. Box 1006, New Haven, CT 06504. (203) 672-5907. www.osearth.com/ws-history.shtml

Websites of Global Service Organizations

Albert Schweitzer Institute
www.iseps.org.uk/contact/htm

Digit Fund (renamed Dian Fossey Gorilla Fund in 1992)
www.dian-fossey.com

Educators for Social Responsibility
www.esrnational.org/home.htm

Heifer Foundation International
www.Heifer.org

Human Rights USA
www.hrusa.org

The Nature Conservancy
www.nature.org

Oxfam America
www.oxfamamerica.org

Solar Box Cookers International
www.solarcookers.org/basics/how.html

World Wildlife Fund
www.worldwildlife.org/about

Websites

www.americanhistory.si.edu/sweatshops/index.htm
Smithsonian Institution's exhibits related to history of United States sweatshops as well as the global production game

www.amnesty.org
Sponsors the work of the Human Rights Educators' Network

www.citizen.org/pctrde/tradehome.html
Global Trade Watch: part of Ralph Nader's Public Citizen devoted to promoting government and corporate accountability in the world economy

www.globaled.org
American Forum for Global Education

www.gesdb.cdie.org/ged/index.htm
USAID: Global Education Database

http://gig.org/Departments/gig.k12.php
Global Issues Gateway K–12

http://java.nationalgeographic.com/studentatlas
The Map Machine, a feature of National Geographic's website, offering an atlas of the world, continent, regional, and country maps for printing, as well as photos, cultural profiles, and geographic facts

www.metmuseum.org/toah
The Metropolitan Museum of Art's "Timeline of Art History"

www.peacecorps.gov.wws
Peace Corps World Wise Schools

www.smithsonianeducation.org/mywonderfulworld
Smithsonian's Geographic Resources

www.stanleyfdn.org
The Stanley Foundation convenes global education programs that involve educators, administrators and students on all levels

www.uis.unesco.org
UNESCO Publications

www.undp.org/indexalt.html
United Nations Development Program (UNDP): known for its work on global inequality by income, region, and gender

www.worldbank.org/poverty/index.htm
Poverty Net: Resources to Support People Working to Understand and Alleviate Poverty (World Bank poverty page with data, interviews, and program descriptions)

Appendixes

Appendix A
Key to National Standards Issued by Professional Organizations Representing Major Disciplines

The following national and educational organizations are among those that have issued content standards or guidelines to be used on the national level:

- International Reading Association (IRA) and National Council of Teachers of English (NCTE)
- National Council of Teachers of Mathematics (NCTM)
- Center for Civic Education
- National Center for History in the Schools
- National Council on Economic Eductaion
- National Geographic Society
- National Academies of Science
- International Society for Technology in Education
- Consortium of National Arts Education Associations

The key to national content standards in the major disciplines below includes those standards that have been matched with objectives listed in each of the lesson plans in this primer:

International Reading Association (IRA) and National Council of Teachers of English (NCTE)

ELA: English and Language Arts Standards K–12

ELA 1: Reading for Perspective
ELA 2: Understanding the Human Experience
ELA 3: Evaluation Strategies
ELA 4: Communication Skills
ELA 5: Communication Strategies
ELA 6: Applying Knowledge
ELA 7: Evaluating Data
ELA 8: Developing Research Skills
ELA 9: Multicultural Understanding
ELA 10: Applying Non-English Perspectives
ELA 11: Participating in Society
ELA 12: Applying Language Skills

National Council of Teachers of Mathematics (NCTM)

MAT-N/O: Mathematics—Numbers and Operations (K–12)

MAT-N/O 1: Understand numbers, ways of representing numbers, relationships among numbers, and number systems.

MAT-N/O 2: Understand meanings of operations and how they relate to one another.
MAT-N/O 3: Compute fluently and make reasonable estimates.

MAT-MEA: Mathematics and Measurement (K–12)

MAT-MEA 1: Understand measurable attributes of objects and the units, systems, and processes of measurement.
MAT-MEA 2: Apply appropriate techniques, tools, and formulas to determine measurements.

MAT-PS: Problem Solving (K–12)

MAT-PS 1: Build new mathematical knowledge through problem solving.
MAT-PS 2: Solve problems that arise in mathematics in other contexts.
MAT-PS 3: Apply and adapt a variety of appropriate strategies to solve problems.
MAT-PS 4: Monitor and reflect on the process of mathematical problem solving.

MAT-COM: Communication (K–12)

MAT-COM 1: Organize and consolidate their mathematical thinking through communication.
MAT-COM 2: Communicate their mathematical thinking coherently and clearly to peers, teachers, and others.
MAT-COM 3: Analyze and evaluate the mathematical thinking and strategies of others.
MAT-COM 4: Use the language of mathematics to express mathematical ideas precisely.

MAT-CONN: Connections (K–12)

MAT-CONN 1: Reorganize and use connections among mathematical ideas.
MAT-CONN 2: Understand how mathematical ideas interconnect and build on one another to produce a coherent whole.
MAT-CONN 3: Recognize and apply mathematics in contexts outside of mathematics.

MAT-REP: Representation (K–12)

MAT-REP 1: Create and use representations to organize, record, and communicate mathematical ideas.

MAT-REP 2: Select, apply, and translate among mathematical representations to solve problems.

MAT-REP 3: Use representations to model and interpret physical, social, and mathematical phenomena.

Center for Civic Education

Civics and Government (K–12)

SOCS-C 1: What is government and what should it do?

SOCS-C 2: What are the basic values and principles of American democracy (includes diversity).

SOCS-C 3: How does the government established by the Constitution embody the purposes and principles of American democracy?

SOCS-C 4: What is the relationship of the United States to other nations and to world affairs?

SOCS-C 5: What are the roles of the citizen in American democracy?

National Center for History in the Schools

U.S. History (K–4)

SOCS-USH 1: Living and working together in families and communities, now and long ago.

SOCS-USH 2: The history of students' own state or region.

SOCS-USH 3: The history of the United States: Democratic principles and values and the people from many cultures who contributed to its cultural, economic, and political heritage.

SOCS-USH 4: The history of peoples of many cultures around the world.

U.S. History (5–12)

SOCS-USH 1: Era 1: Three worlds meet (beginnings to 1620).

SOCS-USH 2: Era 2: Colonization and settlement (1585–1763).

SOCS-USH 3: Era 3: Revolution and the new nation (1754–1820s)

SOCS-USH 4: Era 4: Expression and reform (1801–1861)

SOCS-USH 5: Era 5: Civil war and reconstruction (1850–1877)

SOCS-USH 6: Era 6: The development of the industrial United States (1870–1900)

SOCS-USH 7: Era 7: The emergence of modern America (1890–1930)

SOCS-USH 8: Era 8: The Great Depression and World War II (1929–1945)

SOCS-USH 9: Era 9: Postwar United States (1945–early 1970s)

SOCS-USH 10: Era 10: Contemporary United States (1968–present)

World History (5–12)

SOCS-WH 1: Era 1: The beginning of human society

SOCS-WH 2: Era 2: Early civilizations and the emergence of pastoral peoples (4000–1000 BCE)

SOCS-WH 3: Era 3: Classical traditions, major religions, and giant empires (1000 BCE–300 CE)

SOCS-WH 4: Era 4: Expanding zones of exchange and encounter (300–1000 CE)

SOCS-WH 5: Era 5: Intensified hemispheric interactions (1000–1500 CE)

SOCS-WH 6: Era 6: The emergence of the first Global Age (1450–1770)

SOCS-WH 7: Era 7: An age of revolutions (1750–1914)

SOCS-WH 8: Era 8: A half-century of crisis and achievement (1900–1945)

SOCS-WH 9: Era 9: The 20th century since 1945: Promises and paradoxes

National Council on Economic Education

SOC-EC: Economics (K–12)

SOCS-EC 1: Scarcity

SOCS-EC 2: Marginal cost/benefit

SOCS-EC 3: Allocation of goods and services

SOCS-EC 4: Role of incentives

SOCS-EC 5: Gain from trade

SOCS-EC 6: Specialization and trade

SOCS-EC 7: Markets—Price and quantity determination

SOCS-EC 8: Role of price in market system

SOCS-EC 9: Role of competition

SOCS-EC 10: Role of economic institutions

SOCS-EC 11: Role of money

SOCS-EC 12: Role of resources in determining income

SOCS-EC 13: Profit and the entrepreneurs

SOCS-EC 14: Growth

SOCS-EC 15: Role of government

SOCS-EC 16: Unemployment and inflation

National Geographic Society

Geography (K–12)

SOCS-GEO 1: The world in spatial terms

SOCS-GEO 2: Places and regions

SOCS-GEO 3: Physical systems

SOCS-GEO 4: Human systems

SOCS-GEO 5: Environment and society

SOCS-GEO 6: Uses of geography

National Academies of Science

NS: National Science Standards (K–12)

NS 1: Science as inquiry

NS 2: Physical science
NS 3: Life science
NS 4: Earth and space science
NS 5: Science and technology
NS 6: Personal and social perspectives
NS 7: History of nature and science

International Society for Technology in Education

NT (or NTECH): National Technology Standards (K–12)

NT 1: Creativity and innovation
NT 2: Communication and collaboration
NT 3: Research and information fluency
NT 4: Critical thinking, problem solving, and decision making
NT 5: Digital citizenship
NT 6: Technology operations and concepts

National Arts Education Associations (K–12)

Dance (K–12)

NA-D 1: Identifying and demonstrating movement elements and skills in performing dance
NA-D 2: Understanding choreographic principles, processes, and structures
NA-D 3: Understanding dance as a way to create and communicate meaning
NA-D 4: Applying and demonstrating critical and creative thinking skills in dance
NA-D 5: Demonstrating and understanding dance in various cultures and historical periods
NA-D 6: Making connections between dance and healthful living
NA-D 7: Making connections between dance and other disciplines

Music (K–12)

NA-M 1: Singing alone and with others, a varied repertoire of music
NA-M 2: Performing on instruments, alone and with others, a varied repertoire of music
NA-M 3: Improvising melodies, variations, and accompaniments
NA-M 4: Composing and arranging music within specified guidelines
NA-M 5: Reading and notating music
NA-M 6: Listening to, analyzing, and describing music
NA-M 7: Evaluating music and music performances
NA-M 8: Understanding relationships between music, the other arts, and disciplines outside the arts
NA-M 9: Understanding music in relation to history and culture

Theater (K–12)

NA-T 1: Script writing by planning and recording improvisations based on personal experience and heritage, imagination, literature, and history
NA-T 2: Acting by assuming roles and interacting in improvisations
NA-T 3: Designing by visualizing and arranging environments for classroom dramatizations
NA-T 4: Directing by planning classroom dramatizations
NA-T 5: Researching by finding information to support classroom dramatizations
NA-T 6: Comparing and connecting art forms by describing theater, dramatic media (such as film, television, and electronic media), and other art forms
NA-T 7: Analyzing and explaining personal preferences and constructing meanings from classroom dramatizations and from theater, film, television, and electronic media productions
NA-T 8: Understanding context by recognizing the role of theater, film, television, and electronic media in daily life

Visual Arts (K–12)

NA-VA 1: Understanding and applying media, techniques, and processes
NA-VA 2: Using knowledge of structures and functions
NA-VA 3: Choosing and evaluating a range of subject matter, symbols, and ideas
NA-VA 4: Understanding the visual arts in relation to history and cultures
NA-VA 5: Reflecting upon and assessing the characteristics and merits of their work and the work of others
NA-VA 6: Making connections between the visual arts and other disciplines

Sources:

International Reading Association and National Council of Teachers of English. (1996). *Standards for the English Language Arts.* Urbana, IL: Authors. Copyright 1996 by the International Reading Association and the National Council of Teachers of English. Reprinted by permission.

National Council of Teachers of Mathematics. (2000). *Principles and Standards for School Mathematics.* Reston, VA: Author. Reprinted by permission of the National Council of Teachers of Mathematics.

Center for Civic Education. (1994). *National Standards for Civics and Government.* Washington, DC: Author. © 1994. Center for Civic Education. Calabasas, CA. www.civiced.org. Reprinted by permission.

National Center for History in the Schools. (1996). *National Standards for History, Basic Edition.* Los Angeles: University of California. Courtesy of National Center for History in the Schools, UCLA, http://nchs.ucla.edu.

National Council on Economic Education. (1997). *Voluntary National Content Standards in Economics*. New York: Author. Copyright © 1997 Council for Economic Education, New York, NY. All rights reserved. For more information, visit www.councilforeconed.org or call 1-800-338-1192. Reprinted by permission.

National Geographic Society. (1994). *U.S. National Geography Standards*. Washington, DC: Author. Reprinted by permission.

National Academies of Science. (1997). *National Science Education Standards*. Washington, DC: National Academies Press. Courtesy of the National Academies Press, Washington, DC.

International Society for Technology in Education. (2007). *National Educational Technology Standards for Students*. Washington, DC: Author. © 2007, ISTE (International Society for Technology in Education), www.iste.org. All rights reserved. Reprinted by permission.

Consortium of National Arts Education Associations. (1994). *National Standards for Arts Education*. Reston, VA: National Association for Music Education. Copyright © 1994 by MENC: The National Association for Music Education. Listed with permission. For more information on these standards and how to achieve or assess them, please visit www.menc.org, www.aapherd.org/NDA, www.aate.com, and www.naca-reston.org.

Interstate New Teacher Assessment and Support Consortium (INTASC) Standards

(This text was constructed with INTASC standards in mind. You will be able to observe their applications in the principles listed in each chapter as well as within the lesson plans and units of instruction herein.)

A program of the Council of Chief State School Officers, the INTASC standards reflect the requisite knowledge, skills, and attitudes necessary for teachers starting their careers. INTASC, created in 1987, is a consortium of state education agencies and national educational organizations dedicated to the reform of the preparation, licensing, and professional development of our teaching corps. INTASC standards emphasize how teachers need to integrate content knowledge and leverage the strengths and address the needs of individual students so that each and every student can reach his or her academic and social potential.

These standards address the knowledge, dispositions, and performances deemed essential for all teachers regardless of their specialty area. They were developed to be compatible with the advanced certification standards of the new National Board for Professional Teaching Standards (K–12).

INTASC Principles

Principle 1: Making Content Meaningful

The teacher understands the central concepts, tools of inquiry, and structures of the discipline(s) he or she teaches and creates learning experiences that make these aspects of subject matter meaningful for students.

Principle 2: Child Development and Learning Theory

The teacher understands how children learn and develop and can provide learning opportunities that support their intellectual, social, and personal development.

Principle 3: Learning Styles and Diversity

The teacher understands how students differ in their approaches to learning and creates instructional opportunities that are adapted to diverse learners.

Principle 4: Instructional Strategies and Problem Solving

The teacher understands and uses a variety of instructional strategies to encourage students' development of critical thinking, problem solving, and performance skills.

Principle 5: Motivation and Behavior

The teacher uses an understanding of individual and group motivation and behavior to create a learning environment that encourages positive social interaction, active engagement in learning, and self-motivation.

Principle 6: Communication and Knowledge

The teacher uses knowledge of effective verbal, nonverbal, and media communication techniques to foster active inquiry, collaboration, and supportive interaction in the classroom.

Principle 7: Planning for Instruction

The teacher plans instruction based upon knowledge of subject matter, students, the community, and curriculum goals.

Principle 8: Assessment

The teacher understands and uses formal and informal assessment strategies to evaluate and ensure the continuous intellectual, social, and physical development of the learner.

Principle 9: Professional Growth and Reflection

The teacher is a reflective practitioner who continually evaluates the effects of his or her choices and actions on others (students, parents, and other professionals in the learning community) and who actively seeks out opportunities to grow professionally.

Principle 10: Interpersonal Relationships

The teacher fosters relationships with school colleagues, parents, and agencies in the larger community to support students' learning and well-being.

Source: Council of Chief State School Officers. (1992). *Model Standards for Beginning Teachers Licensing, Assessment and Development: A Resource for State Dialogue.* Washington, DC: INTASC. Reprinted by permission.

Appendix C
Gardner's Multiple Intelligences

According to Howard Gardner, Professor of Cognition and Education and Adjunct Professor of Psychology at Harvard University, all human beings possess at least eight quite separate forms of intelligence and possibly a ninth. "Each intelligence reflects the potential to solve problems . . . in one or more cultural settings" (Gardner, 1999, pp. 71–72).

Intelligence tests typically tap *linguistic/verbal* and *logical/mathematical* intelligences, but as a species we also possess *visual/spatial* intelligence, *musical/rhythmic* intelligence (artistic), *bodily/kinesthetic* intelligence (movement), *naturalistic* intelligence (the natural world), intelligence about ourselves (*intrapersonal* intelligence), intelligence about other persons (*interpersonal* intelligence), and possibly *existential* intelligence—"the proclivity to pose (and ponder) questions about life, death, and ultimate realities. Each of these intelligences features its own distinctive form of mental representation; in fact, it is equally accurate to say that each intelligence *is* a form of mental representation" (Gardner, 1999, p. 72).

In the same way that students in a classroom may differ in terms of race, religion, class, ethnicity, gender, and ability, they also may differ in terms of their intelligences, that is, the particular strength(s) they bring to problem solving. In the same way that honoring their individuality in terms of cultural differences helps students gain confidence academically and socially within the school environment, so too when teachers recognize and tap into students' inherent intelligence(s), the greater is the likelihood that content, methods, and assessment techniques administered by teachers will be more just and fair in meeting the interests and needs of each student. Gardner, for example, describes for readers how teachers might acknowledge their students' differences as they study the subject of the Nazi Holocaust. He identifies the content, questions, and approaches that a teacher might apply in terms of each point of entry, from the linguistic to the existential (Gardner, 1999, pp. 186–213). (His use of this particular subject matter is relevant to the topic of this text, culturally responsive teaching, as the Holocaust refers to the genocide of over six million Jews and thousands of others because of their differences, and, of course, the political and economic purposes to which Hitler put scapegoating and stereotyping are equally important to recognize here).

Reference

Gardner, H. (1999). *The Disciplined Mind: What All Students Should Understand.* New York: Simon and Schuster.

Appendix D
Bloom's Taxonomy of Educational Objectives

Hierarchy of objectives in three domains for use in designing lessons that promote critical thinking.

Cognitive Domain

1. *Knowledge*
   - List
   - Identify
   - Define
2. *Comprehension*
   - Compare/contrast
   - Explain
   - Provide an example
3. *Application*
   - Apply the idea to
   - Develop
4. *Analysis*
   - Classify
   - Compare/contrast
5. *Synthesis*
   - Draw conclusion
   - Predict
6. *Evaluation*
   - Agree/disagree and explain why
   - Select

Affective Domain

1. *Receiving*
   Demonstrates attention
2. *Responding*
   Responds in acceptable way
3. *Valuing*
   Shows preference and defends position
4. *Organizing*
   - Sees relationships
   - Develops a value system
5. *Characterizing by a value*
   Acts in ways consistent with values (demonstrates)

Psychomotor Domain

1. *Perception* (attending)
   Recognizes cues and relates them to action
2. *Set*
   Displays mental, physical, and emotional readiness to perform
3. *Guided response*
   Imitates a response
4. *Mechanism*
   Performs task habitually
5. *Complex or overt response*
   Performs with confidence and proficiency
6. *Adaptation*
   Adapts skills to fit situation
7. *Origination*
   Creates new performance

Index

Credits

Classroom Applications and Strategies on pp. 85–86 are from Teaching Tolerance. (2000). *101 Tools for Tolerance: Simple Ideas for Promoting Equity and Celebrating Diversity.* Montgomery, AL: Southern Poverty Law Center. Reprinted by permission of Teaching Tolerance, www.tolerance.org.

Classroom Applications and Strategies on p. 87 were compiled by Pat Griffin in Governor's Commission on Gay and Lesbian Youth. (1993). *Making Schools Safe for Gay and Lesbian Youth.* Boston: Massachusetts Department of Education. Reprinted by permission.

Standards on p. 147 are from Illinois State Board of Education. (2002). *Illinois Professional Teaching Standards* (2nd ed.), p. 4. Available at www.isbe.state.il.us. Copyright © 2000–2009, Illinois State Board of Education, republished by permission. All rights reserved.

Standards on pp. 155 and 156 are from Teachers of English to Speakers of Other Languages. (2006). *Pre-K–12 English Language Proficiency Standards.* Alexandria, VA: Author. Copyright © 2006. Used with permission of Teachers of English to Speakers of Other Languages.